EditWell

Final Cut Studio Techniques from the Pros

Peachpit
Press

LARRY JORDAN, ed.

Edit Well: Final Cut Studio Techniques from the Pros
Larry Jordan, ed.

Peachpit Press
1249 Eighth Street
Berkeley, CA 94710
510/524-2178
Fax: 510/524-2221

Find us on the Web at: www.peachpit.com
To report errors, please send a note to errata@peachpit.com
Peachpit Press is a division of Pearson Education

Copyright ©2009 by Peachpit Press

Editor: Larry Jordan
Senior Editor: Karyn Johnson
Technical Editor: Graeme Nattress
Production Editor: Cory Borman
Copyeditor: Darren Meiss, Robin Drake
Proofreader: Scout Festa
Composition: WolfsonDesign
Indexer: Jack Lewis
Cover Design: Mike Tanamachi

ISBN-13: 978-0-321-61218-2

ISBN-10: 0-321-61218-3

9 8 7 6 5 4 3 2 1

Printed and bound in the United States of America

EditWell

About the Contributors

Larry Jordan

Larry Jordan, the editor of *Edit Well*, is a consultant and Apple Certified Trainer in Digital Media with more than 25 years' experience as a television producer, director, and editor with national broadcast and corporate credits. Based in Los Angeles, he's a member of both the Directors Guild of America and the Producers Guild of America. Larry has also been recognized as one of the Top 100 Corporate Producers in America. He has written two books on Final Cut Pro for Peachpit Press and is the executive producer and host of Digital Production BuZZ. Visit his web site at **www.larryjordan.biz**.

Clay Asbury

Clay Asbury is a freelance editor and instructor in Atlanta, Georgia. His clients include well-known companies such as Turner Networks, CNN, and Crawford Communications. His approachable and effective teaching style has developed from having over a decade of experience as an educator with such institutions as Fordham University and The Art Institute of Atlanta. He is certified in both Final Cut Studio and Adobe Photoshop. In addition, he worked as a broadband video editor for Weather.com and as a quality assurance tester for Apple Computer.

Matthew Geller

Matthew Geller is the principal at Meta Media Creative Technologies, a firm dedicated to providing consulting, integration services, training, and support to facilities in postproduction and broadcast. He is also an Apple Mentor Trainer and has taught courses for system integrators and channel partners worldwide. His book *Apple Pro Training Series: Getting Started with Final Cut Server* is now available from Peachpit.

Noah Kadner

Noah Kadner graduated from the USC film school with an MFA in production. He runs High Road Productions, a film, television, production, and post-production company. Noah is also an Apple Certified Pro experienced in building editing suites and training users on Final Cut Pro, Motion, and DVD Studio Pro. He hosts and produces Call Box (**www.callboxlive.com**), a series of digital filmmaker training courses on DVD. Noah also works as a forum administrator for 2-pop.com, Creative-Cow.com, and DVXuser.com

Stephen Kanter

Stephen Kanter is an Avid and Apple Certified editor who has worked in television, documentaries, and feature films as an editor, producer, and post-production supervisor. An Apple Certified Trainer since the program began, he is the technical editor for much of the Apple Pro Training Series, including Final Cut Pro, Final Cut Pro for Avid Editors, DVD Studio Pro, and Soundtrack Pro. Based in Los Angeles, Mr. Kanter currently works as a freelance editor and trainer for UCLA, Moviola, and Weynand Training. He is a member of the Editors Guild. Visit his web site at web.mac.com/editdog.

Mike Krause

Mike Krause is a Los Angeles-based Apple Certified editor with experience in television and independent film and music, as well as DVD production. Previously an Avid Assistant Editor and ACSR technician, Mike made the jump to Final Cut Pro three years ago. He is currently the lead editor at one of the largest DVD production facilities in the world. Mike's current favorite program is LiveType.

Tom Meegan

Tom Meegan is the creative director of Woven Pixels Productions, a media production and consulting business in Central New Hampshire. He has been in broadcast television production for 20 years and has won 2 New England Emmy Awards for lighting design, and he was nominated for his work as a coordinating producer. He edits for the MLB World Series on Fox Network, the NBA Finals, the Olympics, and Wimbledon. He is an Apple Certified Trainer for Final Cut Pro. Visit his web site at **www.wovenpixels.com**.

Kevin Monahan

Kevin Monahan is a video editor and motion graphics artist living in San Francisco. He is the president and cofounder of the world's first FCP User Group, SF Cutters. Kevin has worked on projects at such companies as Apple, Electronic Arts, and Pixar. He is also the author of *Motion Graphics and Effects in Final Cut Pro* (Peachpit). Visit Kevin at **www.sfcutters.org**.

Graeme Nattress

Graeme Nattress, the technical editor of *Edit Well*, is a software developer who specializes in cutting-edge algorithms for the improvement of video quality. Nattress Productions, Inc. offers special-effects filters and plug-ins for Final Cut Pro. Graeme is a frequent contributor to kenstone.net, LAFCPUG, DV Info Net, and DVXuser.com and is the **www.red.com** Problem Solver. Visit his web site at **www.nattress.com**.

Bruce Nazarian

Bruce Nazarian is an award-winning DVD producer and author, and the newly-elected president of the DVD Association. Bruce recently completed *DVD Studio Pro 4: The Complete Guide to DVD Authoring with Macintosh* (McGraw-Hill). He is president of Gnome Digital Media, his DVD and media production company in Los Angeles. Visit his web site at **www.Recipe4DVD.com**.

Bryan Peel

Bryan Peel is a producer and editor, as well as the owner of Keyframe Communications Inc. TV broadcasting has been in his family for years. Bryan self-taught himself when introduced to one of the first non-linear editing systems. His past projects include local and national TV commercials, infomercials, documentaries, and series programs. Some of his current work is available online at **www.keyframeinc.com**.

Mary Plummer

Mary Plummer has been editing and composing music professionally for more than 16 years. An Apple Certified Master Trainer, she has authored Apple Pro Training Series books on Soundtrack, Soundtrack Pro, and Motion, as well as books on Final Cut Studio and GarageBand. She is co-owner of InVision Digital and Media Arts, Inc., an Apple Authorized Training Center located at Universal Studios in Orlando, Florida. Visit her web site at **www.invisiondigital.com**.

Kevin Shea

Kevin Shea is a graduate of Northern Illinois University. He has a B.A. in Art with a minor in Communications, with concentrations on video production and graphic design. Kevin has been using Final Cut for six years and is an Apple Certified Trainer in Digital Media. Kevin is a creative engineer with MacSpecialist, an Apple Specialist reseller in the Chicago area. He has also taught video editing for the University of St. Francis in Joliet, Illinois.

Mark Spencer

Mark Spencer is a freelance producer, editor, teacher, and author working in the San Francisco Bay Area. He is an Apple-Certified Master Trainer for Final Cut Pro, Motion, and DVD Studio Pro; is a coauthor of the Apple Pro Training Series books: *Motion 3* and *Motion Graphics and Effects in Final Cut Studio 2* from Peachpit; is the host of the Motion Fast Forward and Motion Deep Dive tutorials from Ripple Training; and maintains the Motion-dedicated site **applemotion.net**.

Alexis Van Hurkman

Alexis Van Hurkman is a writer, director, colorist, and effects artist. As a postproduction artist, Alexis has created effects for the award-winning short subject Artistic License, and color-corrected the feature *Souvenir* and the television pilot "FBI Guys." As a filmmaker, Alexis's feature debut, *Four Weeks, Four Hours,* has screened at the 2006 San Fernando Valley, Portland Longbaugh, and Toronto ReelHeART film festivals. His written work includes several Apple Pro Training Series titles including *Encyclopedia of Color Correction,* as well as contributions to the Final Cut Pro, Color, and Shake User Manuals. Visit his web site at **www.alexisvanhurkman.com**.

Tom Wolsky

Tom Wolsky is a former ABC News producer and operations manager in London and New York. He now has a boutique production company in northern California and has been teaching Final Cut Pro since it came out. He teaches for Digital Media Academy and has written a number of books, articles, and DVDs on Final Cut Pro, Final Cut Express, video production, and video journalism. Visit his web site at **www.SouthCoastTV.com**.

Introduction

I first started thinking about creating Edit Well in August of 2005. I had been training editors in Final Cut Pro for two years as an Apple Certified Trainer and had begun traveling around North America on seminar tours.

Everywhere I went, I met people with a real hunger to learn more about the finer points of editing with Final Cut Pro. I was struck by the incredible range of projects they were working on—from home movies for the family, to broadcast television and feature films. By far, the majority of those I met were self-employed editors working on documentaries, events, and corporate productions.

As individuals, they needed a fast way to stay current in the industry and improve their skills. And from that need, Edit Well was born.

After putting out the publication alone the first year, I eventually found a home for Edit Well with Peachpit, the publisher of computer graphics, design, and digital video books. Many of the contributors of Edit Well are esteemed authors of books in the Apple Pro Training Series and are top-notch in their fields—they constitute a Who's Who of experts and practicing professionals. Check out their bios on the preceding pages.

We launched the first issue of Edit Well on June 26, 2006, as a PDF delivered via e-mail: five articles covering the applications contained in Final Cut Studio, at least two audio interviews, one video tutorial, at least a dozen keyboard shortcuts, and lots of interesting odds and ends all revolving around Final Cut Studio. As of this writing, we have published 155 articles, 80 interviews, and hundreds of keyboard shortcuts.

What's in the Book and at the Companion Web Site

This book contains some of the top articles featured in Edit Well that are as current today as when we originally published them. It's packed with step-by-step instructions on using the tools in Final Cut Studio, tips and techniques from in-the-trenches editors, and keyboard shortcuts to make your work smoother and faster.

Throughout the book are sidebars that point to the companion Web site at:

www.peachpit.com/editwellbook

Here you can download video tutorials and fascinating audio interviews with industry leaders and editors from all around the world.

This book is divided into six sections, representing the key areas we cover:

- Editing in Final Cut Pro

- Effects in Final Cut Pro

- Motion 3D

- Soundtrack Pro

- Color

- Everything else

Whether you decide to read the entire book from cover to cover, or just skip around picking the subjects you are interested in, I guarantee you'll learn something that will be useful to you on just about every page.

Taking It Further

I encourage you to check the Edit Well Web page frequently and take advantage of the information you'll find there. While we no longer publish the magazine as a PDF, Edit Well continues to thrive on the Web. When there are updates in Final Cut Studio, we're often the first to publish on topics that editors care most about. Hopefully, if you like what you see, you'll join our community. You can find the details at www.peachpit.com/editwell.

Creating each issue of Edit Well has been a labor of love and deadlines and a fair amount of stress, but basically a great time. I hope you enjoy reading our favorite articles.

Take care and edit well.

—Larry Jordan
  Founder & Editor-in-Chief

Part 1
Final Cut Pro Editing

At its heart, Final Cut Pro is a video editor. More specifically, it is a QuickTime movie editor. Even though Final Cut Pro has more bells and whistles than a steam calliope, the reason that hundreds of thousands of editors turn to it every day is because they want to edit their video.

So that seems like a good place to start for us as well.

There is a flow—a process—to editing. It starts with planning what you want to do, followed by editing the story, adding transitions and effects, sweetening the audio, correcting the color, and producing the output. When you're in the thick of a project, it's easy to get distracted and waste time. Keeping these steps in mind allows you to focus on the task at hand.

To this end, the first chapter in this part tackles the process of building your story. Kevin Shea explains how to customize the interface of Final Cut Pro. Like any working environment, it is more fun, and faster, to work in a space where you feel comfortable.

Clay Asbury then gets right to the core: how to edit and trim your clips faster. There are tips in this chapter that can save you up to five seconds per edit. This chapter alone can save you hours in every project!

Once the story is built, Kevin Monahan shares his ideas on how to create more interesting transitions. More importantly, he explains when and why to use transitions effectively.

Tom Wolsky then answers a perennial question from new Final Cut users: How do I export a still frame? He has a step-by-step approach that provides the answers, including a few tips on manipulating your images in Photoshop, as well.

Film is shot at 24 frames per second. Video in North America is viewed at 30 frames per second (29.97 frames per second to be technically accurate). The difference between these two frame rates is handled by pull-down frames. Sometimes you want them, sometimes you don't. Noah Kadner shows you how to get rid of them when you don't want them.

Finally, as the video industry continues its transition from recording images on videotape to digital, the issue of how to archive media becomes increasingly important. Ah, make that vital. There's nothing worse than losing all your media, and the final chapter from Bryan Peel will help prevent that trauma.

Throughout this section you'll discover links to some interesting audio interviews, video tutorials, and some helpful keyboard shortcuts.

Chapter 1

Customizing the Final Cut Pro Interface

KEVIN SHEA

The best part about moving into a new office is customizing it so it feels comfortable to work in. Final Cut Pro is just the same. It's more fun, and efficient, to work with when you customize it. Best of all, there's no limit to the number of customized settings you can create.

Customize Your Workflow

A Final Cut instructor once addressed the members of a class I attended by saying, "Final Cut was designed specifically for you." What he meant was that while there is a default layout to everything in the interface, almost the entire interface can be customized. Therefore, Final Cut was designed with you specifically in mind. It can adapt to your idiosyncrasies.

Let's say you come to the stage in your workflow where you need to begin building a rough cut. Wouldn't it be great if you could click a few times and call up a specific list of Browser columns, a series of button bars with all your favorite commands, an intuitive set of track heights, a workflow-specific set of keyboard shortcuts, and an aesthetically-pleasing window arrangement that fits your own personal needs? You can! It's all there, waiting for you to pick and choose your favorites in each category.

Who knows what impact a more intuitively laid-out interface could have on your editing. You'll discover that customizing the interface can actually save you a lot of time. For instance, what if you were able to shave two seconds off each action you execute thanks to customization? How many actions does it take to complete a simple project? Let's say, for the sake of argument, the answer is

5,000 actions. Well, two seconds times 5,000 equals almost three hours per project. What if you did one simple project a week? That would mean you saved almost four weeks of time each year—time you could use for more projects, or sleep, or perhaps a well-deserved week's vacation!

There are five main areas of customization:

- Window layouts
- Button bars
- Browser layouts
- Track heights
- Keyboard layouts

Window Layouts

You can reposition, resize, close, minimize, or optimize each of the main windows of the Final Cut interface. Multiple windows can be synchronously resized by dragging the border between any two windows. For instance, dragging the border between the Browser and the Viewer in the default window layout will resize the Browser inversely to the Viewer and Canvas. Increase the size of the Browser, and the Viewer and Canvas will decrease in size. The same resizing rules apply when you drag the border between the Timeline and the Browser, Viewer, and Canvas.

Your cursor indicates when it is in the right place to resize a window by turning into a double-pointing arrow.

You can load and save custom window layouts by choosing **Window > Arrange**. There are several preset window layouts from which to choose (the list expands when you add a second monitor to your workstation). Since you have the freedom to rearrange and resize the windows in the interface, feel free to make your own window layouts.

Audio Profile

ED KAUFHOLZ
Freelance editor, **ESPN**

What do a golf ball and Final Cut Studio have in common? They both regularly appear at ESPN golf tournaments. Working Final Cut's controls right in the television remote truck is Ed Kaufholz, long-time video editor on the Masters Golf circuit. Visit the companion Web site to hear this audio profile.

If you choose **Window > Arrange > Save Window Layout**, you can save your custom window layouts. Window layouts are saved in the folder at the end of this file path: /Users/[username]/Library/Preferences/Final Cut Pro User Data/ Window Layouts. Once you save a custom window layout, you can call it up by choosing Window > Arrange, as you would call up the preset layouts.

Saved window layouts are set according to the screen resolution in which they are created. You can make the proportions of the layout automatically adjust to different resolutions by choosing **Auto-Aspect Layout** from the Format pop-up menu in the window layout Save dialog (**FIGURE 1.1**).

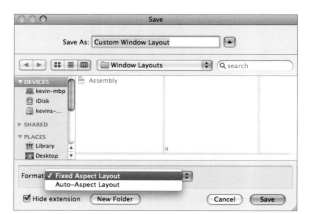

FIGURE 1.1: Custom window layout Save dialog.

Video Tutorial: Troubleshooting Your Final Cut Pro System

To see how you can optimize and troubleshoot your Final Cut system, please visit the book's companion Web site.

Button Bars

There are plenty of handy tools to be found in the Tools menu. One of these is the button bars function. Every window of Final Cut's interface has a button bar. By default, the only windows that contain populated button bars are the Timeline and Audio Mixer. But we can place buttons for just about any command in these button bars.

NOTE: Buttons can only contain menu choices. They can't contain clips, effects, or scripts.

Button bars are nothing without the Button List (**FIGURE 1.2**), also found in the Tools menu. (See the sidebar, "The Button List," for information.) Find a command in the Button List, and then drag the command into any of the button bars in the interface. The bar will open to receive the button as you drag it in (**FIGURE 1.3**). Repeat as necessary.

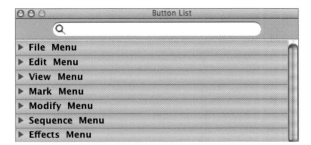

FIGURE 1.2:
The Button List.

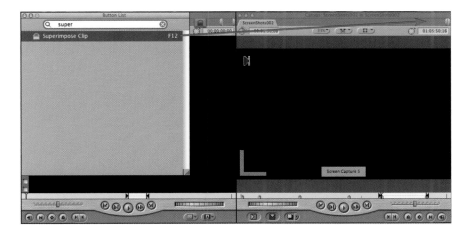

FIGURE 1.3: Adding buttons to button bars is as easy as dragging them from the Button List to the button container in the upper-right corner of every Final Cut window.

Audio Profile

PHILIP BLOOM
Director of Photography, Editor, Director, **www.philipbloom.co.uk**

 Philip Bloom is a UK-based DP, editor, and director with credits on the BBC and SkyOne, among many others. Visit the companion Web site to discover more about his process of shooting and editing XDCAM HD using Final Cut Pro.

The Button List

The Tools menu houses a wonderful tool called the Button List, an often-underestimated tool for Final Cut users. The Button List is an index of every menu command in Final Cut Pro, presented with corresponding keyboard shortcuts and button icons. You can search through commands grouped according to the menu in which they reside or in collections of relative items. You can also type either the command or its shortcut into the search bar at the top of the Button List window. As you type, the list refines to display only commands that contain what you have typed thus far.

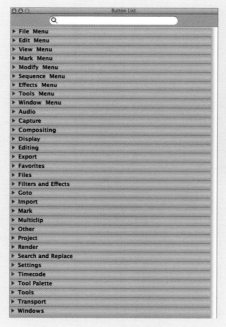

Because each command is listed with its shortcut, the Button List also works great as a "command-to-shortcut" dictionary. Let's say you can't remember the shortcut for Superimpose. Type superimpose into the search bar, and by the time you get to the "r" in superimpose, there is only one line item displayed. And right there, next to the command name, is the shortcut.

Once a button is in a button bar, it can be further customized by right-clicking to reveal a shortcut menu with the options to change the button's color or add a spacer (**FIGURE 1.4**). You can remove a button or an entire button bar by right-clicking it and choosing **Remove > Button or Remove > All Buttons**.

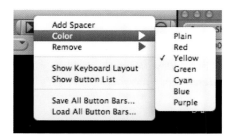

FIGURE 1.4: This contextual menu displays for buttons.

Button bars are saved globally (all button bars from every window save in one preference file). Whether you choose **Tool > Button Bars** or right-click any button bar in the interface, when you choose to save your button bars, they are saved in the folder /Users/[username]/Library/Preferences/Final Cut Pro User Data/Button Bars.

Browser Layouts

The Browser contains over 50 columns storing data about the clips and sequences in your project. This information (also called "metadata") is sorted into vertical columns when the Browser is displayed in List view.

NOTE: List view is the default view for items in the Browser. Browser items can also be displayed as icons of various sizes. You can switch between the different views by choosing View > Browser Items or by right-clicking in the Name column of the Browser.

Dragging column headers left or right can reorganize columns in the Browser, which helps to place the most pertinent information where you need it. However, not all Browser columns are visible all the time. To discover more than 20 hidden columns, Control-click any column header except the Name column.

NOTE: Any column with the word "Comment" in its name (Master Comment 1, for example), can be renamed. Simply right-click that column's header and choose Edit Heading. There are six columns in the Browser that can be renamed this way. However, if you attempt to find something in a renamed column, you will need to use the original name in the Find window for it to work. Also, the original name of the column is used in batch lists.

Once you reorganize your Browser's columns, right-click any column header and choose **Save Column Layout** (**FIGURE 1.5**). Column layouts are saved in the folder /Users/[username]/Library/Preferences/Final Cut Pro User Data/Column Layouts. Once a layout is saved, it can be accessed from the same shortcut menu where you can show/hide columns, rename column headers, and save layouts.

Timeline Track Heights

You can choose from four preset track heights by toggling the Timeline Track Heights button (or by pressing **Shift+T**), or you can choose one from the Time-line Layout pop-up menu (**FIGURE 1.6**). Did you know that each track could be made a different height? Or that you can make all of the video tracks one cus-tom height and all of the audio tracks a different custom height in a few simple steps? And then save your custom track heights for recall at any time?

FIGURE 1.6: To access the Timeline controls, you can toggle the Timeline Track Heights button or Control-click the small right-pointing arrow labeled "Timeline Layout Popup."

It all starts in the Timeline patch panel in the left of the Timeline. Drag the horizontal boundary between two tracks to resize individual tracks to custom heights. Using this method you could resize each track to a different custom height.

If you want all the tracks to be the same custom height, press and hold **Shift** as you resize a single track. All tracks inherit your custom height. If you would like your video tracks to be one custom height and your audio tracks to be a differ-ent custom height, press and hold **Option** as you drag to resize a single track. If the track you resized was a video track, all of your video tracks will inherit the custom track height you just set.

Once you have set your tracks to custom heights, you can save the track heights as a Track Layout in the Timeline Layout pop-up menu. Track Layouts are saved in the folder /Users/[username]/Library/Preferences/Final Cut Pro User Data/Track Layouts.

FIGURE 1.5: Browser column shortcut menu. You can access this by Control-click-ing any column heading except the Name column. This menu illustrates the additional fields of data that are tracked for each clip but hidden in the default layout of the Browser.

Keyboard Layouts

Did you know there are over 650 menu choices inside Final Cut? And there are hundreds of default keyboard shortcuts. But not all menu choices have keyboard shortcuts created by default.

All of that can change when you choose **Tools > Keyboard Layout**. A dialog opens that displays a model of your keyboard, a series of tabs representing nearly every modifier key combination, and a representation of the Button List, used to look up commands for assignment (**FIGURE 1.7**). Remember, before you can make any changes, you have to unlock the window by clicking the Lock button in the lower-left corner.

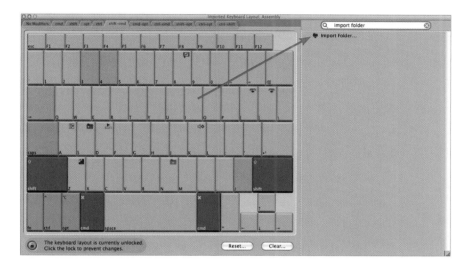

FIGURE 1.7: Customizing keyboard layouts. The keyboard layout will change, depending upon what keyboard you have connected to your Mac.

In the search field in the right pane of the dialog, you can search to find a command and its keyboard shortcut, if there is one. Click one of the modifier tabs at the top of the left pane to target that specific combination of keystrokes. At this point, you can drag the command from your search results in the right pane and drop it on a key in the keyboard display to assign that keystroke to that command.

After completing a number of keyboard customizations, you can save your customized keyboard layout by choosing **Tools > Keyboard Layouts > Save Keyboard Layout**. Keyboard layouts are saved in the folder /Users/[username]/ Library/Preferences/Final Cut Pro User Data/Keyboard Layouts.

Don't Lose Your Preferences

What is one of the first troubleshooting steps for when Final Cut goes awry? Trash your preferences. But trashing your preferences means trashing your customizations. There goes that week's vacation, right? Wrong.

As long as you save your customizations to disk, they will always be available to you. The only time you need to worry about losing a customized setting is when you don't save it to disk and you trash your Final Cut preferences, because unsaved custom settings are stored in your preference files.

I always tell my students, "There is no wrong way of doing something, so long as the project gets done." There is no wrong way to use Final Cut. And there is no wrong way to set up the Final Cut interface. They call these "preferences" for a reason: Because it sets the system to look and act as you prefer.

So go ahead, customize the interface. Remember what my own instructor said, "Final Cut was designed specifically for you." Use these tools to make it your own.

Chapter 2

Techniques for Smarter Selection and Trimming

CLAY ASBURY

During a rough edit, you are not worried about the exact length of each clip; you are focusing on telling the story. From there you tighten up your story with each editing pass, working from the rough cut to the fine cut. With each pass you finesse and refine the edit.

Final Cut Pro has a wide array of selection tools at your disposal, the key is to find ways to get your work done faster using the right selection tool or a few handy keyboard shortcuts. The goal is to work smarter not harder.

Faster Selections

Selection comes before trimming, so here are some techniques to help you make faster selections.

> ### Video: Selecting
>
> To see a short video demonstration of selections, please visit the book's companion Web site.

An often-forgotten tool is the Edit Selection tool (**FIGURE 2.1**). It is located directly below the Selection tool in the Tool palette, and really consists of three tools:

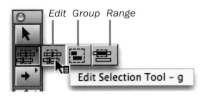

- Edit Selection tool (G)

- Group Selection tool (GG)

- Range Selection tool (GGG)

FIGURE 2.1: The three selection tools: Edit (left), Group (center), and Range (right)

To use the Edit Selection tool, press **G**, then click and drag over the ends of a clip to select it (in effect, lassoing the end of the clip).

NOTE: When you use a specialized tool, always remember to switch back to the Selection tool by pressing A.

Here's another technique you can use to select an edit point:

1. Move the playhead close to the edit point you want to select.

2. Press **V**, and the playhead jumps to the nearest edit point.

3. Press **U** to toggle between selecting the In point and the Out point (**FIGURE 2.2**).

FIGURE 2.2: Pressing U toggles between selecting the In point, the Out point (shown on left), or both (shown on right). In the left example, the Out point is selected, which allows you to ripple trim the Out point.

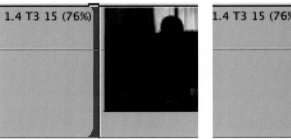
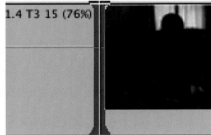

To preview an edit:

1. Turn on loop playback by pressing **Control+L**, or choose **View > Loop Playback**.

2. Press \, or click the Play Around Current Frame button (see **FIGURE 2.3**).

3. Press the < or > keys to trim as the edit loops in real time.

FIGURE 2.3: The Play Around Current Frame button.

Faster Trimming

Once you have the edit point selected, it's time to trim. There are a variety of techniques you can use to speed your trimming, such as using the extend edit and trimming numerically, which we'll discuss next.

NOTE: To get the most accurate trims, be sure snapping is turned off (choose View > Snapping to turn off snapping if it's selected, or press N). Also, in order to trim any clip, it needs to have handles—extra video before the In or after the Out.

Keyboard Shortcuts for Trimming Left and Right

SHORTCUT	FUNCTION
V	Moves the playhead to the nearest edit point
U	Toggles between selecting the In point, the Out point, or both
Comma	Trims the selected edit point left one frame at a time
Period	Trims the selected edit point right one frame at a time
Shift+< or Shift+>	Trims left or right multiple frames. By default, this trims in five-frame increments. The number of frames can be changed by choosing Final Cut Pro > User Preferences, and entering the number of frames in the Editing tab.

User Preferences

| General | Editing | Labels | Timeline Options | Render Control | Audio Outputs |

Still/Freeze Duration:	00:00:10:00
Preview Pre-roll:	00:00:02:00
Preview Post-roll:	00:00:02:00

☐ Dynamic Trimming
☑ Trim with Sequence Audio
☐ Trim with Edit Selection Audio (Mute Others)
Multi-Frame Trim Size: ☐ 5 ☐ frames

In the Editing tab, you can change the number of frames trimmed ("5" is shown here) using the shortcuts Shift+< or Shift+>.

> ### Video: Trimming
>
> To see a short demonstration of trimming, please visit the book's companion Web site.

The Extend Edit

The extend edit is a high-speed roll edit, except instead of using the Roll tool, we are using a keystroke. When we perform a roll, we are making one clip longer and the other clip shorter. We are not affecting the overall length of the sequence.

> ### Video: The Extend Edit
>
> To see a short demonstration of the extend edit, please visit the book's companion Web site.

Here are the steps:

1. Press **A** to access the Selection tool.

2. Select the edit point you want to trim.

3. Move the playhead to where you want the new edit to occur.

4. Press **E** to perform the edit.

You can also perform the extend edit "on the fly" while you play the footage. Here's how:

1. Press **A** to access the Selection tool.

2. Select the edit point you want to trim.

3. Move the playhead prior to where you want the edit to occur.

4. Play the sequence, and press **E** when the playhead is where you want the new edit.

The extend edit also works well for making several clips on multiple tracks the same length—for instance, when you want all the clips in a multi-layer effect to end at the same time. To create this, do the following:

1. Select either the In or Out point of a clip.

2. Use the Edit Selection tool (G), or press and hold the **Command** key, and select the other edit points you want to move (**FIGURE 2.4**).

3. Move the playhead where you want the selected edit points to roll, and press **E**.

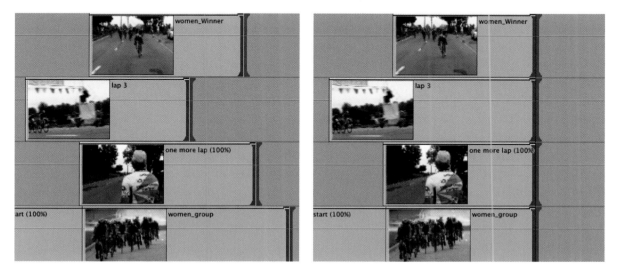

FIGURE 2.4: You can use the extend edit to roll all selected edit points to the position of the playhead by pressing **E**.

Keyboard Shortcuts for Marking In and Out Points

SHORTCUT	FUNCTION
I	Sets the In point
O	Sets the Out point
Shift+I	Jumps the playhead to the In point
Shift+O	Jumps the playhead to the Out point
Option+I	Clears the In point
Option+O	Clears the Out point
Option+X	Clears both In and Out points

Trimming by Numbers

If you liked trimming with the < and the > keys, you're gonna love trimming numerically, which is a very fast way to work.

1. Select an edit point.

REMINDER: If both sides of the edit point are selected, you are performing a roll. If you select the left side of the edit, the clip ripples the Out of the preceding clip. If you select the right side, the clip ripples the In of the following clip.

2. Press the plus sign (+), then enter a number, which shifts the selected edit point to the right.

3. Press the minus sign (-), then enter a number, which shifts the selected edit point to the left.

Trimming in the Viewer

You can also trim in the Viewer. To do so, double-click a clip from the Timeline to load it into the Viewer. Using the Ripple or Roll tool, grab the edit point you want to trim and drag it. The large image in the Viewer shows the In point, and the Canvas shows the Out.

The benefit to trimming in the Viewer is that you get larger images, plus the ability to see how much handle you have to work with for the clip.

Slipping a Clip

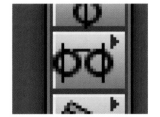

Slipping is a way to trim the contents of a clip, rather than just the In or the Out points. Slipping a clip changes the contents of a clip but not its duration or position in the Timeline (**FIGURE 2.5**).

> ### Video: Slipping
>
> To see a short demonstration of slipping a clip, please visit the book's companion Web site.

FIGURE 2.5: The Slip tool (S).

There are lots of uses for a slip edit—especially for music, sports highlights, and placing B-roll. Let's say you have edited a clip to the Timeline but need to slip it slightly to get it into the beat of the music. With the Slip tool, this is a simple task. Another use is adjusting the timing so you "cut on action"; for instance, cutting from one shot of a baseball player starting to swing to a shot of a player hitting the ball (the second clip finishes the action of the first). You can use the Slip tool to retime the clips so the first shot ends right before the ball is hit and the second shot starts when the ball is hit.

Here's one way to do a slip edit:

1. Double-click a clip to load it into the Viewer.

2. Move the playhead to the frame where you want the shot to start.

3. Select the Slip tool by pressing **S**.

4. Position the pointer over the In point. The pointer changes to the Slip tool.

5. Click and drag the edit point to match the position of the playhead.

6. You can also turn the Selection tool into the Slip tool by pressing and hold-ing **Shift**, then dragging the clip to a new position. This technique works in both the Viewer and the Timeline.

Here's another way to slip a clip. Let's say the clip is in the Timeline, and you want to change the In point:

1. Double-click the clip in the Timeline to load it into the Viewer. You'll see two rows of dots in the Viewer (**FIGURE 2.6**).

2. Press and hold **Shift**, and drag the In or the Out with the playhead. The duration of the clip remains constant, but the content changes.

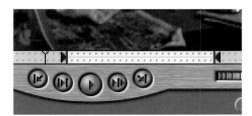

FIGURE 2.6: The two rows of gray dots in the playhead scrubber bar of the Viewer indicate that a clip has been loaded into the Viewer from the Timeline.

Trimming with Final Cut Pro is the fine-tuning that gives you the power to polish your story. The point of these techniques is to make you a quicker, more effi-cient editor, allowing you to spend more time telling your story.

Audio Profile

SHANE ROSS
Editor, **lfhd.net**

 Shane Ross edits high-profile documentaries for the Discovery and History Channels. In this interview (on the companion Web site), discover how he works with really big projects and the techniques he uses to bring his documentaries to life.

Keyboard Shortcuts for Selection Tools

SHORTCUT	FUNCTION
A	Selects the Arrow tool
G	Selects edit points only
G+G	Selects a clip(s) without being able to move a clip
G+G+G	Selects a portion of a video or audio clip
T	Selects all clips on the same track to the right of where this tool is clicked (including audio, if linked)
T+T	Selects all clips on the same track to the left of where this tool is clicked (including audio, if linked)
T+T+T	Selects all clips on the same track to the right and left of where this tool is clicked (including audio, if linked)
T+T+T+T	Selects all clips on all tracks to the right of where this tool is clicked
T+T+T+T+T	Selects all clips on all tracks to the left of where this tool is clicked
Option-click with Selection tool	Selects just the audio or just the video of a linked clip
Control-click the red flag of an out-of-sync clip with Selection tool	Selects "Move into Sync" to move an out-of-sync clip back into sync
Command+A	Selects all clips in sequences
Shift+Command+A	Deselects all selected clips in sequences

Chapter 3

Transitions: Beyond the Straight Cut

KEVIN MONAHAN

Dissolves are but one of many transitions found in Final Cut Pro. However, that doesn't mean you should use every transition in a single production. In fact, as a rule of thumb, transitions should be used very sparingly. Of course, you probably already know this, so I won't go into detail about the pros and cons of using transitions (**FIGURE 3.1**). Instead, I will try to give you new tips on using transitions. But first, let's review how to apply them.

FIGURE 3.1: If you pick your images wisely, a dissolve can be very effective.

Applying Transitions

Transitions are easy enough to apply. In fact, there are three different ways you can apply a transition:

- Select the edit point and use a keyboard shortcut.

- Select the edit point, choose **Effect > Video Transitions**, and select your transition from the menu.

- Drag the transition you want from the Effects tab of the Browser.

If you cannot apply the transition with any of these methods, then you don't have enough media "handles" (**FIGURE 3.2**). Handles are extra video before the In and after the Out. When you have a handle on only one side of the cut, you can still apply the transition but you'll need to adjust it so that it either starts or ends on the edit point.

How do you get handles? Just ripple-trim back one or both sides of the edit and then you'll have handles to add the transition to the cut.

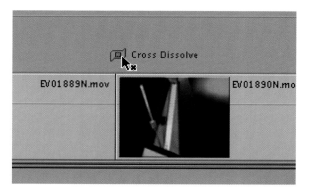

FIGURE 3.2: If you attempt to drag and drop a transition to a cut, and an "X" appears, you don't have sufficient handles.

Video Tutorial: Open Format Timeline

New with Final Cut Pro 6 is the ability to conform, or change, the sequence to match the video format of the first clip you edit into it, then conform every succeeding clip to match the sequence. Please visit the book's companion Web site to see a demonstration of this powerful new feature.

Changing the Default Transition

Want a fast way to add a video transition? Just select an edit by clicking it (or press V if the playhead is near the edit) and press **Cmd+T**. This adds the default video transition to the cut, which is a 30-frame cross-dissolve. To apply the default audio transition, press **Option+Cmd+T**.

To change the default transition, locate the transition you want to use as a new default in the Effects tab of the Browser, then Control-click it. In the shortcut menu that appears, choose Set Default Transition, and then the new default transition will be applied whenever you select a cut and press **Cmd+T** (or **Option+Cmd+T**).

Insert and Overwrite with Transition

You may already be aware that using the Insert with Transition and Overwrite with Transition drop zones in the Canvas Overlay menu allows you to edit a clip into the Timeline with the default transition intact. But did you know that there are keyboard shortcuts that also perform these edits, as well? For a quick way to add an Insert with Transition, press **Shift+F9**; for Overwrite with Transition, press **Shift+F10**.

Creating a montage with a transition between each shot? If so, you can group a set of clips in storyboard order using Icon view in the Browser (**FIGURE 3.3**), then drag them all into one of the Edit with Transition overlays (**FIGURE 3.4**). In the Timeline, a transition is added to each clip in the group, provided, of course, that each clip has sufficient handles.

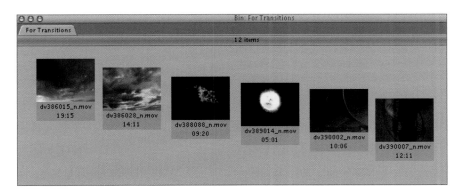

FIGURE 3.3: To edit clips from the Browser to the Canvas, stagger the clips from left to right in a "stair-step" pattern to force the clips to edit into the Timeline in the proper order.

FIGURE 3.4: Drag the clips from the Timeline into the Overwrite with Transition overlay to add multiple transitions to existing cuts.

Adding the Default Transition to Multiple Clips on the Same Video Track

What if you edit many clips into the Timeline, all using cuts, and now want the default transition applied after the fact? Easily done! Just do the following:

1. Make sure all clips have handles.

2. Select the Timeline.

3. Press **Option+X** to remove any Timeline edit points.

4. Place the playhead at the In of the first clip in the group.

5. Select all the clips to which you want to add the transition.

6. Drag the clips into the Canvas and drop them onto the Insert with Transition or Overwrite with Transition overlay menu.

Your edit now has the default transition applied between every cut. Pretty cool, huh?

Adding the Default Transition to Multiple Clips on Different Video Tracks

If you've ever stacked up clips on different video tracks and then wanted to add the default transition to each clip, you probably applied it one edit point at a time. A better method involves using the Edit Selection tool to marquee around the edit points to which you wish to add transitions (**FIGURE 3.5**). The Trim Edit window launches, but you won't need it, so close the window by pressing **Cmd+W**. Note that your edits are still selected after the window closes. Since your edits are selected, just press **Cmd+T** to add the default video transition to all selected edit points.

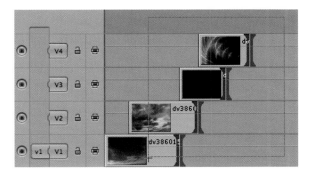

FIGURE 3.5: Select multiple edits across multiple tracks with the Edit Selection tool (press G).

NOTE: You can also select multiple edits points on different tracks by Cmd-clicking them.

Modifying a Transition's Parameters

It's simple to modify a transition. All you need to do is double-click the transition icon to open the Transition Editor inside the Viewer. You can also Control-click the transition icon and choose **Open "Transition Name"** from the shortcut menu.

Once in the Transition Editor (**FIGURE 3.6**), you can adjust parameters until you get the desired effect. Here you can also reset the transition back to its defaults by clicking the small red "X" in a circle. The small button with an arrow over a transition icon will reverse a transition's motion, and the upper section of the window will allow you to trim the transition to adjust its timing.

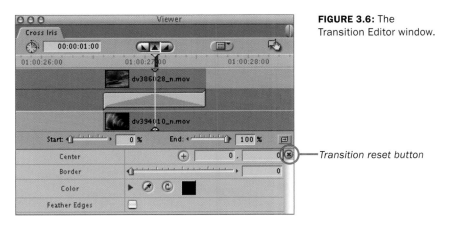

FIGURE 3.6: The Transition Editor window.

Transition reset button

Modifying a Transition's Timing

After you've added a transition, oftentimes you will want to slightly alter the timing to make it move faster or slower. There are several ways to do this, mostly having to do with trimming the transition or changing the duration of the transition itself.

Here is one way to change the duration of the transition:

1.   Control-click the transition and choose **Duration** from the shortcut menu.

2.   In the pop-up window that appears, enter the new duration and then click **OK**.

NOTE: A variation on this is to click the transition icon and press Control+D. This opens the Duration dialog, where you can change the duration.

Second, you can drag the edges of the transition icon to make it shorter or longer.

A third way is to open the transition in the Transition Editor by double-clicking the transition icon, entering a new value in the Duration field (found in the upper-left corner of the window), and pressing **Enter**.

Another way is to trim the transition. To move the transition to a new place in the Timeline:

1.   Select the Roll tool (or press **R**).

2.   Click the center of the transition icon to select the edit point.

3.   If necessary, turn off snapping (press **N**).

4.   Drag the transition to a new position, up to the limit of the handles on each side of the edit point.

NOTE: You can also select the edit point and use the bracket keys [] to reposition the transition on a frame-by-frame basis.

If you want to alter the beginning and/or ending frames within a transition, you can use the Ripple Trim tool. Select the edit with the Ripple Trim tool and drag it to a new position, or press the bracket keys to trim frame by frame (**FIGURE 3.7**).

FIGURE 3.7: Click and drag the dark blue bars above or below the transition icon to ripple trim the transition. The light blue portion of the bar indicates the clip's handle.

In the Transition Editor window, you can also drag the transition icon to roll the edit point, or drag the dark blue bars above or below the transition icon to ripple the edit point. The two-up window will be your guide as you tweak the new position (with a Roll edit) of the transition or the new images for the outgoing and incoming frames (with a Ripple edit). You can also use the Trim Edit window to fine-tune the timing of your transition.

TIP: It's always a good idea to preview your effect before you render it. I usually preview my effects right in the Canvas in real time. To do this, set the RT pop-up menu in the upper-left corner of the Timeline to Unlimited RT with the Playback Quality and Frame Rate set to Dynamic. Even cooler, you can choose Tools > Quickview if you like to adjust the effect as the transition loops.

Adding a Custom Transition to Another Cut

Once you've dialed-in your transition, you'll often want to add it to another cut. There are a few ways to do this: Use the Drag Hand in the Transition Editor, the copy and paste method, or save the transition as a Favorite and drag and drop it to the desired cut.

The Drag Hand feature (**FIGURE 3.8**) is the simplest way to copy a custom transition. Just open the transition into the Transition Editor and then drag the transition from the Drag Hand icon (it looks like a hand holding a transition) in the upper-right corner of the window to the new cut.

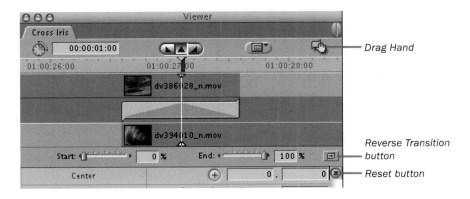

Drag Hand

Reverse Transition button

Reset button

FIGURE 3.8: The Drag Hand icon, the Reverse Transition button and the Reset button.

You can copy and paste the transition to a new cut as well. Just select the transition and press **Cmd+C**. Make sure to place the playhead and then select the edit (press **V** to move the playhead to the nearest edit point and select it) where you wish to place the custom transition, and then press **Cmd+V** to paste the transition into place. Want something even easier? Just Option-drag the transition to a new edit point to copy your transition.

If you've created a cool transition, want to add it to another cut, and then save it for later, you can create a favorite transition and drag and drop it to a new cut. To do this, open it into the Transition Editor, and with the Viewer still selected, choose **Effects > Make Favorite Effect**. Your customized transition is now stored in the Favorites bin in the Effects tab. Rename it if you like. To apply your carefully crafted transition, just click and drag it to the new cut.

NOTE: Favorite transitions are stored in your Final Cut Preferences files. Trashing preferences will delete all favorite transitions and effects. To save a favorite permanently, drag it into the Project folder in the Browser.

Organizing Custom Transitions

Now that you know how to make custom transitions, wouldn't it be nice if they were neatly organized instead of splayed all over the Favorites bin? And you can't make bins in the Favorites bin to keep them organized—or can you?

Although you can't physically create a bin in the Favorites bin, you can create one in the Project tab and drag it over into the Favorites bin. You can drag in new bins as needed to hold different categories of custom transitions (**FIGURE 3.9**). This way, you can keep all your custom dissolves, wipes, or slides in their rightful places.

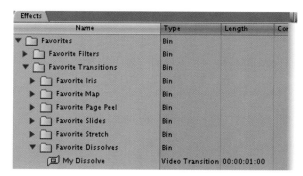

FIGURE 3.9: Organize your favorites by creating new bins in the Project tab and dragging them into Effects > Favorites.

Using a Transition as a Compositing Tool

One cool trick you can do with transitions is to turn a simple transition into a compositing tool. This way, you can create a multi-layer composition quickly and easily. Here's how to do it:

1. Make sure you have plenty of handles for both clips.

2. Apply the transition to your edit point.

3. Change the duration of the transition to the length you desire for your composite.

4. In the Transition Editor, set the Start and End sliders to the same numbers (like 50 for Start and 50 for End). Experiment until you get the desired results.

5. To cleanly edit into and out of this composite, zoom in and use the Razor Blade tool (B) to trim off any excess frames.

Here, an Edge Wipe is used to make a split-screen effect. This is one of the only ways you can make a split screen with a soft edge at the center.

After your composite is cleanly bladed, you will have a solid edit point for your transition composite.

Aligning Transitions

Usually, transitions are centered on the cut by default. But you can change the alignment of the transition to start on the cut or end on the cut as well. Sometimes it's an aesthetic choice and other times by necessity, as adequate handles may not be available on one side of the cut.

To change the alignment of the transition, just Control-click the transition and choose the alignment you desire from the shortcut menu. Another way is to load the transition into the Transition Editor in the Viewer and click one of the Transition Alignment buttons at the top-center of the interface. A third way is to select the transition and type **Option+1**, **Option+2**, or **Option+3** to start the transition at the edit, center it at the edit, or end it at the edit, respectively.

Duplicating Transitions

Once you create a custom transition, you may need to alter a parameter or two to create a desired effect. Rather than altering an existing custom transition, a better method is to duplicate the transition and make the changes for your desired effect. This method allows you to keep the transition and then add a new one based upon the original.

Swapping Transitions

Since there are so many transitions to choose from, it's fun to experiment to see which transition works the best. To replace the existing transition, simply drag and drop the new transition on top of the existing one (**FIGURE 3.10**). Your transition will immediately be replaced with the new one.

FIGURE 3.10: Drag and drop a new transition on top of an existing one to replace it.

Never forget that your transitions should be restrained and classy. There is a right way and a wrong way to use them. If a transition seems overblown, try to alter the transition's parameters or timing, try a new transition, or revert to a simple dissolve. If that still doesn't work, there's always the straight cut.

Chapter 4

Exporting Still Images from Final Cut Pro

TOM WOLSKY

Exporting still frames from FCP has puzzled many people, if for no other reason than there is no Export > Still Image function in Final Cut as you might expect there to be. There are also a number of gotchas to be aware of, not least of which is the difference in pixel aspect ratios between television formats and computer graphics.

First Steps

So how do you export a still frame from Final Cut? Well, the first thing you do not have to do is make a freeze frame. Instead, all you need to do is place the playhead over the frame you want to export, whether in the Viewer, Canvas, or Timeline. This can be a frame of a clip or of a sequence. It can even contain a multiple layer stack of videos with effects combined including transparency (**FIGURE 4.1**). Here are the steps:

1. Place the playhead (either in the Viewer or in the Canvas) on what you want to export, select the window the playhead is in, and choose **File > Export > Using QuickTime Conversion.**

   Whoa! You're thinking: I don't want to have to send a whole clip out. You don't have to.

FIGURE 4.1: Here's a multi-layer image from the Timeline that we want to export as a still frame.

2. From the Format pop-up menu, choose **Still Image** (**FIGURE 4.2**).

FIGURE 4.2: To export a still frame, rather than a movie, change the Format to Still Image.

Notice also the Image Sequence option—this is exactly the same as Still Image. You can use either.

3. Next click the Options button.

4. If you want to create an image sequence—one still image for every frame of video—simply enter a frame rate, but be careful because this can generate an enormous number of files. Make sure you have only a limited selection if you want to do this.

   To export just one frame, simply leave the frame rate value box empty. That's the only difference between exporting a sequence of images and a single image.

5. From the Format pop-up menu in that window, you can choose what type of file you want to export. If you want to export with transparency, pick a file format like Photoshop or TIFF or PNG (**FIGURE 4.3**).

FIGURE 4.3: To maintain both high quality and transparency information, choose either Photoshop, PNG, or TIFF formats. (If you want to output an image sequence, rather than a still, enter a frame rate for Frames per second.)

Personally I like to export in PNG because it exports transparency as a Photoshop layer rather than with an alpha channel (**FIGURE 4.4**). I then usually save the file in Photoshop as a Photoshop file with multiple layers. Although other people prefer TIFFs, I think their file sizes are larger than necessary. If you just need a flattened image, and minimum file size is important, you can save as JPEG, which is substantially more compressed than other formats.

FIGURE 4.4: Exporting an image as a PNG maintains transparency information by creating a separate Photoshop layer. Exporting as a TIFF maintains transparency in the alpha channel of the image.

If you choose JPEG, make sure you click the Options button in this window and set the Quality slider to Best (**FIGURE 4.5**). Do this every time because the setting is not "sticky," and it will revert to the default Medium every time you do it (see the sidebar, "Still No Still Export").

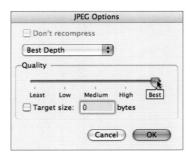

FIGURE 4.5: Only select JPEG when you need the image to be as small as possible. Remember to set the Quality to Best before clicking OK.

Still No Still Export

Because there is no Still Export function in Final Cut, one very annoying "feature" is that every time you choose Export > Using QuickTime Conversion, you have to reselect the Format pop-up. It's not sticky; it doesn't retain its settings. So, it always reverts to QuickTime Movie. If you have a lot of images to export, as I did writing this article, this becomes really annoying.

The file type in the Options button, however, is sticky, so once you've selected Photoshop, for instance, the next time you want to export it will still be set to Photoshop.

Removing Interlacing

Creating the still frame is only the first part of this process. It's time to open it in Photoshop to finish the process. Most video formats produce images by interlacing fields. For an image of a static object, this isn't a problem because both fields are identical. When the object is in motion, however, portions of the image will show combing from the interlacing, as in **FIGURE 4.6**.

Notice the shoulder of the figure on the left, or the hat of the figure on the right in particular. If you look closely at the full-size image, you'll notice the combing caused by interlacing.

FIGURE 4.6: Those small horizontal lines radiating off moving objects are caused by interlacing. These need to be removed before you print or post the image.

You could fix this by deinterlacing the image in Final Cut before you export it, but don't. Final Cut's deinterlacing is pretty crude, and the whole image doesn't need to be processed with the deinterlacing filter, only the portions that show the combing.

A better way to fix this is in Photoshop:

1. Select the Lasso tool.

2. In the Options bar, set the Feather to something like **10** pixels to soften the edges of your selection.

3. With the Lasso tool, loosely draw a selection around the moving portion.

4. Choose **Filter > Video > De-interlace**.

I usually start with the default settings for this filter: Odd field using Interpolation. Sometimes the Even field will produce a better result because of how the object was recorded while it was moving. **FIGURE 4.7** shows the selection around the figure: the original combing showing on the left and the filtered figure on the right. Removing interlacing like this allows the rest of the image to be unaffected and left as pristine as digital video can provide.

EDITOR'S NOTE: There are also a number of third-party Final Cut Pro deinterlace filters—from companies such as Joe's Filters, Digital Anarchy, and Graeme Nattress—that can automate this process. The benefit of using these filters is that you don't need to deinterlace in Photoshop at all.

FIGURE 4.7: Note the horizontal interlacing lines at the edges of the hat, or the shoulder in front of the window. These interlace artifacts disappear on the right after the filter is applied.

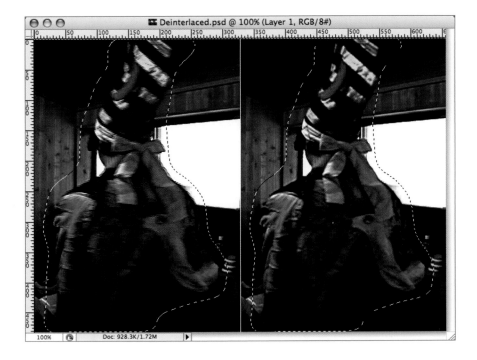

Sizing Your Images

Now that we've got our frame in, say, Photoshop it might look like **FIGURE 4.8**. This was a circle created in a Final Cut Pro DV sequence. DV, and uncompressed standard definition video, don't use the square pixels that computers use, but instead they use rectangular pixels; specifically, narrow, tall pixels for NTSC 4:3 and wide, short pixels for PAL.

Square pixels are described as having an aspect ratio of 1, meaning 1:1. CCIR-601 (NTSC 4:3) digital video pixels are described as having an aspect ratio 0.9; that is 1 unit high and 0.906 units wide. When your rectangular NTSC pixel image is displayed on a computer screen, it looks like the one shown in Figure 4.8.

Recent versions of Photoshop have an option under the Image menu to set the pixel aspect ratio. This is similar to the pixel aspect ratio adjustment that's normally on in the Final Cut Viewer and Canvas. Fixing that adjustment makes the image look right, but don't be fooled. The image is still in the wrong aspect. If you print it out, or put it on the web, or take it to some other application that doesn't understand pixel aspect ratio adjustment you'll still see the pretty oval in Figure 4.8, not the circle you should get.

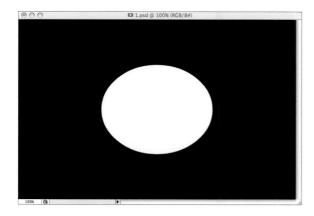

FIGURE 4.8: Displaying a video image on a computer monitor illustrates the differences in aspect ratio between video (rectangular pixels) and computer (square pixels). For instance, this is a circle in Final Cut, but an oval when displayed in Photoshop.

So how do we adjust this? The simplest way is to change the image size of the your picture. In Photoshop, you can do this by choosing **Image > Image Size (Cmd+Option+I)**. For a DV NTSC 4:3 image such as this one, you would deselect Constraint Proportions and set Resample Image to Bicubic Sharper (see **FIGURE 4.9**). Set the width of Pixel Dimensions to 640.

There is a long debate about whether you should resize to 640 x 480 by changing the horizontal dimension or to scale to 720 x 540 by changing the vertical dimension. I prefer the former. If you use the latter, set Resample Image to **Bicubic Smoother.** Either way you end up with a square pixel 4:3 image.

EDITOR'S NOTE: Because video has so few pixels to work with, my preference is to always scale smaller as it holds image quality better. So, my vote is to scale to 640 x 480 as well.

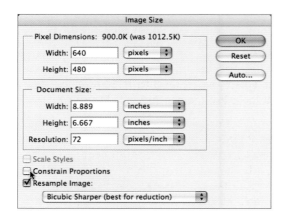

FIGURE 4.9: To convert a still frame from rectangular to square pixels, select Image > Image Size, turn off Constrain Proportions, and set the Width to 640.

PAL uses a different aspect ratio pixel, 1.07. (1 unit high by 1.07 units wide.) PAL video images should be resized in Photoshop to 768 x 576. See **TABLE 4.1** for a resizing chart of different aspect ratios.

What about anamorphic material? Anamorphic NTSC DV uses yet another pixel aspect ratio of 1.25. For this material, I would resize horizontally to 863 x 480 using Bicubic Smoother to create a widescreen image. PAL anamorphic should be resized to 1024 x 576 to bring it back to widescreen square pixel aspect.

FOOTAGE	SOURCE	SCALE TO	FUNCTION
DV NTSC	720 x 480	640 x 480	720 x 540
SD NTSC	720 x 486	640 x 486	720 x 546
DV NTSC Anamorphic	720 x 480	864 x 480	
SD NTSC Anamorphic	720 x 486	864 x 486	
PAL	720 x 576	768 x 576	
PAL Anamorphic	720 x 576	1024 x 576	
All 1080 HD formats	Varies	1920 x 1080	
All 720 HD formats	Varies	1280 x 720	

TABLE 4.1: Resizing chart for a variety of still image formats.

High-Definition Formats

We thought pixel aspect problems would be all behind us when we went to the square pixel world of high definition. Not so. Many HD formats use pixel aspect compression to compress their media. For instance, 1920 x 1080 in DVCPRO HD is actually 1280 x 1080 in NTSC (1440 x 1080 in PAL). DVCPRO HD in the 720p format is 960 x 720. So in Photoshop (using square pixels), your circle looks like the one shown in **FIGURE 4.10**.

NOTE: In HDV, the image size for 1080i is 1440 x 1080; for 720p, the image is 1280 x 720.

The good news is that with HD, there are only two image sizes: 1920 x 1080 or 1280 x 720. Regardless of your source footage, you can regain the correct pixel aspect ratio by scaling all HD still images to one of these two sizes.

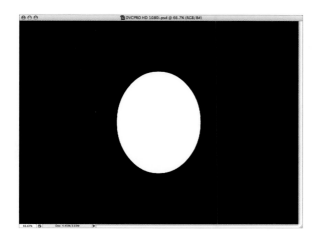

FIGURE 4.10: Even HD uses non-square pixels in some formats, as does this DVCPRO HD example here.

Resolution

One more thing that people always ask about is how to print this material. There is no good answer to this. Video is fixed resolution, with fixed pixels. It's not like print where the more pixels you can jam into an inch the better the print quality. Video is equivalent to 72 dpi, which is pretty poor for printing.

You have a couple of options. The simplest way is to let Photoshop do it. In the Image Size dialog, set Resample Image to Bicubic Smoother (because the image is going to be scaled up). Set the resolution to 150 dpi to make your 640 x 480 image 1333 x 1000 or set it to 300 dpi to make it 2666 x 2000. This used to create images that looked pretty ropy, but improvements have made this work very well.

NOTE: Third-party software, such as Genuine Fractals from onOne Software or PhotoZoom Pro 2, give you great control over the finished image size. PhotoZoom Pro also has excellent sharpen features that produce excellent results.

Exporting still images has traditionally been frustrating because we needed to convert the image from a video format into a computer format. Now that you know what to do, exporting your images should be a piece of cake.

Chapter 5

Removing Pulldown Frames with Cinema Tools

NOAH KADNER

Cinema Tools was once a third-party application used primarily to ingest material shot on film and telecined to video into Final Cut Pro. Foreseeing that this program could have many additional uses, Apple bought Cinema Tools and incorporated it into FCP. One of the most important features of Cinema Tools is the ability to work with the 3:2 pulldown frames created by 24p cameras.

First, let's review why you would want to remove pulldown frames from your video. Material shot on a 24p DV camera is actually 24 progressive frames per second plus a 3:2 pulldown. 3:2 pulldown is a method of adding interlaced frames to the progressive footage in order to create standard 29.97 NTSC-compatible video.

In post, you have the option to leave this pulldown intact and edit at 29.97. The result is footage with a "film look" that behaves like standard DV video.

The other option is to remove the pulldown and edit at true 23.98, known as native progressive editing. The advantages of native progressive editing primarily deal with image quality. You gain the option to create a native 24 fps DVD for display on computers and progressive displays such as plasma monitors and overhead projectors. Also, you can film at a 1:1 ratio without any of the usual tricks required to fit 29.97 video onto 24 frames per second film.

NOTE: The process of removing pulldown frames from video is also called "reverse telecine." The reason these are called "pulldown" frames is that when film is transferred to videotape in a telecine projector, the teeth in the telecine engage with the sprocket holes in the film to "pull it down" to the next frame.

Understanding Cadences and Pulldown

Removing pulldown frames can be easy or tricky, depending on how the pull-down frames are sequenced into the video. The reason that pulldown frames exist is that all televisions in North America display video at 30 frames per second (29.97 fps, for you engineering types). So, if you shoot 24 fps, 6 frames need to be "invented" every second to allow your video to play properly. These invented frames are called pulldown frames, and they're created in either Standard cadence (2:3:2:3) or Advanced cadence (2:3:3:2).

Cadences

Pulldown frames take advantage of the fact that each NTSC video frame is composed of two fields—the odd lines (field 1) and the even lines (field 2). (For this illustration, we can ignore field dominance.) A pulldown frame adds extra fields that duplicate the existing image, so that 24 frames per second can be stretched to 30 frames without slowing the playback speed.

Here's how it works. Take four frames of 24 fps video: A, B, C, and D (**FIGURE 5.1**). Spread each frame across two fields (because film is shot progressively, meaning all at once, the image for both fields is identical):

Frame A   Frame B   Frame C   Frame D

FIGURE 5.1 Twenty-four frames per second can be stretched to thirty frames without slowing the playback speed.

If we make no changes, it will take six sets of four frames to make one second of film (6 × 4 = 24). However, if we add one frame—two fields—to this sequence, those four frames become five frames, which, when we do the math, perfectly fills one second of 30 fps NTSC video (6 × 5 = 30).

The way in which those pulldown fields are created is the cadence. The Standard (traditional telecine) cadence is 2:3:2:3 (**FIGURE 5.2**). The B, C, and D frames are spread across eight fields, and the third frame (C) doesn't exist as a single frame—it's shared between frames three and four. This cadence makes removing pulldown frames complicated because the C frame needs to be constructed from two different frames; hence, it requires manual intervention in Cinema Tools.

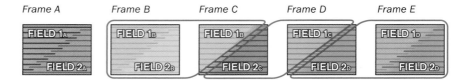

FIGURE 5.2: A standard 2:3:2:3 cadence.

The Advanced cadence solves the problem that was created by splitting the C frame across two frames. This cadence uses a 2:3:3:2 format. Here only one frame shares images. This cadence makes it easy for the computer to remove the pulldown frames—it's a simple process of automatically deleting the third frame in each five-frame set.

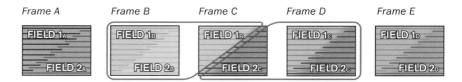

FIGURE 5.3: The Advanced 2:3:3:2 cadence.

The Panasonic DVX100 camera added a video format called 24p Advanced to take advantage of this Advanced cadence. (The Canon XL2 offers a similar mode.) The key benefit is that the 24p Advanced pulldown frames can be removed automatically by FCP without any loss of image quality.

The 24p Advanced mode accomplishes this trick by adding an electronic flag to the footage, which can be detected during capture, so that FCP can automatically remove the pulldown frames from 24p Advanced footage as it's captured. The process is simple and straightforward, with little or no attention required.

The number one benefit of 24p Advanced handling is that it doesn't require a recompression step, which causes a slight decrease in quality. Again, this improvement is due to the discrete nature of the pulldown pattern, in which interlaced frames are kept completely separate from progressive frames.

But what happens when you forget to shoot in 24p Advanced? Or you shoot in 24p Standard with a 29.97 finish in mind, but suddenly plans change and you want a 23.98 edit? It ends up being more work than 24p Advanced capture, but with a little bit of manual labor and Cinema Tools, 24p Standard footage can be resolved to 23.98 without too much trouble.

Determining the Type of Pulldown Frames

How can you find out whether the pulldown frames in a clip use the Standard or Advanced cadence? There are two ways to figure out whether a clip is actually 24p Standard. The simplest is to play the tape in a Panasonic DVX100 and toggle the counter button. You'll see an indicator that shows the mode in which the footage was shot.

If you don't happen to have a DVX100 handy, you can use Cinema Tools to determine the pulldown mode of a clip. Cinema Tools is included as part of the Final Cut Pro installation, and you can find it in your Applications folder. Let's launch Cinema Tools and get started:

1. Open the clip in Cinema Tools. If Cinema Tools asks you to open a database, click Cancel (we don't need a database).

2. Step through the clip frame by frame with the arrow keys until you hit an interlaced frame.

3. If two interlaced frames are followed by three progressive frames, the clip is 24p Standard (**FIGURE 5.4**) If there's one interlaced frame every fifth frame, it's 24p Advanced (**FIGURE 5.5**).

FIGURE 5.4: This interlaced image is shot in 24p Standard. Note the soft edges around the moving car, which indicate interlacing. We're literally seeing two fields of action overlaid to create a single frame of video.

FIGURE 5.5: This interlaced frame is shot in 24p Advanced. The key difference is whether the interlaced frame occurs every five frames or every three frames.

Once you've determined that your clip is 24p Standard, you can manually remove the pulldown frames by using Cinema Tools.

Video Tutorial: Improving Capture

Please visit the book's companion Web site to download a video tutorial that shows how you can improve your log and capture skills.

Identifying the A-Frame

Before we begin the process of deleting interlaced frames, we need to determine which frames are to be deleted. We start by identifying what's known as the A-frame. Doing this properly will instruct Cinema Tools where the cadence begins and ends and will determine which frames are removed.

Begin by launching Cinema Tools, and then choose **File > Open** and select your clip (**FIGURE 5.6**)

The A-frame is the start of the pulldown cadence. As I mentioned earlier, the pulldown is simply a pattern for laying down 24-frame footage into a 29.97 video stream. The pattern repeats itself every five frames, but we have to tell Cinema Tools where the pattern starts (in other words, where the "A" is). The trick is that every clip's first frame has a 1 in 5 chance of being an A-frame, depending on where the clip's In point falls. The main difference between standard and advanced cadences is that an advanced cadence can be removed automatically within FCP, while a standard cadence requires the sort of manual removal that we're doing in Cinema Tools. You determine which mode as you shoot, so it's crucial to make this determination during preproduction.

FIGURE 5.6: The Cinema Tools window, with the video clip open.

WARNING: If you don't get the right A-frame, Cinema Tools will throw out the progressive frames you need and keep the interlaced frames you don't. You'll wind up with a 23.98 clip with some progressive frames deleted and some interlaced frames still in the clip. When played, the footage will jump and strobe.

Audio Profile

VICKI PARKS-MURPHY AND LUKE MCMANUS
Dublin, Ireland, Final Cut Pro User Group,
http://web.mac.com/vparks/FCP_User_Group/

  What's it like to start a Final Cut user group in a country where user groups are very, very rare? Visit the companion Web site and discover the impact Final Cut is making internationally.

Luckily, it's quite easy to find the A-frame. Set the Canvas or Viewer to 100% scale. Go frame by frame from the start of the clip until you find the first interlaced frame. It looks like a sawtooth pattern around objects in motion (**FIGURE 5.7**). Now, from the first of the two interlaced frames, go back two frames (**FIGURE 5.8**). You are now "parked" on the A-frame, which should be progressive; that is, it has no interlace lines.

FIGURE 5.7: When looking for the A-frame, first look for the interlaced frame that follows it.

FIGURE 5.8: The A-frame is two frames back from the first interlaced frame.

The Reverse Telecine Process

You don't need to set the A-frame as the first image in a clip; you can mark the A-frame at any point during the clip. For instance, if the clip begins on an interlaced frame, keep going until you see the next set. If there's no motion early in the clip, keep stepping forward. I picked the frame shown in Figure 5.7 because it's easier to spot the interlacing there than earlier in the clip. At the beginning of the take, there might be very little motion. But once action begins to happen it's easier to see the telltale signs of interlacing, which is more pronounced on things moving quickly.

1. Click the Rev Telecine button. ("Rev Telecine" is short for reverse telecine—we're reversing the process of inserting those interlaced frames.)

   Confirm the settings you see in **FIGURE 5.9**.

FIGURE 5.9: Use this dialog to confirm that you're parked on the A-frame and that you want to remove frames, not fields.

2. Click **OK** to begin processing.

3. When Cinema Tools finishes reversing the telecine, it opens the conformed clip. Go through the clip frame by frame to confirm that all interlaced frames have been removed (**FIGURE 5.10**). The new file has been saved automatically by Cinema Tools.

FIGURE 5.10: The finished movie (note the .rev extension in the title bar) with all pulldown frames removed.

4. Try opening the clip in FCP and playing it out to FireWire in Final Cut Pro. Don't worry that it now has a .rev file extension; it's still a QuickTime movie file that can be opened in any QT-compatible application. The REV extension simply means that the clip has been reverse-telecined.

The motion of the clip should be smooth, without interlacing artifacts or strobing. If you see anything that doesn't look right, try running through the steps again. Because you're creating a new clip during the reverse-telecine process, you'll always have the original 29.97 clip to go back to if you find any problems.

Traditionally, Cinema Tools is used to reconcile film negative to videotape. However, as illustrated here, Cinema Tools comes in handy for removing pull-down frames from 24-frame video, even when no film is involved.

Chapter 6

An Archiving Solution for Final Cut Studio 2

BRYAN PEEL

I n the postproduction work we do at my company, we deal with a variety of formats, which can be either tape-based or tapeless. Once the project is complete and the client or the network has the final materials, we are faced with a mountain of files used to create the final product (taking up valuable storage space). How do we archive?

NOTE: Before I jump into our solution for archiving, I recommend that you include archiving in the quote stage to your client. Ask them if they would like the project to be permanently archived for future re-edits and then build the archive fee as a separate item on the quote. Almost every time, they will want their project stored in a state that can be retrieved easily without having to reload camera tapes (taking up more edit time) and worry about missing elements.

There are many items to take into consideration when choosing your method of archiving, and I would suggest that you spend the time researching various archiving solutions, searching the forums, and speaking with your insurance company to decide how important a safe and secure archive is for you and your clients.

If you choose Blu-ray or external FireWire as your backup choice, I suggest that you also make a clone of your backup and store it offsite so that you're prepared for the worst. Also, make sure to purchase "archival-quality" Blu-ray media. Not all optical discs are created the same.

We have had our own share of external FireWire drive failures, and the final straw was having one self-destruct while it sat on a desk. We were making a clone of that drive, and it died during the copy process. Luckily, all the build files (graphics and so on) were already moved over, and it was just the camera footage that was lost.

We began to research tape backups as a result. In the past, DLT and AIT tape drives were good solutions for us, but we needed a tape solution that would hold hundreds of GB per tape.

Finding the Hardware

First, we experimented with the Quantum LTO-3 (400 GB) connected via gigabit Ethernet. For various reasons, this product didn't leave us feeling secure with archiving our projects, so we turned to the Tandberg LTO-4 with Retrospect. There was only one minor snag with this method in that it connects via SCSI, requiring us to add an Atto ExpressPCI UL5D card into our Mac Pro. The problem with this, however, was that our main system already had a Fibre Channel card, Radeon X1900, and Kona. As a result, we were only able to give that lane 1x using the Expansion Slot Utility, which severely restricted the data transfer speed.

Instead, we installed the Tandberg LTO-4 into our other Mac Pro, which was an identical unit, less the Kona. We made sure to assign the correct lane configuration, and that's it for the install. After that, we installed Retrospect, read the manual, and were all set to archive.

NOTE: Our three edit suites all share the XRaid via Metasan with the LTO-4 system connected to one machine.

Preparing for Backup

Here are the steps to follow to begin the backup process:

1. Once you begin an editing project, assign a job number, let's say 080243, in our Excel archive log file (**FIGURE 6.1**).

   This number will be needed for the archive at the end of the project. Then the Final Cut project is built, edited, and approved.

2. Run Media Manager and include all media outside the edit by deselecting "Delete unused media from duplicated items." This assures that you'll archive all project media in the event you need to make changes in the future.

   All of the media-managed files and any other loose items you may want to include are stored in a folder tagged with the job number and the project name; for example, 080243 "CREATIVE DONKEYS KAWASAKI - GOOD TIMES AD."

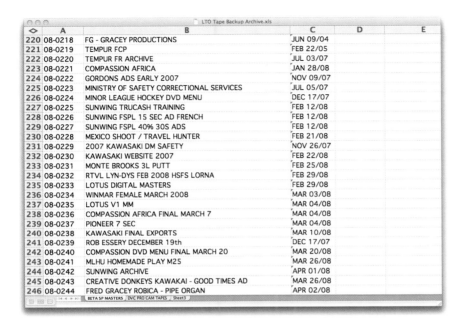

FIGURE 6.1: All jobs are assigned a job number in our Excel database.

3. Once the contents of the project folder are complete, open the project file from another edit suite to confirm that all media connects properly. Then move that folder into the Archive folder on the XRaid, in our case, or other large hard drive.

4. Launch Retrospect and select the Immediate tab (**FIGURE 6.2**). This tab contains the heart of the backup process that Retrospect offers.

FIGURE 6.2: To start a backup immediately, select the Immediate tab. Click the Backup button to launch the archiving process.

5. Click the Backup button (shown in Figure 6.2). The Immediate Backup pop-up menu appears (**FIGURE 6.3**).

FIGURE 6.3: These are the settings you need to configure so Retrospect knows how to process your backup. When all settings are complete, backup is ready to begin. Click Backup to start.

Sources tells Retrospect what folder you want to back up. We have set a specific folder on our XRaid named Archive, which helps keep the catalog files (explained below) organized. If you decide to back up the files straight from the original source, you'll notice that the catalog file will get messy quite quickly, with many folders.

Destination tells Retrospect where you want to back up. I recommend keeping two catalog files, one for onsite and another for offsite. This will be explained later.

Selecting is more of a preference option, but it's easier to keep it at "All Files" to cover all your bases.

Preview is where you view and select the files you want to back up from your Archive folder. You can use the mark and unmark options to tell Retrospect what files you want to back up.

Options describes what kind of backup you want to create. We select Normal Backup with Verification on. Verification is good because it goes through after your backup and compares the files on the LTO-4 tape with the original files on the HD. This option adds a second level of comfort when you back up your files.

The Archiving Process

Now that these steps are taken care of, it's time to start the backing up process. Notice that Retrospect tells you that it's ready to start (see callout in **FIGURE 6.3**). Follow these steps to begin the backup:

1. Click **Backup**.

    A progress bar pops up that shows how fast you are backing up your data. Once Retrospect starts verifying, it will show you a second progress bar.

2. Once the backup is complete, you are rewarded with a sound. I recommend changing the default sound in **Special > Preferences > Sounds**. The default sound sounds like the buzzer when someone loses a game show or when a serious system error occurs.

3. Retrospect makes the backup process easy and does a great job of securing the backups of your projects (**FIGURE 6.4**). It's a good idea to go through this process again, but this time select the destination to an offsite catalog and the media to a new tape.

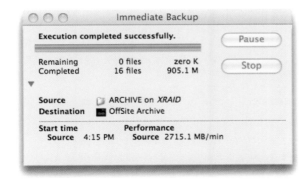

FIGURE 6.4: After verification, Retrospect shows you the statistics from your backup. It's a good idea to have two copies—one onsite and one offsite.

NOTE: Retrospect will fill the tape. So, Retrospect handles the file structure and will ask you to insert a new tape when full. Projects can span multiple tapes as necessary.

Once the onsite and offsite archives are complete, we store the tapes in molded turtle cases and keep the onsite tapes in the studio. I keep the offsite at home. This is a good idea in case of theft, fire, or an unexpected Godzilla attack that leaves the studio in shambles.

Our archive solution costs came in around $5,500. Each 800 GB LTO-4 tape costs around $100; it seems to be the best archive method and most cost-effective per GB. The security of this system helps us sleep at night, and having a second copy of each backup at a separate location is a double layer of comfort. The Retrospect software is very user-friendly and has many more options that can be customized for any user.

Additional Notes on Archiving

LTO-4 tapes hold 800 GB of data. Video files may not compress much more than their current size, but other data files can compress significantly. However, we don't use the Compression option inside Retrospect, mainly to reduce possible compression errors and to maintain a fast transfer speed.

When archiving/restoring, we have seen speeds of up to 7 GB per minute.

Check with your insurance company to find if you have coverage for your projects beyond camera tapes. There are many uncomfortable gray areas; a clone of your backup set is an added insurance policy on its own.

The Restore Process

Let's say the time has come to restore your project. This process is very similar to the backup process:

1. In the Immediate tab, click **Restore** (**FIGURE 6.5**).

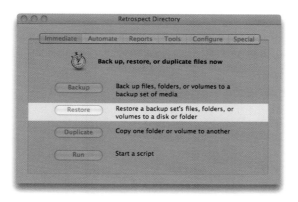

FIGURE 6.5: Click Restore to begin the process.

2. Select the Search for files and folders option (see **FIGURE 6.6**).

This option is great because it lets you view all the files on a backup set. The next step shows all your backup sets.

FIGURE 6.6: Click Search for files and folders to locate the specific files you want to restore.

3. Select the backup set you want to restore and click **OK** (**FIGURE 6.7**).

FIGURE 6.7: Select the archive you want to restore.

Retrospect then lets you select where you want to restore the project files. I created a folder on our RAID named Restore. This process is very similar to what we did in the backup process. By making a restore folder, you know exactly where the files are going to go when the process is finished.

4. Once you have your restore folder selected, click **OK**.

5. In the next dialog, shown in **FIGURE 6.8**, you can select what you want to include and exclude. It's best to include everything and exclude nothing. Click **OK** to move on.

FIGURE 6.8: To make sure all files are transferred, make sure to include everything and exclude nothing.

6. The Searching & Retrieval dialog appears, which is identical to the backup window except most of the selections are already made for you (**FIGURE 6.9**). The main concern here is to make sure you select the project you want to restore. Do this by selecting the **Files Chosen** option and click the Unmark button so you don't restore terabytes of material you don't need (**FIGURE 6.10**).

7. Open the archive folder, find your project, then highlight the files you want to restore and click the Mark button (**FIGURE 6.11**).

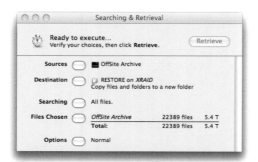

FIGURE 6.9: Like the similar screen in Backup, this screen allows you to configure exactly how your files are restored.

FIGURE 6.10: Click the Unmark button to be sure that you don't copy everything back to your hard disk.

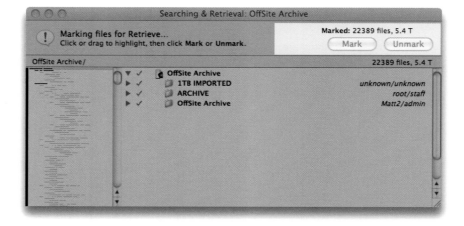

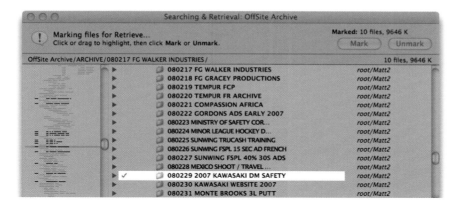

FIGURE 6.11: Mark the files you want to restore by clicking to the left of the folder name. When you have selected everything you need, you are ready to start the process.

Archiving is critical now that we don't have video tape anymore. After a lot of experimentation, this is the system that works the best for us. We are really focused on our archives and also store a backup of the catalog file and client/project spreadsheet on our iDisk as a backup. Believe me, you can rest a lot easier at night knowing your assets are safe.

Final Cut Pro Editing Shortcuts

SHORTCUT	WHAT IT DOES	
Option+P	Plays unrendered sequence in Timeline	
Ctrl+U	Resets windows to default layout	
Shift+Z	Fits image/sequence into window	
Option+up arrow / Option+down arrow	Moves selected clip up/down track	
Cmd+Option+[or]	Moves between tabs in active window (FCP 5.1.2 or later)	
M	Sets clip or Timeline marker	
Shift+M / Option+M	Moves playhead to next/previous marker	
Q	Toggles between selecting Canvas or Viewer	
W	Toggles Canvas or Viewer between Image, Image/Wireframe, and Wireframe display modes	
Option+= (equals sign)	Zooms into Timeline	
Option+− (hyphen)	Zooms out of Timeline	
\	Plays around playhead	
Shift+\	Plays from In to Out	

Part 2

Final Cut Pro Effects

Editing is a craft that requires a balance between the logical and creative sides of our brain. Strong organization and technical skills are balanced by creative storytelling and visualization.

In the previous section, we looked at editing. This is the key place to begin. First, you have to tell your story. Until the story is locked in, it is a waste of time to work on effects. Once the story is complete, then you can make it look as good as possible. That's what this section is about—effects.

Final Cut Pro has an almost limitless number of effects, but we decided to focus on four that are lesser known.

Kevin Monahan leads off with an overview of composite modes. These are the heart and soul of effects compositing in Photoshop or After Effects, but they aren't well understood by many video editors.

Tom Meegan follows Kevin's overview with some very specific uses of composite modes to create a "film-look" with video. Tom's effects work has been seen in the highly stylized openings to NFL, NBA, and Major League Baseball broadcasts.

Kevin's discussion of mattes and masks points to another key challenge in editing. Many times, we only need to see a portion of an image, or, more likely, we need to hide a portion of the image because there's something in it such as a light stand or microphone, that we don't want the audience to see. Kevin shows how you can do this easily in Final Cut Pro.

Finally, as we move into the realm of higher-resolution images in HD, it becomes even more important to avoid hand-held, jerky camera work. The lower the resolution of the image, the more violently you can move the camera. Higher resolutions require smoother camera work. The last chapter in this section talks about how to stabilize your clips.

Throughout this section you'll discover links to some interesting audio interviews and video tutorials, as well as some helpful keyboard shortcuts.

Chapter 7

Blending the Light Away with Composite Modes

KEVIN MONAHAN

I'm sure many of you have tried blending images by dropping the opacity on an overlapping clip. It looks OK, but each clip gets a bit dim. Final Cut Pro offers a cool method to blend clips in a better way: These secret weapons are called *composite modes*. If you're familiar with transfer modes in Adobe After Effects or Photoshop, then you should have no trouble with composite modes in Final Cut Pro; they behave in precisely the same way. If you've never experimented with them, you'll wonder why you waited so long.

You probably already know that the colors found in video are made up of pixels displaying some combination of red, green, and blue, each with a certain brightness level. Knowing that, it's easier to understand just how composite modes do the job of blending. Put simply, composite modes do their blending duty by using mathematical calculations that operate on brightness values within these color channels. These calculations can turn a couple of stacked images into a single blended image (**FIGURE 7.1**).

NOTE: Don't worry about actually having to do any math; your trusty Mac will do that for you. For most effects, it's very simple. You just apply the mode; if you like the effect, you're in the zone.

FIGURE 7.1: Composite modes allow you to blend images in unique ways. Here, Overlay mode was enabled in the film clutter clip, lending a unique texture to the text.

Video: Overlay Composite Mode

To see a short video demonstration, please visit the book's companion Web site.

Creating a Basic Composite Mode Effect

Composite modes work only if you have two (or more) stacked clips with the mode applied to the top layer. Let's experiment with composite modes before we get into the specifics of each blending mode.

To create a composite mode effect, follow these steps:

1. Stack two clips on V1 and V2.

2. Select the V2 clip.

3. Choose **Modify > Composite Modes**.

4. Select a mode from the submenu.

Or try this alternative technique:

1. Control-click the V2 clip.

2. From the pop-up menu, select **Composite Mode**.

3. Select a mode from the submenu (**FIGURE 7.2**).

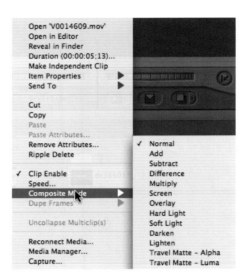

FIGURE 7.2: FCP submenu for composite modes.

Typically, you add composite modes only to the top clip on V2. There is no practical reason to add a composite mode to the clip on V1, because it won't have any effect. Furthermore, if you add a clip to V3 and modify its composite mode from Normal, it will be included in the blend.

TIP: In some cases, the stacking order of the two clips won't matter. In other cases, changing the stacking order will give you a significantly different kind of blend. When it matters to the mode, you can flop the layer order to see even more choices.

How does your blended image look? Great? Not so good? Often, you can't predict what the final image will look like. If you don't like the result of the mode you chose, simply try another until you get the desired result. There is a method to choosing the right mode for the job, but quite honestly, I cycle through a number of different modes to see what my choices are. The only problem with this approach is that it takes time to explore each mode, in part because you must return to the Modify or contextual menu each time you want to try a different mode. So I've developed a cool technique for cruising through all the composite modes in rapid-fire fashion:

1. Choose **Tools > Keyboard Layout > Customize**. The Keyboard Layout window launches.

2. Click the lock in the lower-left corner of the Keyboard Layout window to unlock the keyboard to allow you to make changes.

3. Type the word **Composite** in the search field. The composite modes are displayed.

4. Click the **Command** and **Option** keys in the Keyboard Layout window. You should see a bunch of empty places where you can drag and drop your modes.

5. Drag and drop each mode to another key. I like to use the numeric keypad, but you can use whatever buttons you want (**FIGURE 7.3**).

6. Select **Tools > Keyboard Layout > Save Keyboard Layout**. Name the layout **Composite Modes** and click **Save**.

7. Close the Keyboard Layout window. It's not necessary to relock the lock.

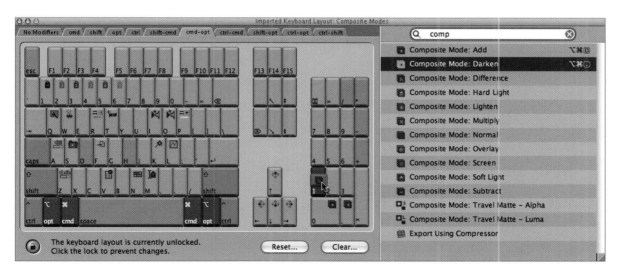

FIGURE 7.3: You can map composite modes to your keyboard for speedy comparisons between modes.

Having a keyboard layout for modes allows me to cycle through the various modes much more quickly. Give it a try and see how fast you can check out the modes. As you can see, different modes create radically different effects. Which one looks best now? I'm rather partial to Add, Screen, Overlay, Soft Light, and Hard Light.

TIP: Be very careful using Add mode. It's the only composite mode that can drive your white levels over 100%. A safer choice is Screen, which creates a similar look to Add, but clamps white levels at 100%.

Behavior of Composite Modes

Although I'm a mode-cycling junkie, sometimes I limit myself to just a few modes, as I know that there are some I would never use for a certain effect. Knowing a bit about how each mode affects color can help you narrow down those choices. Let's take a brief look at the behavior of each composite mode.

NOTE: Final Cut Express shares all of the composite modes available in Final Cut Pro.

Normal: Normal mode is the default composite mode of all clips. No blending takes place.

Add: Color values are combined, lending a blown-out (overexposed) look to blended footage. A cool use of Add mode is to use one image to texturize another selectively based on its highlights (**FIGURE 7.4**). You need to be careful here, though—Add can make your whites travel into illegal brightness values.

FIGURE 7.4: An example of Add mode. This clip of a jet landing takes on a "damaged" texture when overlaid with a grainy clip of a brick wall.

EDITOR'S NOTE: Be VERY careful when using the Add composite mode as it will almost always drive white levels into dangerous superwhite territory. A much better approach is to use the Screen composite mode, which provides a similar effect while clamping white levels at a safe 100%.

Video: Add Composite Mode

To see a short video demonstration, please visit the book's companion Web site.

Screen: Screen creates a harmonious blend that's brighter overall, with whites clipped at 100%. Rather like Add mode, Screen is not quite as strong. Because Screen mode knocks out blacks in an image (**FIGURE 7.5**), it's great for restoring highlights in underexposed footage.

FIGURE 7.5: In this black-and-white silhouetted clip, Screen has totally knocked out the blacks, revealing a busy graphics background.

Video: Screen Composite Mode

To see a short video demonstration, please visit the book's companion Web site.

Overlay: Overlay is another of my favorites. It's like a combination of Screen and Multiply in that it emphasizes the midtones. Stacking order matters, as the underlying image tends to dominate the blend.

Multiply: When I want dark tones, I usually use Multiply instead of Subtract. It can also stand in as a rudimentary luma key, as it knocks out the whites. Multiply is also good for restoring blacks in overexposed footage. Layer order doesn't matter here.

Subtract: Color values are subtracted from each other. You'll get very dark, rich, overlapping tones with this mode. It's not my favorite, but you should always give it a look. Keep in mind that it can create illegal blacks, but you can guard against this possibility by using the Broadcast Safe filter.

Difference: This mode is very similar to Subtract mode, but instead of all the deep blacks you get vivid, almost psychedelic tones. If that's your bag, go for it. I don't use it much.

Hard Light: If you like a dark and oversaturated blend, Hard Light mode is for you (**FIGURE 7.6**). Hard Light functions like a more intense version of Overlay.

FIGURE 7.6: If you want to reveal an image within a flame, use Hard Light. Layer order matters, so be sure to place the fire clip on V2: and the burning image on V1. The composite mode is applied to V2.

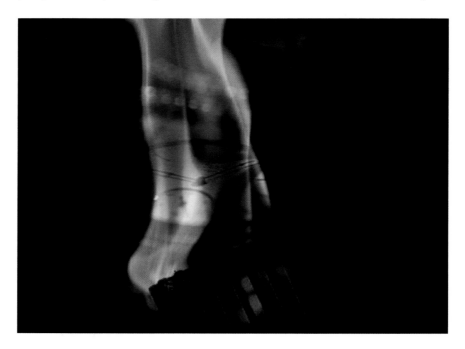

Video: Hard Light Composite Mode

To see a short video demonstration, please visit the book's companion Web site.

Soft Light: This mode is like a less intense version of Overlay. If you want an understated lighting effect with a minimum of contrast, go with Soft Light.

Darken: This mode creates new colors in the blends, as color channels are selectively blended, with the darker colors dominating. Layer order doesn't matter.

Lighten: Blending with Lighten lends an even lighter image than with Soft Light. The inverse of Darken mode, Lighten is likely to give you new colors in the image, as color channels are selectively blended based on their luminance.

Take some time to explore different kinds of footage with composite modes. Blend black-and-white footage with an oversaturated RGB clip. Swap the order of the clips on different tracks and see what happens. Go hog wild! You'll often be surprised at the results.

More Composite Mode Effects

Now that you have a basic grip on what all the modes do, it's time to put them into practice with some more-advanced composite mode effects.

Toning It Down

The problem with composite modes is that they don't come with controls or an interface, so they're either off or on. How do you tame them?

The best way to tone down the intensity of modes is simply to raise or lower the opacity of the overlying clip. If you love the mix that Hard Light gives, but it's too strong for you, just lower the opacity to reduce its intensity.

Pumping It Up

Converse to taming a composite, sometimes you want to make it more intense, so how do you do that? Just stack identical clips with the same mode applied to each. Select the clip and then repeatedly Shift-Option-drag the clip to the track above. The result is that you make the blend even stronger.

Final Cut Pro Keyframing Shortcuts

SHORTCUT	FUNCTION
Control+K	Adds keyframe at current playhead position to all motion parameters
Option+Command+K	Adds audio-level keyframe at current playhead position to currently selected audio clip
Shift+K	Jumps playhead to next keyframe
Option+K	Jumps playhead to previous keyframe
Shift+Command+K	Toggles recording of audio keyframes on or off
Option+T	Toggles display of Timeline keyframes
Shift+I	Jumps playhead to In point of clip
Shift+O	Jumps playhead to Out point of clip

Keyframing Mode to Mode

It's a shame that there's no real way to keyframe from one mode to another; however, here's a trick to work around that problem, as illustrated in **FIGURE 7.7**:

1. On V2 and V3, stack identical clips over a different background on V1.

2. Apply different modes to the V3 and V2 clips.

3. Keyframe the V3 opacity down from opaque to transparent.

4. Trim the V2 clip so it starts at the first opacity keyframe on V3.

It's simple, but it works like a charm!

FIGURE 7.7: Fade identical clips with different modes for a unique effect.

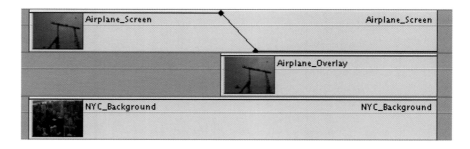

Video Tutorial: Four Quick Keyframe Effects

Visit the companion Web site to learn four quick motion-effect keyframe techniques you can use as building blocks for creating your own effects.

Controlling the Area of the Mode

When you apply a composite mode to a clip, you're applying it to the entire frame, and that's not always warranted in a video composite. More often than not, you'll want to mask a clip that contains a composite mode. **FIGURE 7.8** illustrates this principle.

FIGURE 7.8: Masking an image provides a way to control the area of the blend.

Try this: Stack two clips, one on V1 and the other on V2. Apply a composite mode to the V2 clip. Here are four different ways to get the effect into only a portion of the image:

- Scale down the V2 clip a bit.

- Move the V2 wireframe to another part of the Canvas.

- Add a Matte filter to the V2 clip.

- Select **Matte > Mask Feather** and feather the result to taste.

Video: Mask a Clip with a Composite Mode

To see a short video demonstration, please visit the book's companion Web site.

You can also use a luma key, chroma key, or travel matte to limit the area of a mode-affected clip. By experimenting, you'll come up with new ways to harness and control your composite modes.

TIP: You can blend two grayscale images using the mode of your choice, and then nest them. The result can be used for a mask in a Travel Matte – Luma effect.

Heavenly Blend

One of the coolest things you can do is create a "heavenly blend" with duplicated footage, as illustrated in **FIGURE 7.9**. Follow these steps:

1. Place a clip on V1.

2. Shift+Option-drag the clip up to V2. You should now have a stack of two identical clips—one on V1, the other on V2.

3. Select the V2 clip and then apply the composite mode of your choice. Try **Soft Light**, **Screen**, or **Overlay** to start. You can also cycle modes on your custom keyboard.

You can stop right there if you're satisfied with the resulting "heavenly blend," or continue with a soft, glowing effect.

FIGURE 7.9: An example of "heavenly blend." The image has been altered by duplicating it and applying Hard Light to the V2 copy. The inset clip is the original.

Video: Heavenly Blend Effect

To see a short video demonstration, please visit the book's companion Web site.

Audio Profile

TRACEY GLYNN
Editor, Wheel of Fortune/Jeopardy

Visit the companion Web site to hear some editing secrets from this busy editor who works on two popular U.S. game shows.

Glow Effect

FIGURE 7.10 shows a modified version of the "heavenly blend." Keep in mind that you use composite modes to create different "looks." If you like it, great. If not, try something else.

1. With the clip on V2 still selected, select **Effects > Video Filters > Blur > Gaussian Blur.**

2. Double-click the clip to reload it into the Viewer.

3. Start with a Radius setting of **8.**

4. On the Motion tab, or with Clip Overlays turned on, reduce the opacity to taste.

You can take this look even further:

1. Stack a Noise Generator on V3 at very low opacity.

2. Apply **Strobe**, **Blink**, and/or **Deinterlace** filters.

FIGURE 7.10: This glow effect was created with Screen mode and a Gaussian blur.

These effects give the footage a totally different texture. Now that's what I call heavenly!

Video: Glow Effect

To see a short video demonstration, please visit the book's companion Web site.

Color Correction and Modes

Another cool trick is to use color correction filters to enhance modal looks. With this technique, you can alter the blends that you make with composite modes. Here's how:

1. Stack two clips—one on V1 and the other on V2.

2. Apply a composite mode to the V2 clip.

3. Apply a color correction filter to both clips.

4. Manipulate either the foreground and/or background image to get the desired result (see **FIGURE 7.11**).

FIGURE 7.11: Sometimes you need to color-correct one clip or the other to achieve the blend you want.

Take some time to explore this idea. For instance, if you have two pieces of stock footage that have vastly different color palettes, you can use the Color

Corrector 3-way filter to bring them into the same color range and then blend them. Conversely, if the two images have the same color palette, you can alter them to create a wholly different-looking blend.

Video: Color Correction Filter

To see a short video demonstration, please visit the book's companion Web site.

Blending Text with Modes

One final idea is to try out combinations of composite modes and titles that blend the text in with the background in new and unique ways (**FIGURE 7.12**). You can see this technique in many advanced motion-graphics compositions.

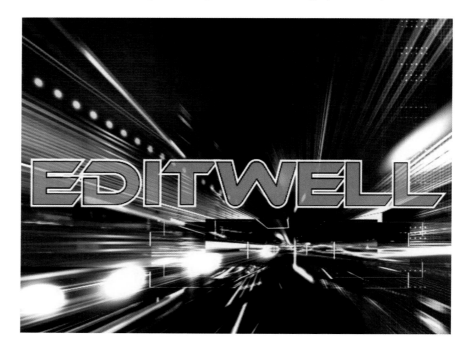

FIGURE 7.12: You can blend text with modes. Text can take on textures from the background with a composite mode enabled.

Video: Text and Composite Modes

To see a short video demonstration, please visit the book's companion Web site.

Of course, each mode has almost infinite possibilities, so it's impossible to bring up every scenario in which you would use a particular one. Are you still curious? You can find even more information about the behavior modes in the Final Cut Pro manual. Have some fun with composite modes. It's really a treat to have them on board.

Chapter 8

"Film It Up" with Composite Modes and Filters

TOM MEEGAN

Good, clean footage is a joy to work with, but producers and clients often ask for a look that is... well, less than clean. For instance: "Make it sweet, glowy, you know, satiny," or maybe, "grungy and industrial," or the ever popular, "Just film it up."

I imagine responding with, "The colorist will take care of that. Let's just get the content down for the online edit." However, in real life the effects are all up to me.

I work on events with a short turnaround time: The project that starts in the afternoon often airs at eight. I am logger, editor, audio mixer, graphic designer, edit maintenance, and colorist. Most of you know what I'm talking about. FedEx waits for no one. Tight deadlines and shrinking budgets are a fact of life.

I employ several techniques to achieve a "sweet and glowy" look and other effects quickly by using composite modes, Gaussian Blur, and the Color Corrector 3-way filters.

Composite modes, sometimes called *blend modes* in other programs, are settings that control how the luma, chroma, and hue of one clip interact with those of the clip layered below it. When you composite a clip with these techniques, the results are immediate and interesting. Stir in some Gaussian Blur, color correct to taste, and you get wonderful visual soup.

So let's get started with some recipes for good soup!

The Basics

By using different composite modes, you achieve a variety of looks (**FIGURE 8.1A–D**).

FIGURE 8.1A Here's the original image.

FIGURE 8.1B Here's the same image with a Soft Light composite mode applied.

FIGURE 8.1C Here's the image with an Overlay composite mode applied.

FIGURE 8.1D Here's the image with a Screen composite mode applied.

Curious about how to achieve these looks? Here is a quick overview of the basic steps:

1. Find a clip and edit it into a sequence.

2. Duplicate the footage and move it to a second layer (**Shift+Option-drag**).

3. Add a Gaussian Blur filter to the top layer with a Blur Radius of **10**.

4. Set the Composite mode of the top layer to **Soft Light**.

5. If the footage is excessively bright or dark, add a Color Corrector 3-way filter to the top clip and adjust the mids and white levels to taste.

Dupe the Clip

The first steps can be summarized as follows:

1. In Final Cut Pro, create a new sequence and edit a clip to the Timeline.

2. Position the pointer over the video portion of the Timeline clip, and press and hold **Shift+Option** as you drag the clip up one layer to duplicate it.

3. Release the mouse before you let go of Shift+Option, which leaves you with the duplicate video on top of the original (**FIGURE 8.2**).

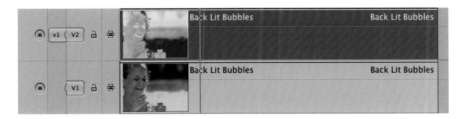

FIGURE 8.2: Here's what our sample clips look like when stacked.

Audio Profile

TOM MEEGAN
Creative director, **wovenpixels.com**

Visit the companion Web site to hear Tom Meegan discuss how he uses Final Cut Studio to cover some of the largest sporting events in the U.S.

Blur the Top! My Favorite!

You probably already know how to add a filter via the Effects menu or the Effects tab, so let's build a favorite so a specific blur setting will be available as a keyboard shortcut.

1. In the Browser, click the Effects tab.

2. Choose **Video Filters** > **Blur**, and then drag Gaussian Blur to the Favorites bin (**FIGURE 8.3**). A copy is created because the master effects in the bins are locked.

FIGURE 8.3: One way to make an effects favorite is to drag it from the Effects bin to the Favorites bin.

1. Rename your new filter **Gaussian Blur 10**.

2. Double-click the icon of Gaussian Blur 10 to load it into the Viewer. Adjust the Radius setting to **10** (**FIGURE 8.4**).

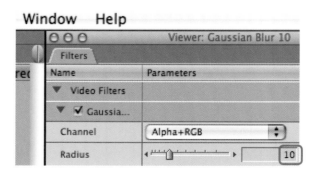

FIGURE 8.4: Change the Radius to 10.

Now here's the cool part:

1. Choose **Effects > Favorites** and, voilá, your new filter is listed with a keyboard shortcut—and its default Radius setting is 10! (**FIGURE 8.5.**)

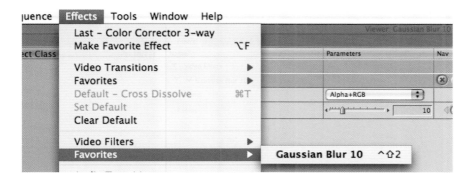

FIGURE 8.5: The Gaussian Blur filter is now stored in the Favorites folder, with the Radius set to 10.

There are keyboard shortcuts for the first four favorites, mapped to **Control+ Shift+2**, **Control+Shift+W**, **Control+Shift+S**, and **Control+Shift+X**. This doesn't make much sense until you notice the location of the keys on the keyboard (**FIGURE 8.6**).

FIGURE 8.6: Note the pattern of keys assigned to the favorite filters.

For a list of all keyboard shortcuts used by your favorites, see the sidebar "Picking Your Favorites."

Let's Take a Shortcut!

To test out the new filter favorite, follow these steps:

1. Click the top layer to select it.

2. Press **Control+Shift+2**.

Picking Your Favorites

You can create favorites for video transitions, audio transitions, motion effects, video filter effects, and audio filter effects.

Here are the keyboard shortcuts for:

Video transition favorites

Audio transition favorites

Motion effect favorites

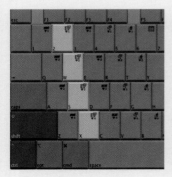
Video filter favorites

Audio filter favorites

That should do it; however, let's double-check.

3. Double-click the video on Track 2 to load it into the Viewer window.

4. Click the Filters tab to make sure the Gaussian Blur is applied with a radius of 10 (see **FIGURE 8.7**).

Here is what the image on V2 looks like now:

FIGURE 8.7: Here's the V2 clip with a Gaussian Blur (with a Radius of 10) applied.

OK, I know, it's blurry, but wait!

Audio Profile

EDDIE KILGALLON

Keyboardist, Montgomery Gentry, **www.montgomerygentry.com**

Eddie Kilgallon is keyboardist for the top country band Montgomery Gentry. But when he's not playing for 50,000 fans, he's editing videos of the band on the bus. Visit the companion Web site to hear an interview with this multi-talented editor.

Creating a Keyboard Shortcut for a Composite Mode

If you find yourself needing a particular composite mode often enough, turn it into a keyboard shortcut.

Creating keyboard shortcuts for common filters can make your whole workflow flow much faster.

1. Choose **Tools > Keyboard Layout > Customize** (or press **Option+H**).

2. Click the padlock icon to allow changes.

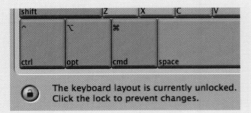

3. Type **soft** into the search window.

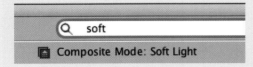

4. Using your mouse, click the **Shift** key, then the **Control** key on the virtual keyboard (or click the **Ctrl+Shift** tab).

5. Drag the **Soft Light** icon in the search window onto the Y key. (You can pick your own keyboard combo, but this is where I put it.)

Soft Light Makes Everything Better

1. Right-click or Control-click the clip on the top layer to open a shortcut menu (**FIGURE 8.8**).

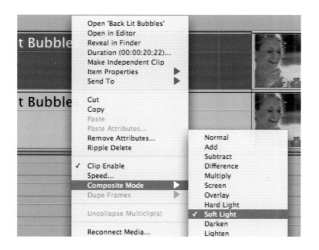

FIGURE 8.8: Control-click a clip to apply the Soft Light composite mode.

2. Choose **Composite Mode > Soft Light** (**FIGURE 8.9**).

FIGURE 8.9: The image with both Gaussian Blur and Soft Light applied.

Use Color Correction to Adjust the Image

The image is better, but it's still a little dark. To fix that, you can add a Color Corrector 3-way filter.

1. Select the top clip and apply Effects > Video Filters > Color Correction > Color Corrector 3-way.

2. Adjust the mids and the white levels to taste to get an image like **FIGURE 8.10**.

FIGURE 8.10: Our finished image.

Audio Profile

STEVE OLSWANG
Editor, Dan Rather Reports

Steve Olswang edits for Dan Rather Reports, working exclusively with HDCAM. Visit the companion Web site to hear how his workflow meets the demanding deadlines of a news magazine.

Using Composite Modes

There's a lot of room for experimentation. For instance, I changed the composite mode to Overlay and reduced the Opacity of the top layer to 73%. Then, I pulled the blacks and the whites toward warmer tones and reduced the saturation (**FIGURE 8.11**).

Gaussian Blur 10 combined with Soft Light consistently produces pleasant results—it is a great place to start, and often is exactly what the producer means by "silky and satiny," or the slightly more technical "deep blacks and glowing highlights."

FIGURE 8.11: A different example, using the Overlay composite mode.

Playing with these techniques will yield rewards. Before long you will have recipes for a variety of moods.

Here is one more: For weddings or romantic footage, try the composite mode Screen with the Gaussian Blur cranked up to 30 and the blacks pulled down a little bit. **FIGURE 8.12** shows how the footage looks after this treatment:

FIGURE 8.12: A different look, using Screen and adjustments to Gaussian Blur and the blacks.

Let's push this a little bit further by limiting where the composite mode is applied.

Vignetting

Using vignetting—limiting your effect to the center of the frame and letting the edges fall off—tends to focus the viewer's attention and lend a feeling of nostalgia.

Here's the CliffsNotes version of the step-by-step:

1. Create a custom gradient using a radial effect.

2. Slide your two-track composite effect up to Tracks 3 and 4.

3. Duplicate Track 3 and place it on Track 1.

4. Place your gradient on Track 2.

5. Nest Tracks 3 and 4.

6. Apply the Travel Matte – Luma composite mode to Track 3.

7. Apply the Color Corrector 3-way filter to Track 1, and darken to taste.

8. Tweak everything until you and your client are happy.

FIGURE 8.13 illustrates the final effect.

FIGURE 8.13: A vignette allows the viewer to focus on the brightest portion of the image.

Customize Your Gradient and Place It

This gradient will determine where the composited effect will be applied. White will be the full effect, and black will be none.

1. From the Generator menu (the menu with the letter A in the lower-right corner of the Viewer), choose **Render > Custom Gradient**.

2. Edit the gradient into the sequence, and then double-click the gradient from the Timeline to load it into the Viewer.

3. Park your playhead within the gradient and then click the Control tab in the Viewer. This allows you to make modifications in the Viewer while observing the effects in the Canvas.

4. Change the Shape field from **Linear** to **Radial** by clicking the Shape pop-up menu.

5. Change the Start fields from 360, 0 to **0, 0** (**FIGURE 8.14**).

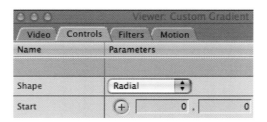

FIGURE 8.14: Configure the gradient's settings to Radial, with a center at 0,0.

6. Reorganize your clips so that the two clips on Tracks 1 and 2 move up to V3 and V4.

7. Place the gradient on V2 and extend it so it runs the same length as the two clips on V3 and V4 (**FIGURE 8.15**).

8. Copy the original clip from V3 and paste it into V1.

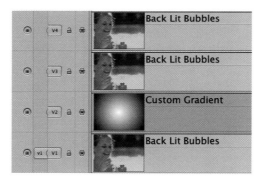

FIGURE 8.15: The final track configuration of your clips. V1 is a copy of V3.

Build a Nest and Apply Travel Matte – Luma

Now that you've placed your gradient, it's time apply the composite mode:

1. Select Tracks 3 and 4.

2. Press **Option+C**.

3. Name your nest **Nested Composite**, or something equally memorable.

4. Right-click your nest and choose **Composite > Travel Matte – Luma** from the shortcut menu (**FIGURE 8.16**).

Perhaps you are underwhelmed? I was, too. The vignette isn't working. Time to customize. I added a Color Corrector 3-way to the clip on V1 as well as the nest on V3, darkened V1, then lightened V3 (**FIGURE 8.17**).

FIGURE 8.16: A before-and-after comparison of the four-layer effect so far.

FIGURE 8.17: The end result.

Then, I played with the size, shape, and width of the gradient on Track 2 (**FIGURE 8.18**).

FIGURE 8.18: The final effect.

Try This at Home!

I love the digital nature of composite modes because they are either on or off. There is no initial tweaking to get started. The unexpected looks I see as I turn composite modes on and off open my mind to the possibilities, leading me to try new things with the filters and the parameters I can tweak. Here are some ideas:

- Animate parameters on Radial Blur or apply a Wind Blur to the top layer.

- Apply anything selected in Effects > Video Filters > Stylize to either layer.

- Try the Strobe and Blink filters.

- Nest, then duplicate the nest on top of itself. Add another composite mode and a different filter. Repeat.

Don't be afraid to make the footage look terrible as you experiment. It won't be long before you have a sense of what the different composite modes do and how they interact with different footage and filter mixtures.

Favorites To Go

Because I work on many different systems, I carry some of my settings on a USB thumb drive. I also carry a project that contains my favorites. I call this project *Saved_Effects*.

In Final Cut Pro, drag the Effects tab out of the Browser, and then drag the Favorites bin from the Effects tab into your project. This will save your favorites to a project.

When you use Final Cut on a different system, insert your thumb drive and open your *Saved_Effects* project. Then drag the Effects tab off into its own window.

Check to see if there are favorites already in the Favorites bin in the Effects window of the new system. If there are, be courteous. Create a bin in your *Saved_Effects* project to hold the favorites for the editor who normally works the system. Name it *edit_friend_favorites*. After those older favorites are safe, replace the favorites in the Favorites bin in the Effects window with your own.

Just like a location shoot, always try to leave things the way you found them when you arrive. Don't forget to return the regular editor's favorites to the Effects window when you are finished.

Storing your favorites in a *Saved_Effects* project will also come in handy when you have to trash your FCP preferences. Trashing preferences trashes favorites as well—but if you follow this procedure, you will be backed up!

Chapter 9

Using Masks and Mattes in Final Cut Pro

KEVIN MONAHAN

At the very heart of video effects creation, you'll find masks and mattes. Masks and mattes give you the power to shape and blend clips to form wholly new images, more commonly known as *composites*.

Mattes Vs. Masks

You may be wondering, "What's the difference between a matte and a mask?" The answer is "Not much." Mattes and masks both have the same effect: They create and control the areas of transparency in a clip. But there are two crucial differences between these two features:

• A *matte* is most commonly a filter that controls areas of transparency within a clip. These filters define areas of transparency with parameters such as sliders and point controls. You activate mattes by choosing **Effects > Video Filters > Mattes**. Use mattes if you need a filter with a simple shape.

• A mask is an independent graphic or video clip (usually grayscale) lying on a video track between the foreground and background images. The mask serves the same purpose as a matte. To "unlock" this mask, you must use a composite mode such as Travel Matte — Luma or Travel Matte — Alpha. You can use a mask to create a more custom look than you can get with a matte, which has predefined parameters (**FIGURE 9.1**).

FIGURE 9.1: This image is a composite made from two separate images. The foreground image (the woman) uses a shape mask and a Mask Feather filter. The clip has also been flopped, repositioned, and tinted.

Matte Filters At a Glance

FCP has a number of filters that you can use to create mattes:

- **Garbage Matte.** Allows you to create shaped mattes by manipulating point controls. There are both four- and eight-point varieties, which are useful for cutting out oddly shaped items.

- **Extract.** Takes the luma information of a clip and allows you to use it as a Travel Matte – Alpha or Travel Matte – Luma mask.

- **Image Mask.** Works like a mask filter, in that you need to supply a separate mask image to make the blend.

- **Mask Shape.** Provides basic matte shapes such as rectangle, rounded rectangle, diamond, and oval.

- **Widescreen.** Used to simulate a widescreen effect with an adjustable viewing area.

- **Soft Edges.** Makes a blended matte with built-in feathering, perfect for a vignette effect with edges that fade to the frame's border.

Now that you're familiar with the major players in matte creation, let's see how mattes create blended video imagery.

Mattes, Masks, and the Alpha Channel

You probably already know that the colors of digital video are created with a combination of red, green, and blue pixels. The red, green, and blue channels control the level at which each pixel displays. Each pixel also has the power to be transparent or opaque (solid). The channel that determines transparency is called the *alpha channel*. The alpha channel uses grayscale values to control whether a pixel is transparent, semi-opaque, or opaque.

When you're manipulating a matte or mask, you're actually controlling the alpha channel of a clip. Three values determine the areas of a clip:

- Black (fully transparent)
- Gray (semi-transparent)
- White (fully opaque)

See the alpha channel in action by doing the following:

1.   Load a clip into the Viewer.

2.   Select **Alpha** in the View pop-up menu (**FIGURE 9.2**).

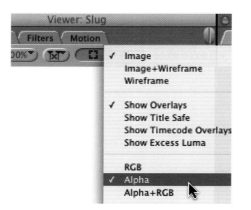

FIGURE 9.2 Select Alpha to view clip transparency.

Your Viewer will now be white, representing the clip's full opacity. (By default, a fully opaque alpha channel is 100% white.)

3.   Choose **Effects > Video Filters > Matte > Mask Shape** (**FIGURE 9.3**).

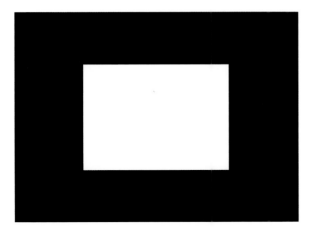

FIGURE 9.3: Black represents 100% transparency in Alpha view. Notice that the alpha channel changes to a white rectangle on a black field.

4. Change the View pop-up menu to RGB and the background to Checkerboard 1 (see **FIGURE 9.4**).

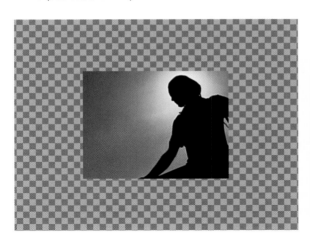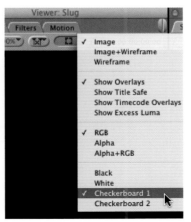

FIGURE 9.4: Viewing black text and effects is easy when the background is changed to Checkerboard 1.

By switching to RGB view, you can easily see how the alpha channel operates. Notice that the area that was black in Alpha view is now transparent, indicated by the checkerboard background. The alpha channel controls the transparency of each pixel in the clip.

NOTE: An interesting piece of trivia is that the alpha channel (along with other computer graphics milestones) was invented by the Lucasfilm Computer Division in the late 1970s.

Using Mattes

Now that you know what's going on behind the scenes, you can create a simple blending technique by putting a matte filter into practice:

1. Place a clip on V1 in the Timeline.

2. Edit a different clip on V2 directly above the V1 clip.

3. Double-click the V2 clip, loading it into the Viewer.

4. Choose **Effects > Video Filters > Matte > Mask Shape**.

5. Experiment with the filter's parameters on the Filters tab and watch what happens (see **FIGURE 9.5**).

FIGURE 9.5: The foreground clip's matte is repositioned and horizontally scaled. The clip is also repositioned and tinted.

You should now see a composite, which displays both the foreground image (defined by the transparency created by the matte) and background image at the same time. By changing the parameters, you can alter the shape and/or the position of the matte. Keep in mind that you can also reposition, scale, rotate, distort, or add a filter to the affected clip.

TIP: To avoid blurring when you reposition an image at 100% scale in interlaced video, be sure to place it on the Canvas, with the vertical value (the right-hand box) set to an even whole number. Set this on the Motion tab by choosing Basic Motion > Center.

Available Masks in Final Cut Pro

Where can you find masks in Final Cut Pro? Actually, you can use generators such as Custom Gradient, Highlight, Particle Noise, Shapes, Boris Vector Shape, or even Title 3D to create a grayscale mask. You can spice up the look of the generators with the addition of a filter (**FIGURE 9.6**), or stack two generators and apply a composite mode (Hard Light, Overlay, etc.) to the overlying clip, and then nest the two into a single graphics track. I've combined filters and composite modes for cool masks inside Final Cut Pro. You can even create more complex static masks in Adobe Photoshop.

FIGURE 9.6: This Circle generator has both Wave and Mask Feather filters added to it. Adding filters to generators is a creative way to make grayscale mattes within Final Cut Pro.

Mask Techniques

We've already seen how to use mattes, so what's the technique for blending images using a mask?

1. Stack two clips on separate video tracks, placing the foreground clip on V3 and the background clip on V1.

2. Place the grayscale generator of your choice on V2 between the edit points of the V3 and V1 clips.

3. Select the V3 clip. Choose **Modify > Composite Modes > Travel Matte – Luma.** (You can also change a composite mode by Control-clicking the clip and choosing the desired mode from the shortcut menu.) **FIGURE 9.7** shows my result.

4. Make any necessary adjustments to the grayscale matte clip.

FIGURE 9.7: Again, a Circle generator with the Wave and Mask Feather filters applied serves as the V2 matte in this composite. The matte's edges undulate, as the Wave filter is self-animating.

NOTE: The stacking order of the clips is important – background on V1, mask on V2, and foreground on V3. A common error occurs in applying the composite mode; you must apply it to the V3 clip (also called graphic fill), not to the mask itself.

Travel Matte Luma vs. Travel Matte Alpha

You may wonder when it's better to use one flavor of travel matte versus another. Here's the general rule: When a mask element has an embedded alpha channel, such as a Title Generator, Title 3D, or Boris Vector Shape, it's better to use Travel Matte – Alpha. This mask is much cleaner than Travel Matte – Luma.

For example, it's possible to create a black-and-white text generator for a mask element on V2 and apply the Travel Matte – Luma composite mode to a clip on V3 for a simple "video in text" effect. If you use Travel Matte – Alpha, however, the edges of the text will be sharper.

Video Tutorial: Creating A Traveling Matte

One of the more flexible layered effects in Final Cut is a traveling matte, where one video plays inside a shape that is inside another video. It sounds complex, but it's easy to create. Visit the companion Web site to see how it's done.

Animated Mattes and Masks

Mattes and masks don't necessarily have to remain static. Matte parameters can be animated with keyframes. Masks can be created with animated grayscale values. Doing either creates an "undulating" blended effect that you can use to create further custom effects. FCP generators combined with animated filters offer some interesting possibilities.

TIP: To readjust a point's position in a Garbage Matte or the position of a Shape Mask, return to the Filters tab and click the point control's button (the cross-hair) to reset it before moving it in the Canvas. Otherwise, you might nudge the entire image.

Feather and Choker Filters

Mask Feather and Matte Choker are two more filters in FCP's collection of matte filters. They aren't actually mattes or masks themselves, but tools to control the edges of the mattes. These filters add and subtract grayscale values from the boundary of the alpha channel, each in a slightly different way:

- **Mask Feather.** Add this filter just *below* any matte filter in the Filters tab to soften the edges surrounding your clip or graphic. This technique lends a vignette effect to any image by adding a gradient ramp at the edges of the alpha channel. Almost every graphic will need at least a little feathering; just make sure that Mask Feather lies at the bottom of the filter stack.

- **Matte Choker.** Add this filter just below any matte filter in the Filters tab, and you can subtly expand and contract the edges of the clip or graphics. This effect is achieved by adding or subtracting solid black or white to the edges of the graphic.

TIP: A matte choker is most commonly used to reduce, or "choke," the matte derived from a chroma key.

Compositing Technique: Blurry Border

Here's a simple technique to add a blurry border to an image:

1. Shift+Option-drag the V1 clip upward to place an identical copy of the clip in the track above.

2. Turn off the visibility of the V1 clip by Control-clicking the clip and choosing **Clip Enable** from the shortcut menu (or press **Control+B**).

3. Apply a matte filter to the V2 clip; for example, **Effects > Matte > Mask Shape**. Try a few different shapes from the Shapes pop-up menu. Adjust the parameters as you see fit.

4. Add a Mask Feather filter to soften the edges.

5. Turn on the visibility of the V1 clip by Control-clicking the clip and choosing **Clip Enable** from the shortcut menu again (or press **Control+B**).

6. Apply a Gaussian Blur filter to the V1 clip (**FIGURE 9.8**).

FIGURE 9.8: Achieve a blurry border effect by stacking identical images and applying a matte to the upper layer and a Blur filter to the lower layer for a simple and elegant look.

The clip appears to have a blurry border, but what's really going on is that the two images have been altered by a matte on V2 and a Blur filter on V1.

TIP: A different look can be achieved in a similar way by using a color correction or tint applied to either or both clips.

Video-in-Text Effect

A simple video-in-text effect has the ability to send two messages at once: a written one and a visual one. Everyone should know how to make the following effect:

1. Place the clip you want to use as the background on V1.

2. Place the text generator you want to use on V2. (I prefer Title 3D and LiveType over the standard Final Cut text generators.)

3. Place the video you want to see within the text on V3.

4. Select the V3 clip.

5. Choose **Modify > Composite Modes > Travel Matte Alpha**. You should now see your video within the matte created by the alpha channel from the text generator.

Add a drop shadow to the video in text. This is normally impossible to do because a drop shadow needs to use the "graphic fill," but is already being used by the V3 clip. You can get around this restriction by nesting the clips.

6. Select the clips on V2 and V3.

7. Nest them by selecting **Sequence > Nest Items (Option+C)**.

8. Name the nest **Video in Text** and click **OK**. The clips collapse into a nest.

9. Option+double-click the nest to load it into the Viewer.

10. On the Motion tab, select the Drop Shadow checkbox and adjust its parameters to get the look you want (**FIGURE 9.9**).

FIGURE 9.9: To add a drop shadow to the effect, nest the travel matte effect first.

You now have a pretty video-in-text effect that was created with the letters of the generator acting as mattes in a Travel Matte – Alpha effect. Experiment with the different elements (such as animating the type or color correcting the graphic fill), if you like. You'll soon have some professional looks going on.

There are literally endless things you can do with mattes, masks, and the techniques with which to exploit them. I covered only three layers of images, but FCP has 99 video tracks available, and nesting increases that number to an astronomical amount. Keep stacking those layers of video and graphics and let your imagination run free.

Chapter 10

Adding Stability with SmoothCam

LARRY JORDAN

You know the drill: There isn't enough time to set up a tripod, so you decide to shoot the scene handheld. Except, once you start editing, you discover the camera is moving so much your viewers are getting motion sickness.

In the past, because there was nothing you could do inside Final Cut to stabilize these shots, you had three choices: not use the shot, use it and hope for the best, or move the clip into another application (such as After Effects or Boris Red) to stabilize it.

With the release of Final Cut Studio 2 and Final Cut Pro 6, you can now stabilize your shots directly in Final Cut using the SmoothCam filter. And this filter is a beauty! Follow along to see how it works, and be sure to check out the accompanying video tutorial to see the SmoothCam filter in action.

Get Your Clip into Analysis

Before Final Cut can work its magic, it needs to analyze the clip to determine how the pixels are moving from one frame to the next. SmoothCam then uses this analysis to determine how to best smooth out the camera movement.

Let's take a look at an example using a clip with some shaky camera movement:

I've loaded a 15-second handheld tracking shot into the Viewer (**FIGURE 10.1**). You can also edit it to the Timeline; the process is the same.

SmoothCam needs to analyze the entire clip, not just the portion from the In to the Out. For this reason, it doesn't make any difference if the filter is applied in the Viewer or the Timeline.

FIGURE 10.1: This 15-second handheld snowboard tracking shot is a perfect candidate for SmoothCam.

With the Viewer selected (or, if you are using the Timeline, with the clip selected), choose **Effects > Video Filters > Video > SmoothCam**.

FIGURE 10.2: Applying the SmoothCam filter.

NOTE: This analysis needs to be done only once. Final Cut creates a data file that is stored in the same folder as the clip. So if you use the clip again, or change the In or Out points, the analysis does not need to be redone.

Keep in mind, this analysis can take a long, LONG time, depending on the length of the clip and the speed of your computer. For instance, on my MacBook Pro, this 15-second DV clip took more than 3 minutes to analyze. During the analysis, a special overlay warning appears over the clip in the Viewer (**FIGURE 10.3**), or Timeline, and the Background Processes window appears, estimating how much time remains for the analysis (**FIGURE 10.4**).

FIGURE 10.3: A warning overlay in the Viewer showing that the clip is being analyzed for SmoothCam.

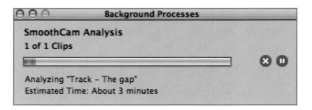

FIGURE 10.4: The Background Processes window.

When the analysis is complete, simply play the clip and marvel at the changes. What used to be shaky is now amazingly smooth!

Getting Everyone into Analysis

You don't need to analyze only one clip at a time. Here's a fast way to move multiple clips into analysis:

1. In the Browser, select all the clips you want to analyze.

2. Control-click the Duration column header at the top of the Browser and choose **Show SmoothCam** from the shortcut menu (it will be way down at the bottom).

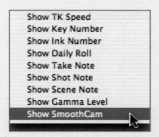

3. The dashed lines indicate that a clip has not been analyzed by SmoothCam. Control-click this dashed line in the SmoothCam column and choose **Run Analysis** from the shortcut menu.

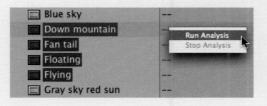

The Background Processes window opens up and shows the analysis status of your selected clips. Analysis takes a long time, but you are still able to edit inside Final Cut. If you need to capture, play back, or output, the Background Process will stop until your actions are complete.

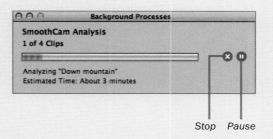

4. If you need to stop or pause the process, click one of the two icons to either stop or temporarily pause the process.

After each clip has been analyzed, the SmoothCam Browser column will display "Analysis completed."

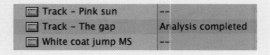

How It Works

SmoothCam calculates movement caused by the shakiness of the camera, rather than the subject of the frame, and shifts the picture by an equal yet opposite amount so that it cancels out the perceived camera shake.

The problem is that when this compensation occurs, black edges appear around your frame—sometimes very big black edges (**FIGURE 10.5**).

FIGURE 10.5: Note how much the picture has been rotated and shifted up and to the right to compensate for the excess camera movement.

SmoothCam zooms into the image to enlarge it enough so that these black edges don't appear; however, if you are working with standard-def video, zooming in runs the risk of making your images blurry.

Later I'll show you one way to deal with this problem by using a compositing solution. For now, though, keep in mind that SmoothCam will work better with HD images than with SD, because HD has more pixels to work with, thus decreasing the apparent softening effect.

Tweaking the Results

Like all good filters, SmoothCam has settings you can tweak to improve the results. Let's take a look at what they are (**FIGURE 10.6**).

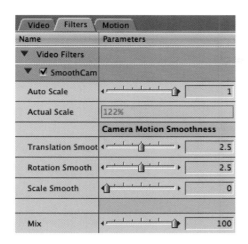

FIGURE 10.6: SmoothCam filter settings in their default state.

- **Auto Scale** lets you determine how much to zoom in your image. When Auto Scale equals 0, all zooming is turned off. When it equals 1, the image is zoomed in such that no black edges appear. You can adjust this to suit your needs.

- **Actual Scale** shows how much the image has been zoomed. You cannot edit this field. Generally, an SD image can be safely zoomed about 105% without showing too much softness. In our example, however, the image needed to be zoomed 122%, causing serious image degradation.

- **Translation Smooth** controls smoothing movement horizontally and vertically; 2.5 is the default setting. The larger this number, the greater the smoothing effect.

- **Rotation Smooth** controls smoothing rotation around a center point; 2.5 is the default setting. The larger this number, the greater the smoothing effect.

- **Scale Smooth** controls smoothing movement to and from the camera—the "z" axis—either from a shaky zoom or the camera moving to or from the subject; 0 is the default setting. The larger this number, the greater the smoothing effect.

- **Mix** determines how much of the effect is applied; 0 applies none of the smoothing effect, 1 applies the full effect. (For some truly weird effects, set Mix to 0.5 to show how much compensation is really applied to your clip.)

NOTE: Keep in mind that this filter won't remove gentle pans or tilts; it just smooths out the jerkiness. Motion, on the other hand, has an additional setting for SmoothCam that can give your video a "locked-on-a-tripod" look. To achieve it, apply the SmoothCam filter to the clip in Final Cut Pro, send your clip to Motion, go to the Inspector > Behaviors tab and change the Method from Smooth to Stabilize.

Using a Compositing Technique to Improve Sharpness

For SD images, the smaller the zoom, the better the images look. Not zooming in at all is ideal. However, that prevents SmoothCam from working.

Here's an alternative to zooming: composite your image into a stable background (**FIGURE 10.7**).

FIGURE 10.7: The snowboarding image composited into a background, with Auto Scale set to 0.

In this example, I set Auto Scale to **0** to turn it off. Then I applied a Mask Shape filter, set it to a rectangular shape, and sized it to 80% of the full image (see the settings in **FIGURE 10.8**). Because I'm cropping all the wildly gyrating black edges, my image looks stable, without any decrease in image quality.

However, the composite looks a bit stiff and geometric. So, in Figure 10.8, I added a Mask Feather filter and adjusted it to add a lot of blur to the edges of the matte by setting Soft to **60**. Now, the snow from the snowboarder and the background all seem to blend to create a much more interesting, organic, and stable look. (If I wanted to blend this further, I'd color correct the background to remove the blue cast.)

FIGURE 10.8: The same composite with a Mask Feather filter added with a Soft setting of 60: to maximize the blur around the edge of the composite and blend it with the background.

If you give it time to analyze your clips, SmoothCam can do magic. Even shaky handheld zooms can be stabilized to look almost as though your camera was on a tripod.

Video Tutorial: Working with SmoothCam

SmoothCam is a new filter in Final Cut Pro 6 that can take truly shaky footage and make it look amazingly smooth. In this tutorial (available on the companion Web site), Larry Jordan shows you how it works, some traps to avoid, and how to get the best out of this filter for either SD or HD video.

Part 3
3D in Motion

Nothing is more confusing to most editors than stepping out of their nice, safe, 2D world into the endless three dimensions found in Motion 3.

In the next chapters, Mark Spencer offers a clear, straightforward approach to working in Motion's 3D world that gives all of us a chance to acclimate. As an added bonus, Mark has made some of his project files available for you to experiment with.

First, though, I'd like to include a couple of thoughts based on my experience teaching Motion to experienced editors. Under the covers, Motion is doing all its calculations in 3D, even when you are looking at a standard 2D graphic. This means that when you switch from 2D to 3D, Motion looks exactly the same. That can greatly reduce the stress of trying to learn a new interface, since it hasn't changed.

Second, as these chapters make clear, you can create successful animated graphics without using every 3D bell and whistle. In fact, throughout this section are some video tutorials that can give you ideas on using 3D space without even going into a 3D environment.

So, take your time, experiment, and give yourself time to understand this new feature of Motion. Because once you understand it, the graphical possibilities are endless.

As usual, throughout this section you'll discover links to some interesting audio interviews and video tutorials, as well as helpful keyboard shortcuts specific to Motion.

Chapter 11

Foundations of 3D in Motion

MARK SPENCER

Working in three dimensions on a two-dimensional computer screen is tricky business, but Motion makes it surprisingly easy. Still, it takes some getting used to. To work in 3D using Motion, it's important to know how Motion "thinks" about the 3D world and then learn how to manipulate objects in that world (**FIGURE 11.1**).

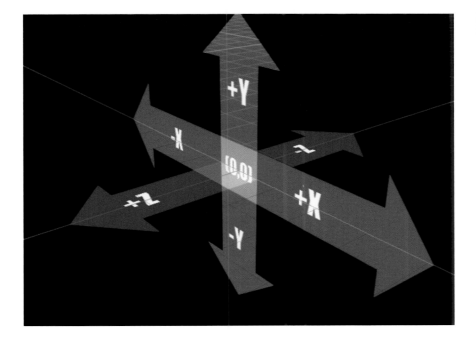

FIGURE 11.1: 3D space in Motion.

3D or 2.5D?

First, let's clarify what Motion means by 3D. Much like in other compositing and motion graphics applications, 3D in Motion means you can change the position and rotation of objects in 3D space (horizontally, vertically, and in Z-depth), but the objects themselves are always two-dimensional. Think of a deck of playing cards. In a 2D environment, cards that lay on a table may be able to be moved or rotated on the table, but they will always appear flat on the table.

In 3D, you can pick up the cards and throw them in the air—they can move and spin on all axes in 3D space but still appear as flat, two-dimensional objects. In Motion, the playing cards represent your objects: movies, graphics, text, shapes, particle emitters, and so on, and they can all be arranged and animated in 3D space. But each object remains a flat, two-dimensional object (**FIGURE 11.2**). That's why this type of 3D environment is sometimes called "2.5D" (**FIGURE 11.3**).

By arranging and animating objects, cameras, and lights in a 3D environment, you can create incredibly engaging, dynamic, motion graphics. You can even create pseudo-3D objects by arranging 2D layers to form basic 3D objects—much as you can build a house out of a deck of cards.

If you want to build models of true volumetric 3D objects that can be textured and animated, you should take a look at a 3D modeling application, such as Cinema 4D (**FIGURE 11.4**).

FIGURE 11.2: 2D in Motion—2D objects on a flat X-Y plane.

FIGURE 11.3: "2.5D" in Motion—2D objects in 3D space.

FIGURE 11.4: Volumetric 3D objects created in Cinema 4D.

Video: An Introduction to 3D Space in Motion 3

If you've never worked in 3D space before, it can be very disorienting. Visit the companion Web site to see a video on creating 3D effects in Motion 3 that doesn't require a complete knowledge of 3D or working in a 3D world.

A Little Terminology

Let's start with the basics regarding 3D in Motion. In 2D space, the horizontal axis is denoted by X and the vertical axis by Y (**FIGURE 11.5**). The very center of Motion's canvas is denoted (0,0), which means X=0 pixels and Y=0 pixels. The X value increases to the right and the Y value increases as you move up.

EDITOR'S NOTE: Objects move along the Y-axis in Motion in the opposite direction to the axis in Final Cut Pro. In Motion, up is denoted by positive numbers, down by negative numbers. In Final Cut Pro, up is negative and down is positive.

FIGURE 11.5: Motion's X-Y axes—the center of the Canvas is (0,0).

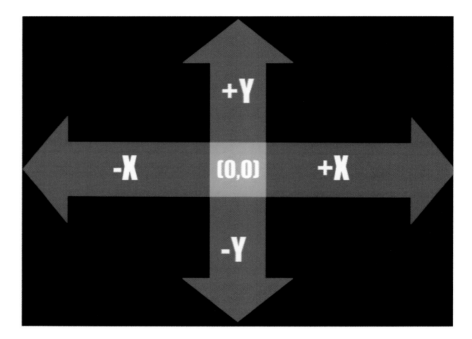

When you move a layer in 2D space, you can only move it horizontally (changing its X position) or vertically (changing its Y position), but when you rotate an object in 2D space, you are actually rotating it around the virtual Z-axis, as if you were spinning it around a pin stuck into the screen (through the layer's anchor point). In both cases, however, the layer stays flat on the X-Y plane. Make sense? This may be simple, but things quickly get complicated once you start moving layers, groups, and cameras in 3D space, so make sure you have a firm grasp of X, horizontal; Y, vertical; and Z, depth.

Stepping into a New Dimension

When you first launch Motion 3, it looks almost identical to Motion 2. The only things that indicate that there is more going on are a new tool in the View bank of tools and the New Camera icon in the toolbar. The developers at Apple have done a great job at hiding the 3D tools and 3D views, therefore keeping the workspace uncluttered. After all, sometimes 2D is all you need.

Let's look at how to manipulate objects in 3D space. First, we'll add two graphics from Motion's Library to the Canvas: a chalkboard and some chalk (**FIGURE 11.6**).

Video: Working in 3D in Motion

To see a video demonstration of what's covered in this section, please visit the book's companion Web site.

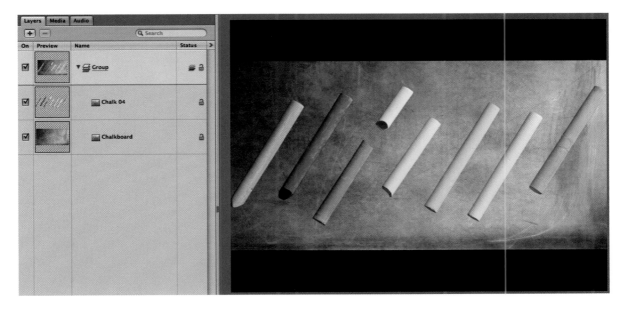

FIGURE 11.6: Two simple graphics from Motion's massive Content folder in the Library. Note the stacking order in the Layers tab matches what you see in the Canvas: The chalk is on top of the chalkboard.

In the Layers tab, we can see that each object is a layer, and the layers are contained in a group. The layer order in the Layers tab determines which layer appears on top in the Canvas.

In the Canvas, we can change the horizontal and vertical position of each layer simply by dragging the layer, and we can rotate each layer by dragging the handle that extends from the layer's anchor point (**FIGURE 11.7**). But the layers still remain flat. How do we change the position and rotation of a layer in 3D space?

FIGURE 11.7: Changing the position and rotation of layers by dragging in the Canvas.

If you've used Motion before, you'll know that, in addition to manipulating layers in the Canvas, you can access all of a layer's parameters in the Inspector. When you look at the Properties tab of the Inspector, you'll find (among other things) controls for a layer's position and rotation (**FIGURE 11.8**). But just as in the Canvas, Position lets you change only X and Y, and Rotation just lets you rotate the layer flat in relation to the screen.

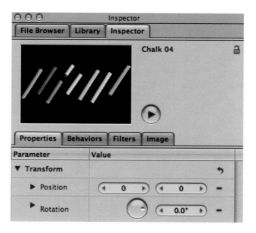

FIGURE 11.8: The Position and Rotation parameters in the Inspector let you enter specific values, but at first it appears you can only manipulate the layer in 2D.

However, if you click the disclosure triangle next to the Position parameter, you will find the Position Z parameter, quietly tucked away (**FIGURE 11.9**). Drag in the value field, and you'll see the layer get larger as it moves towards the screen (a positive value) and smaller as it moves away from the screen (a negative value) (**FIGURE 11.10**).

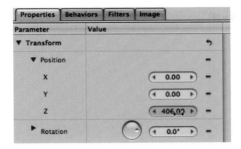

FIGURE 11.9: Changing the Position Z parameter.

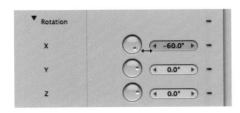

FIGURE 11.10: A positive Z-position value moves the layer "closer" to the screen, making it appear larger.

And if you click the disclosure triangle for Rotation, you'll see three additional parameters: Rotate X, Rotate Y, and Rotate Z (**FIGURE 11.11**).

FIGURE 11.11: Revealing the X, Y, and Z Rotation values and changing the X value.

Drag in each value field and observe how the layer rotates around each axis. When it rotates around the X-axis, for example, it's as if there were a horizontal bar running through the layer's anchor point, and the layer can then spin around the bar (**FIGURE 11.12**).

FIGURE 11.12: A negative X-rotation value tilts the top of the layer "away" from the screen.

Understanding the Anchor Point

A layer's anchor point is the point around which it scales and rotates. By default, it's located at the center of a layer, indicated by the small x with a circle around it (and a handle sticking out of it so you can rotate the layer). You can move the anchor point, which changes how the layer rotates in 3D space.

To move the anchor point, you need to switch to the Anchor Point tool, which is available either in the toolbar (**FIGURE 11.13**), or by right-clicking (or Control-clicking) in the Canvas and choosing it from the shortcut menu (**FIGURE 11.14**).

FIGURE 11.13: Selecting the Anchor Point tool from the toolbar.

FIGURE 11.14: Selecting the Anchor Point tool by right-clicking or Control-clicking in the Canvas and choosing Anchor Point from the shortcut menu.

Once you select the Anchor Point tool, the icon changes to a red arrow pointing right, a green arrow pointing up, and what looks to be a blue dot, but is actually a blue arrow pointing right at you (**FIGURE 11.15**). The three primary colors, R-G-B, are matched to the three axes, X-Y-Z (X is red, Y is green, and Z is blue). This will be very important later on, so keep it in mind.

FIGURE 11.15: The three axes of the anchor point.

You can move the anchor point horizontally by dragging the red arrow or vertically by dragging the green arrow (an arrow turns yellow when you mouse over it). Or, if you click anywhere inside the little white circle *without* touching the blue arrow, you can move in both X and Y at the same time.

Try moving the anchor point to the edge of a layer, and then use the Inspector to rotate it around the different axes (**FIGURE 11.16**). Perhaps you can start to see some interesting creative possibilities?

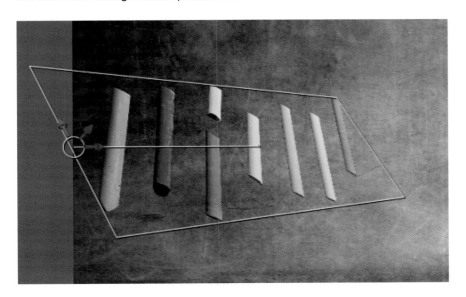

FIGURE 11.16: With the anchor point moved to the left edge of the layer, the layer now rotates around that edge. Note that you can move the anchor point completely off the layer.

When you are done, press **Command+Z** enough times to undo the rotation and move the anchor point back to the center of the layer. Press **Shift+S** to switch back to the default Select/Transform tool.

3D Groups

You may have noticed as you were moving the top chalk layer along its Z-axis, or rotating it around its X- or Y-axis, that it never moved behind the chalkboard layer. Logically, it should—if you move the front layer back in Z-space, it should disappear behind the closer layer, right? But right now, the only way to move one layer in front of another is to change the stacking order in the Layers tab (**FIGURE 11.17**).

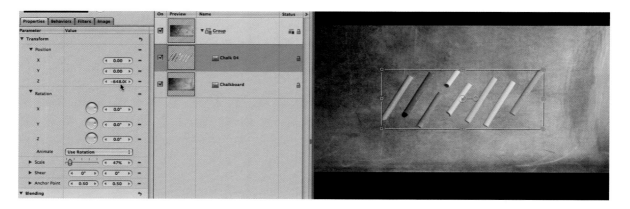

FIGURE 11.17: The layer that appears on top in the Canvas is determined by the stacking order in the Layers tab, no matter how much you move it in Z-space. Here, the chalk layer is more than 400 pixels "behind" the chalkboard, but still appears in front.

By the same token, if you rotate one layer, it should intersect the other layer, shouldn't it (**FIGURE 11.18**)?

That's because by default, the groups that contain layers are 2D groups. This means that layers in 2D groups won't *interact* with each other. Luckily, it's an easy situation to remedy.

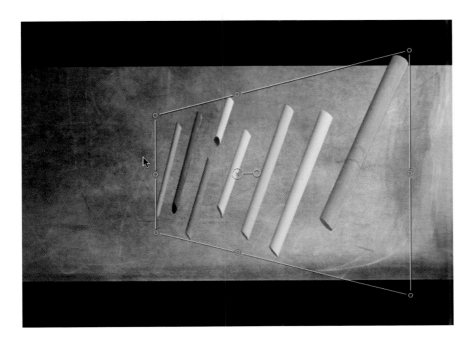

FIGURE 11.18: Here, the two layers are at the same position in Z-space, so when the chalk layer is rotated, you'd think it would intersect the chalkboard, but it doesn't.

In the Layers tab, the far right column is called the Status column, which contains a small 2D/3D icon for each group (see Figure 11.17). To switch the group from a 2D group to a 3D group, just click the icon, which changes from three flat rectangles to a stack of rectangles (**FIGURE 11.19**).

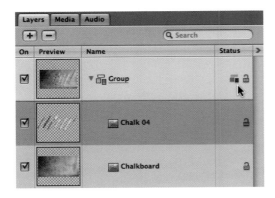

FIGURE 11.19: Clicking the icon switches the group to 3D. Note that you can also select the group and choose Object > 3D Group or press Control+D.

Now that the group is a 3D group, if you move the top chalk layer back in Z-space (in the negative direction), it will move behind the blackboard layer. Therefore (and this is important, so I'll put it in italics), *in a 3D group, it's the Z-position value, not the stacking order of the Layers tab, that determines how layers appear in the Canvas.* Try changing the layer order in the Layers tab—nothing changes in the Canvas (**FIGURE 11.20**).

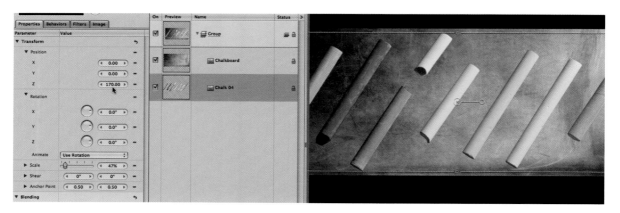

FIGURE 11.20: With a 3D group, even though the chalk layer is below the chalkboard in the Layers tab, it appears on top in the Canvas because its Z-position value is greater than the chalkboard layer, so it is closer to the screen in Z-space.

NOTE: If two layers have the exact same Z-position value (as when you first add objects to the Canvas), then the layer stacking order does determine which layer appears on top.

If you rotate a layer around its X- or Y-axis, it will now intersect the other layer (**FIGURE 11.21**).

FIGURE 11.21: Rotating a layer in a 3D group will cause it to intersect other layers.

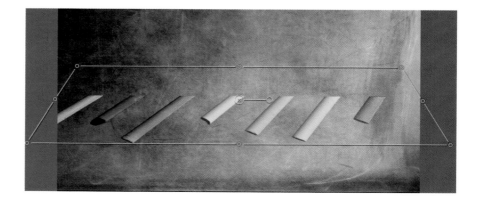

To see this more clearly, you can rotate the group containing the layers
(**FIGURE 11.22**).

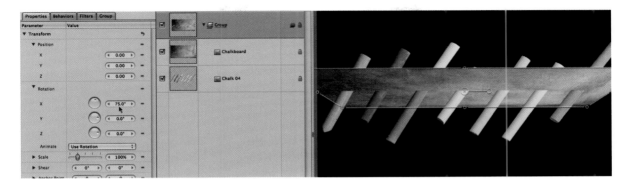

FIGURE 11.22: By first rotating the chalk layer 90 degrees on the X-axis, then rotating the entire group on its X-axis (notice the group is selected in the Layers tab), you can see the chalk layer clearly intersecting the chalkboard.

So this is all well and good, but wouldn't it be nice to be able to change the position and rotation of these layers around all axes directly in the Canvas, rather than resorting to the Inspector? Enter the indispensable, yet awkwardly named, Adjust 3D Transform tool. Undo your changes or click the little reset button (the hooked arrow) at the top right of the Properties tab for each layer and the group before proceeding.

Your New 3D Friend, The Letter Q

In the toolbar, the second button from the left is the Adjust 3D Transform tool (**FIGURE 11.23**). As the tooltip will tell you, its keyboard shortcut is the letter **Q**.

FIGURE 11.23: Pressing Q activates the Adjust 3D Transform tool.

It's a good shortcut to memorize. Select the tool, and two things happen: the contents of the heads-up display (HUD) changes, and the anchor point of the selected layer once again turns into red, green, and blue arrows (**FIGURE 11.24**). But this is NOT the Anchor Point tool, so don't get confused! The arrows are farther apart than on the anchor point tool, and there is a hollow white circle at the end of each arrow.

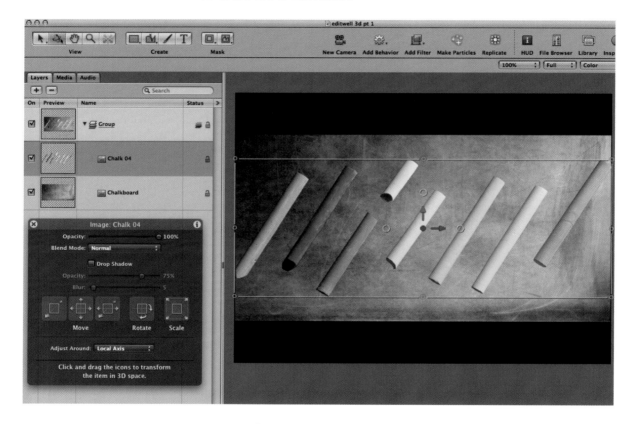

FIGURE 11.24: Selecting the Adjust 3D Transform tool populates the HUD with a set of controls and creates new onscreen controls.

3D Tools in the HUD

Let's start with the HUD (if you don't see it, press **F7**). The HUD contains three Move controls, a Rotate control, and a Scale control. The controls are pretty intuitive, but there are some modifier keys that come in handy. By the way, it can be helpful to have the Properties tab of the Inspector open while you make adjustments in the HUD so you can see exactly which parameters are changing.

The first Move control moves the layer back and forth along its Z-axis—pretty straightforward. If you hold down the Command key while dragging, nothing seems to happen. But if you look at the Inspector, you'll see that indeed the Z-position is changing, but so is the Scale parameter for the layer! In fact, as the layer moves towards the screen, its scale is shrinking just enough to look like it hasn't moved at all. This automatic adjustment allows you to separate elements in Z-space without changing how they look in relationship to each other (see **FIGURE 11.25**). Although it may not make much sense now, keep it in the back of your mind—we'll come back to it in the next chapter.

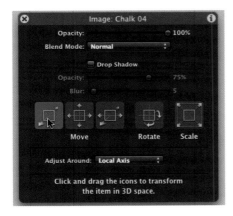

FIGURE 11.25: Using the HUD to move the selected layer in Z-space.

The second Move tool moves the layer in X and Y. If you hold down the Command key while dragging, the movement will be constrained to just X or just Y.

The third Move tool moves the layer along the X-axis (horizontally) by dragging left/right or in Z-space by dragging up/down. Again, you can constrain the movement with the Command key.

Audio Profile

PHILIP OHLER
Senior Editor, McCann Erickson, **www.philipohler.com**

 Philip Ohler is an in-house editor for McCann Erickson, one of the largest advertising agencies in New York City. Philip is part of a team of editors creating in-house promotional and client-service videos. Visit the companion Web site to hear his thoughts on using Final Cut Pro and Final Cut Server.

The Rotate tool rotates around both the X-axis (dragging up/down) and the Y-axis (dragging left/right). With this tool, the Command key doesn't constrain to just X or just Y, but instead forces the layer to rotate around its Z-axis (**FIGURE 11.26**). This modifier will come in handy later when we work with cameras.

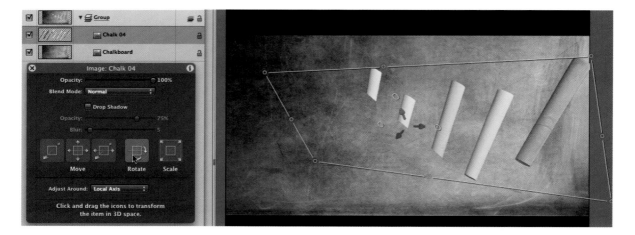

FIGURE 11.26: Freely rotating a layer around both its X and Y axes. Note how the blue arrow now points down to the left—the same direction that we dragged in the HUD.

The Scale tool simply changes the size of the layer. Pressing the Command key constrains the scale change to just horizontal (as you drag left/right) or just vertical (as you drag up/down). The Scale tool is most useful when applied to a camera, as we'll see in the next chapter.

With each of these HUD tools, you can use the same modifier keys for gearing up and gearing down the rate of change as you would in the Inspector: adding the Shift key makes the change much more rapid (or coarse); adding the Option key makes the change much slower (or fine). So, for example, if you wanted to move an object only vertically a very small amount, you'd press Option (to move just a little) and Command (to constrain the movement) and then drag up on the center Move control in the HUD.

Keyboard Shortcuts: Accessing 3D in Motion

SHORTCUT	FUNCTION
Q	Selects 3D Transform tool
Control+A	Sets 3D View to Active Camera
Control+C	Sets 3D View to Next Camera
Control+P	Sets 3D View to Perspective
Cmd+Shift+' (apostrophe)	Toggles 3D grid on and off
Control+D	Creates 3D group of selected objects
D	Cycles HUD properties for selected layer
F8	Shows/Hides Motion interface
X	Exposes all layers at playhead
Shift+X	Exposes all layers in project
W	Exposes all groups at playhead
Shift+W	Exposes all groups in project

Using the Canvas Controls

Everything you can do with the HUD controls you can do in the Canvas as well, but you have a few additional options in the Canvas.

Drag on a red, green, or blue arrow to move just along an X-, Y-, or Z-axis. Just like with the Anchor Point tool, arrows turn yellow when the pointer is placed over them (see **FIGURE 11.27**).

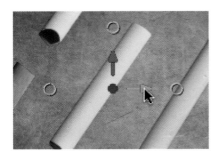

FIGURE 11.27: Dragging the layer along the X-axis. Note how the selected arrow turns yellow.

Moving the cursor over the rotation handles (the white circles) turns on rotation rings—dragging a ring rotates the layer around the selected axis (**FIGURE 11.28**). It might at first seem strange that the rotation handle above the green arrow (Y direction) reveals a red ring, but you are actually rotating around the X-axis. Work with these rings until they makes sense to you.

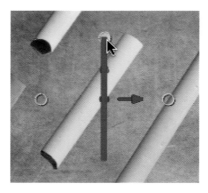

FIGURE 11.28: Rotating a layer in the Canvas.

If you hold down the Shift key *before* you drag on one of the rotation handles, the rotation will be constrained to 45-degree increments (**FIGURE 11.29**).

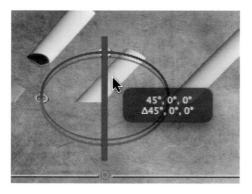

FIGURE 11.29: Using the Shift key when rotating.

Note that if you press Shift *after* you start to drag, Motion will add 45 degrees to however much you have already rotated the layer. This is a different behavior from rotating a layer with the Select/Transform tool, so be careful!

Finally, if you hold down the Command key, all three rotation rings turn on, and you can freely rotate the layer on all axes at the same time (**FIGURE 11.30**).

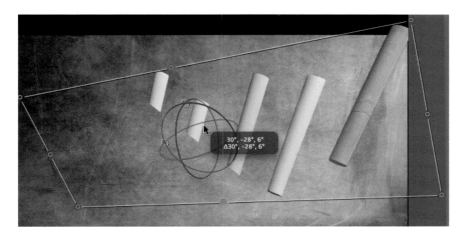

FIGURE 11.30: Free rotation around all axes in the Canvas. Note the tooltip indicates changes in X, Y, and Z.

You can of course animate any of these position and rotation parameters using either keyframes or behaviors. Several behaviors, such as Throw, have 3D buttons that allow you to create animation in 3D space (**FIGURE 11.31**). We'll work with animating layers (and cameras) in the next chapter.

FIGURE 11.31: By clicking the 3D button at the top left of the HUD, you can use the Throw behavior to animate an object in any direction in 3D space.

If you spend some time getting comfortable manipulating layers and groups in 3D space using the Inspector, the HUD, and the Adjust 3D Transform tool in the Canvas, you'll have a strong foundation as you start to add more layers, move them around in 3D space, add cameras and lights, and animate your scene.

Chapter 12

Using Cameras and Navigating in 3D Space

MARK SPENCER

We'll go a bit deeper into Motion's 3D world by adding a camera to a scene and then turning on and working with the various interface elements that allow us to navigate. We'll also build a couple of "sets" in different locations in 3D space and learn how to quickly jump to different elements and adjust them. In Chapter 13, we'll animate the camera to fly to each of these sets, completing the project.

Building a Set

Let's begin by building a little project that will have three "sets." A set is several related objects located in the same general region. Think of it like a Hollywood movie set: a set in Motion can have walls, a floor, a ceiling, and all sorts of actors and props inside it. For our purposes, we'll keep the sets simple.

Our first set will consist of a Photoshop file with two layers and some text. To keep things organized, I've placed the image layers into one group, the text layer into another group, and both those groups into the overall group named Set 1 (**FIGURE 12.1**).

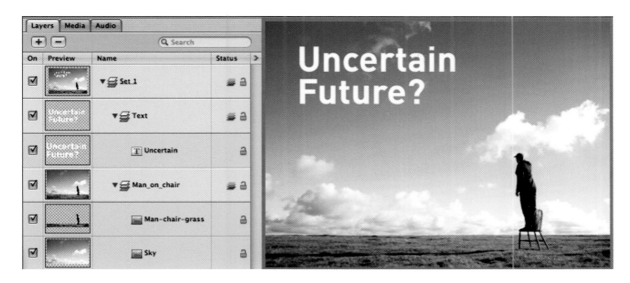

FIGURE 12.1: Our first set includes a photograph made up of two layers and a text layer.

As we saw in the previous chapter, groups are 2D by default and need to be switched to 3D before the layers within them will interact with each other as they are moved and rotated in 3D space. But rather than clicking the 2D/3D icon for every group, you can convert them all to 3D at once simply by adding a camera. To do so, click the **New Camera** icon in the toolbar (**FIGURE 12.2**).

FIGURE 12.2: The left two-thirds of Motion's toolbar, where the New Camera icon resides.

When you click the icon, a dialog appears. It lets you know that cameras won't affect 2D layers, and it gives you the option to switch all your 2D layers to 3D. Click **Switch to 3D** to do it (**FIGURE 12.3**).

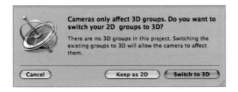

FIGURE 12.3: If none of your project's groups are 3D groups, you'll get this dialog when you try to add a camera. If at least one group is already 3D, the camera is added and any 2D groups are left as 2D.

The camera appears in the Project pane at the top of the Layers tab, and all the groups' 2D/3D icons have switched to 3D (**FIGURE 12.4**).

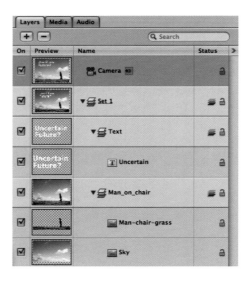

FIGURE 12.4: The Layers tab, with the camera added and the groups changed to 3D.

In the Canvas, our view of the scene hasn't changed at all. This is because a new camera gets added to the same location as the default reference camera: the one through which you were already viewing the scene but couldn't control. It's almost as if you always *were* looking through a camera, but you just didn't know it. But with an explicit camera, there are all sorts of interesting things you can do, like move the camera around or even move away from the camera and look at both the scene *and* the camera from a different viewpoint.

To make these changes, you need to know where the camera's controls are, as well as how to get up and walk away from the camera.

Video: Adding a 3D Camera in Motion 3

Visit the companion Web site to download and watch a video on adding and animating a 3D camera, as well as using light to add movement and visual interest to your Motion 3 projects.

The 3D Overlays

When you add a camera to your project, three new sets of controls appear around the border of the Canvas: the Camera menu, the 3D View tools, and the Compass (**FIGURE 12.5**).

FIGURE 12.5: Three of the 3D overlays: the Camera menu (top left), the 3D View tools (top right), and the Compass (bottom left).

Audio Profile

BRIAN PSHYK

Senior Video Production Coordinator, **www.samaritanspurse.ca**

 Brian Pshyk works for Samaritan's Purse, the Canadian disaster relief charity. As senior video production coordinator, Brian finds himself on the front lines of major disasters worldwide, and Final Cut is right there with him. Visit the companion Web site and discover how he uses the powerful nonlinear editing tool.

By the way, if you don't see these overlays, click the **View** button at the top right of the Canvas and make sure that Show 3D Overlays is selected, and that each of the five items underneath it is selected as well (**FIGURE 12.6**).

FIGURE 12.6: Make sure all the 3D overlays in the View pop-up menu are turned on.

By using these overlays in combination with controls in the Canvas, the HUD, and the Inspector, you have complete creative control over the camera and layers in 3D space.

Video: Moving in Motion's 3D Space

To see a video demonstration of moving in 3D space and positioning a camera, please visit the book's companion Web site.

The 3D View Tools

Let's start with the 3D View tools at the top right of the Canvas. The three icons represent Pan, Orbit, and Dolly. The camera icon to the left of the tools indicates that, right now, these tools control the camera.

Dragging the Pan tool moves the camera left and right (along its X-axis) or up and down (along its Y-axis). Dragging the Orbit tool rotates the camera around its focal plane's X and Y axes (more on this in a moment). The Dolly tool moves the camera forward and backward along its Z-axis, just as if you were standing behind the lens and walking straight forward or straight back. By using all three, you can move the camera anywhere in 3D space and look in any direction (**FIGURE 12.7**).

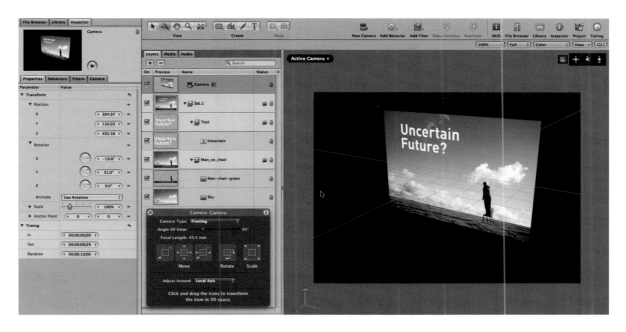

FIGURE 12.7: Panning, orbiting, and dollying the camera with the 3D View tools. Notice how the values for the camera's Position and Rotation in the Properties tab of the Inspector change as you move.

Here's a super-handy tip: If you ever want to move the camera back to its original position and rotation, just double-click any one of the 3D View tools.

When you rotate the camera, the 3D grid appears in the Canvas. This grid represents the "floor" of your virtual world, and it is very helpful for keeping oriented as you add more layers and start to move both the layers and the camera around. The red line represents the horizontal X-axis and the blue line the Z-axis. They intersect at 0,0,0—the center of the virtual world.

The Compass

The three-legged guy at the bottom left of the Canvas is the Compass. As you can probably guess by now, the red axis is X, the green axis is Y, and the blue axis is Z. The Compass provides two functions. First, it lets you know exactly how you are oriented in the virtual world. See how the axes are aligned with the 3D grid axes? They will always match because the Compass always shows you the orientation of the world and not the orientation of the camera or layers in the world, both of which can change.

Second, the Compass lets you choose different points of view from that of the camera. In other words, it lets you step away from the camera lens and move other places in space so you can see both the scene and the camera. You do so by clicking the head of an axis. When you move the pointer over a head, the Compass tells you what the view is (**FIGURE 12.8**). Clicking the head then flies you to that view in a very smooth, elegant fashion (**FIGURE 12.9**).

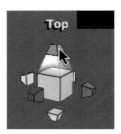

FIGURE 12.8: The Compass, indicating the view angle under the pointer.

FIGURE 12.9: The Canvas in Top view. Notice how the green arrow on the Compass is now pointing at us, because we are looking straight down from above the scene.

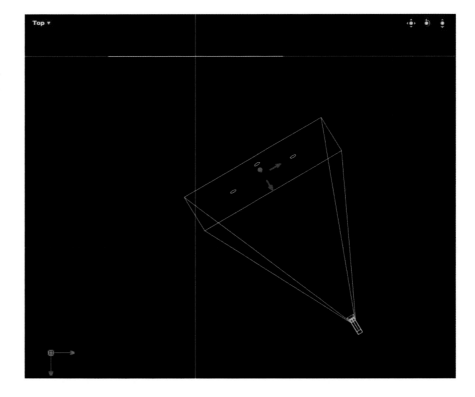

Each view from an axis is called an orthogonal view: It is a view directly along the X-, Y-, or Z-axis, and it doesn't show any perspective. Notice how our text and image layers appear as a single thin white line. This is because they are both currently on the same plane, and they are each two-dimensional objects: Layers in Motion are 2D, arranged in 3D space. From this Top view, we can also see the camera and how it's pointed at the layers. In addition to these orthogonal views (Top, Bottom, Left, Right, Front, and Back), the Compass also gives you an option to choose a Perspective view, which you can choose by clicking near its center.

The Camera Menu

The Camera menu at the top left now tells us we are in Top view. We could probably figure that out by looking at the Compass, but the Camera menu does provide a few other useful features.

Notice that the 3D View tools no longer have a camera icon next to them. This is because they now control our current view, which is not a camera view; changing them will change our view but will have no effect on the camera's view of the scene (**FIGURE 12.10**).

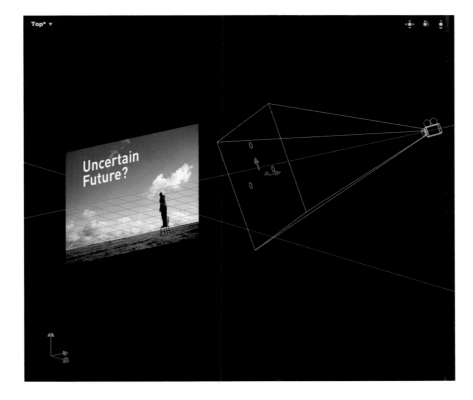

FIGURE 12.10: A modified Top view. Notice there is no longer a camera icon next to the 3D View tools.

In Figure 12.10, I used the Orbit tool to change the view of the scene. When you use the 3D View tools to modify a view, an asterisk appears in the Camera menu to let you know that this is no longer the default view. To reset the view, click the Camera menu, and choose **Reset View** (**FIGURE 12.11**).

In Figure 12.10, notice the yellow lines extending from the camera. They connect to the corners of a rectangle. This is the focal plane of the camera. The anchor point of the camera is located at the center of this focal plane, where you see yet another set of red, green, and blue axes, along with three white circles, which are the rotation handles.

FIGURE 12.11: Using the Camera menu to reset the Top view.

Inset View

If you drag a rotation handle, the camera rotates around its focal plane. In other words, the center of the focal plane stays still while the camera swings around it, maintaining its "point of interest" as it rotates. As you drag, a window pops up to show you how the scene looks through the lens of the camera. This is the fifth and final 3D overlay, and it's called the Inset view (**FIGURE 12.12**).

FIGURE 12.12: Moving the camera with the onscreen controls activates the Inset view, which shows you the scene through the lens of the camera.

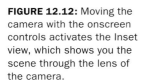

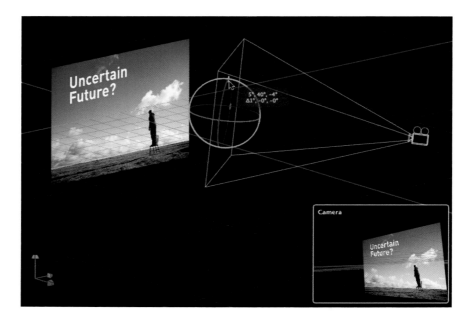

The Inset view is handy, but it pops up only when you are actively changing something. What if you want to look at two different views as you work? Or three? Or four?

At the top right of the toolbar, just under the Timing icon is the View Layouts pop-up menu. Click it, and you can choose from six different layouts that include from one to four separate viewports (**FIGURE 12.13**).

For example, the third one down gives you a split horizontal layout, with two viewports (see **FIGURE 12.14**).

FIGURE 12.13:
The View Layouts option.

FIGURE 12.14: Two horizontal viewports showing a Perspective view on top and the Active Camera view on the bottom. I reset the Active Camera view by double-clicking one of the 3D View tools.

You can set each viewport to its own view. Each viewport has its own camera menu, 3D View tools, and Compass (if you have turned those overlays on). Pressing Shift+Z fits a view to the viewport.

Note the yellow outline around the upper Perspective view in Figure 12.14. This outline tells you that this viewport is the active viewport. The active viewport is the one that will respond to keyboard shortcuts (such as Shift+Z to fit to window, or F, discussed a bit later), shows any motion when you play back the project, and will remain if you switch back to a single viewport layout. You make a viewport active simply by clicking anywhere inside it.

Arranging a Set

With our camera added, our overlays turned on, and our layout showing two viewports, we can now arrange our first set.

If you select the text layer, you'll see the three axes extending out of its anchor point. Its blue axis points perpendicular to the layer, its green axis points up, and its red axis points to the right.

FIGURE 12.15: A layer in Local Axis mode. Note how the text layer is selected in the Layers tab, the HUD indicates Local Axis mode, and the axes in the Canvas are oriented based on the layer.

In the HUD, notice that the Adjust Around menu is set to Local Axis (**FIGURE 12.15**). This means that the axes for the layer are oriented *relative to the layer*: If you rotate the layer, the axes will move with it (**FIGURE 12.16**).

Local Axis is the default and is usually what you want when moving a layer so you can move it forward or back, up or down, and left or right relative to itself.

The Adjust Around menu allows you to change a layer's axis to align with the World axis, or with your point of view, which is called the View axis (**FIGURE 12.17**).

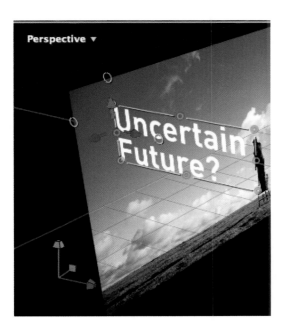

FIGURE 12.16: With the text layer rotated and in Local Axis mode, its axes rotate with it. Notice how they no longer align with the 3D grid axes or the Compass.

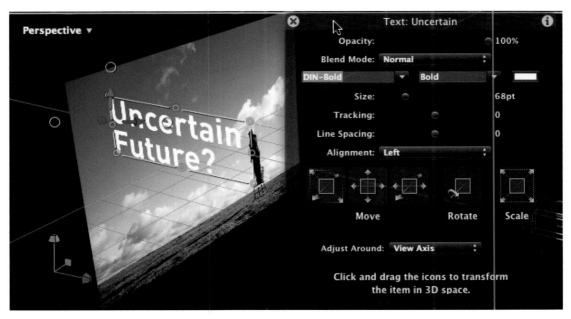

FIGURE 12.17: In View Axis mode, the Z-axis always points straight at the screen, no matter how the layer or the camera is oriented.

The key here is to check the Adjust Around mode before you start moving layers with the Canvas or HUD controls so the layer moves in the way you expect.
Note that the Inspector controls are always based on the World axis.

Let's go back to Local Axis mode and rotate the text back to 0 degrees using
the Inspector. Now we can use the first HUD control to drag the text forward in
Z-space, then down and over a little to reposition, using the Active Camera view
as our guide.

Why are we doing this? Because with the elements spread out from each other
in Z-space, you'll see them shift in relationship to each other as you animate
the camera to move around the set (**FIGURE 12.18**). In other words, because it
will look cool.

FIGURE 12.18: Using the HUD control to separate the text layer from the image.

Of course, with the text layer closer to the camera, it appears larger, so we'll need to scale it down to have it look like it did when it was farther away.

But wait, there's actually a way to do that automatically! Let's try it out with the sky layer. If you select the sky layer and use the HUD to push it back in Z-space, it appears smaller. In the Active Camera view, we can now see black around the edges—not so nice (see **FIGURE 12.19**).

FIGURE 12.19: Pushing the sky back in Z-space reveals its edges.

We could scale it up enough to fill the frame again, but instead, undo the move, then before dragging in the HUD's first control, hold down the Command key. Take a look at the Inspector as you drag (see **FIGURE 12.20**).

FIGURE 12.20: By holding down Command while dragging the HUD's first Move control, the layer automatically scales up as it moves back in Z-space. Note in the Inspector how the Scale changes along with the Position Z value.

The Scale parameter is changing as you drag! In fact, Motion is changing the scale dynamically, just enough to keep the layer looking the same size from the camera's point of view.

If you now use the 3D View tools in the Active Camera view to orbit the camera, you'll see the man on the chair shift in relationship to the clouds behind him, creating a sense of depth.

Adding Another Set

With the first set arranged, let's drop in the second one. The idea is that we'll want to "fly" the camera from the first set to the second. We could put it anywhere in space, but let's say we want it off to the left.

The easiest way to add objects to a different location is to first move the camera to that location, then add them to the Active Camera view. Let's try it.

First, we'll close our Set 1 group to keep the Layers tab tidy. In the Perspective view, we'll dolly way out and over so we can see the first set and lots of space to the left. Then we'll select the camera, and in the Perspective view, drag the red handle to move it to the left (**FIGURE 12.21**).

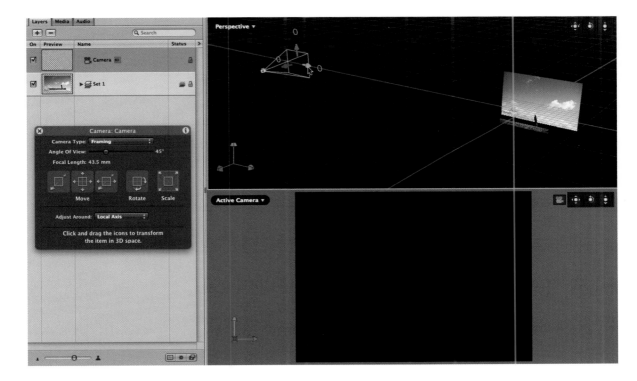

FIGURE 12.21: Positioning the camera at the location for the second set. Note how an axis turns yellow when selected.

The camera faces the same direction, since we didn't rotate it at all, but now it looks out at a vast expanse of nothingness. Now, here's the critical part. If you drag an object directly to a viewport in the Canvas, it will be positioned in 3D space to face that view. For example, if you drag to the Perspective view, the image faces that view (**FIGURE 12.22**).

FIGURE 12.22: Dragging an image to Perspective view.

This is not what we want. And if you drag the image to the Layers tab, it gets positioned in the center of the virtual world; in our case, right in the middle of Set 1 (**FIGURE 12.23**).

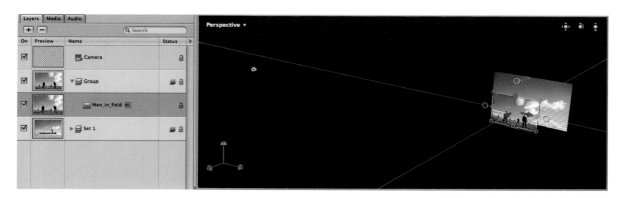

FIGURE 12.23: Dragging an image to the Layers tab, even above the existing group to form its own group, places its anchor point at 0,0,0 in the virtual world.

However, we want it over to the left, where the camera is. So instead, drag the image for the second set from the File Browser *directly* to the Active Camera view in the Canvas (**FIGURE 12.24**). If the file is a multi-layered Photoshop file, as in our case, wait before letting go and choose to Import All Layers so you can manipulate them separately.

FIGURE 12.24: By dragging to the Active Camera view, the image is placed at the focal plane of the camera.

Let's add some text and then spread out these elements. Select the Text tool, click in the Active Camera view, and type "Waiting for what's next?". In the Layers tab, put the text in its own group, and name the group containing the text and the image layers "Set 2" (**FIGURE 12.25**).

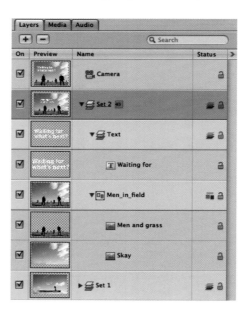

FIGURE 12.25: The layers and groups of the Set 2 group, after a bit of cleanup. I also moved the camera back to the top just to keep things organized.

This process of first moving the camera and then adding elements directly to the Active Camera view makes the process of building multiple sets in 3D space quick and easy.

Now, to spread out the layers of the Set 2 group, it would be helpful to zoom in closer in the Perspective view. You could use the 3D View tools to pan, orbit, and dolly to where you want, but there's a quicker way. Make the Perspective view active, and then in the Layers tab, press the **Command** key, then select both the **Set 2** group and the **Camera**. Now click the Camera menu and choose **Frame Objects**, or simply press the letter **F** (**FIGURE 12.26**).

Motion moves the view to precisely frame just the selected objects. Very nice!

Now it's just a matter of selecting the text and each layer in the image and Command-dragging the first HUD control to move the layers in Z-space to scale them at the same time in order to keep the composition aligned, as we did with the first set. You will probably still need to tweak the position of the elements due to the parallax shift. If an object isn't in the center of the frame, as it moves towards you it also moves off to the edge (**FIGURE 12.27**).

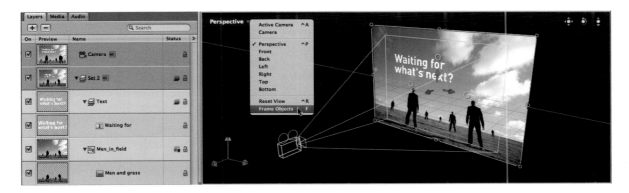

FIGURE 12.26: Framing objects. Note how the selected items in the Layers tab are the ones framed in the viewport.

FIGURE 12.27: Set 2, arranged. You can see the elements spread out in Z-space in Perspective view, and how they are still properly composed in the Active Camera view.

For the final set, let's push the camera straight forward through Set 2 (using the camera's blue Z-axis handle in the Canvas), then move the camera up (with the green Y-axis handle). Now, deselect everything, and in the Active Camera view, add some text with the Text tool. Since nothing is selected, the text gets created in its own new group. Add a rectangle shape around the text, use the HUD to turn on the Outline and turn off the Fill. Set this frame back from the text a little in Z-space. Name the new group **Set 3** (**FIGURE 12.28**).

FIGURE 12.28: The third and final set, placed behind and above Set 2.

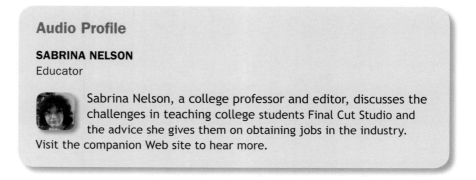

Audio Profile

SABRINA NELSON
Educator

Sabrina Nelson, a college professor and editor, discusses the challenges in teaching college students Final Cut Studio and the advice she gives them on obtaining jobs in the industry. Visit the companion Web site to hear more.

With all sets constructed, close the groups, click below them to deselect every-thing, then in the Active Camera view, double-click any of the 3D View tools to reset the camera to its default location at the center of the virtual world. With the Perspective view active, press **F** to frame all the sets (**FIGURE 12.29**).

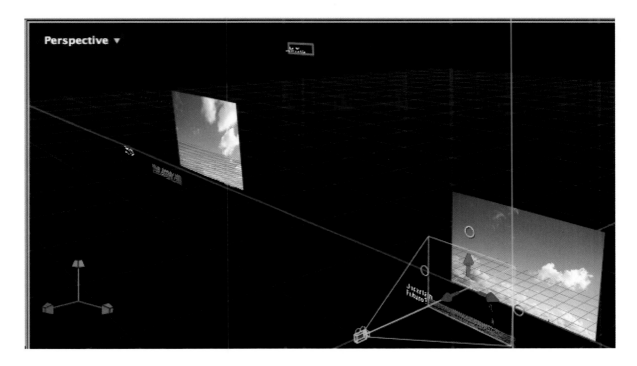

FIGURE 12.29: All three sets framed in Perspective view, with the camera selected and back in the center of the virtual world, framing Set 1.

The F key is a very powerful way to quickly frame an entire scene or selected layers in a scene. If you use the F key in the Active Camera view, it moves the camera; in other views, it just changes the view.

By using the 3D overlays such as the 3D View tools and the Compass, in combi-nation with the onscreen controls and the HUD, you can quickly build sets and move to and adjust any part of a 3D scene.

In the next chapter, we'll look at some options for animating the camera to move from scene to scene, and explore some other ways to quickly select and adjust elements in 3D space.

Chapter 13

Animating Cameras in Motion's 3D Space with Keyframes

MARK SPENCER

Now we get to the (really) fun stuff: flying a camera around in 3D space. We'll start where we left off in the previous chapter—with three sets arranged in 3D space—and then look at how to use keyframes to animate the camera to fly from set to set.

The project we'll use is a short promo for a fictional business news show called "Future News." It consists of three virtual sets—groups of layers each positioned in a different place in 3D space. Using the Camera menu at the top left of the Canvas (discussed in the last article) to go to Perspective view allows you to see all three sets, as well as the location of the camera (**FIGURE 13.1**).

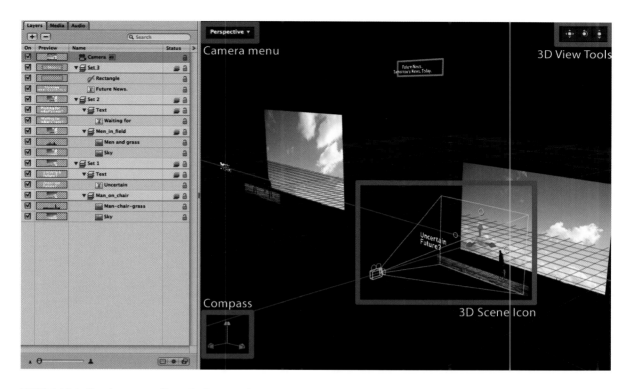

FIGURE 13.1: Our three sets. Note the Perspective view is selected in the Camera menu. Because the camera is selected in the Layers tab, we can see the outline of its focal plane in the Canvas. The names of the 3D overlays are also called out.

Audio Profile

FLORIAN GINTENREITER
Owner, Image/Worxx, **www.thirdeye.at**

 Florian Gintenreiter, based in Austria, is a guerrilla filmmaker who recently completed a horror/western film shot on HDCAM and finished totally in Final Cut Studio. He shares his experiences in this interview on the companion Web site.

Project Files

The project files and the content used in this chapter are available for download. If you'd like to follow along, please visit the book's companion Web site.

So what are we looking at? The first two sets in this project each consist of a two-layer Photoshop file and a text layer, all spread apart from each other along the world's Z-axis. The third set consists of a rectangular blue frame created with a shape and a text layer.

In addition to the layers being spread apart in Z-space, the sets themselves have been separated from each other in X-, Y-, and Z-space. To see this, use the Compass at the bottom left of the Canvas to go to Top view; you'll see each set is located differently in X and Z (**FIGURE 13.2**). Then go to Front view to see how Set 3 is higher in Y (**FIGURE 13.3**).

FIGURE 13.2: Our sets in Top view, which allows us to see how they are arranged along the X-axis (the red line) and the Z-axis (the blue line).

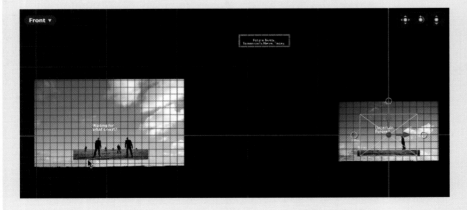

FIGURE 13.3: Our sets in Front view, which allows us to see how they are arranged along the X-axis (again, the red line) and the Y-axis (the green line).

The Three Rules

Now, when building and arranging your sets in 3D, I have three rules that can help make your first camera animation process go smoothly.

Rule 1: Make your starting camera position at 0,0,0.

In other words, have the camera animation start at the very center of the virtual world. To check the location of the camera in this project:

1.   Use the Camera menu to go to the Active Camera view.

2.   Select the camera in the Layers tab.

3.   Go to the Properties tab of the Inspector.

You'll see that our first set is visible through the camera lens, and that the camera is positioned at 0,0,0 with no rotation (**FIGURE 13.4**).

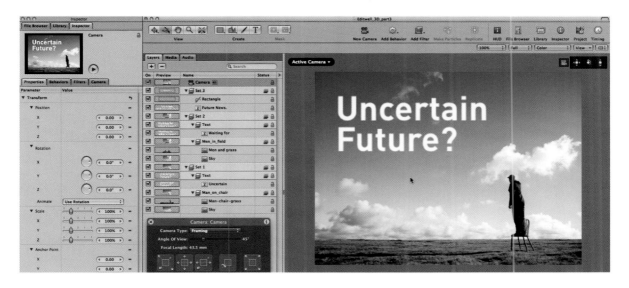

FIGURE 13.4: The camera is in its default location and orientation, with the first set visible in Active Camera view. Note that in the Properties tab, position and rotation are all at zero.

Why is it useful to set up your scene in this way? No matter where you move the camera, you can always move it back to perfectly frame the first set if you reset it, which you can do by clicking the hooked reset arrow next to the Transform properties in the Inspector or double-clicking any one of the 3D View tools in the Canvas.

Rule 2: Keep all your sets facing the same direction along the Z-axis.

As you saw in the Perspective, Top, and Front views, each layer of each of the three sets is flat to the X-Y plane. And the groups the layers are contained in are also oriented in the same way. Also, notice in **FIGURE 13.5** that the Adjust Around option in the HUD is set to Local Axis, and that each of the three groups are oriented with their Z-axis (the blue arrow) aligned to the world's Z-axis (the blue line on the grid).

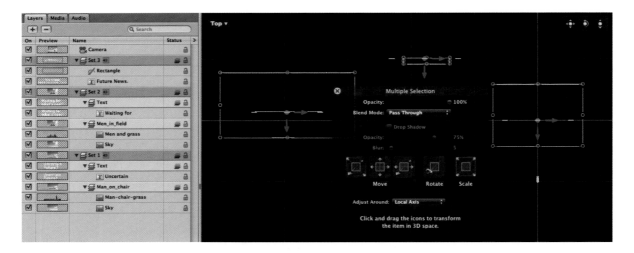

FIGURE 13.5: The groups Set 1, Set 2, and Set 3 are selected in the Layers tab, and therefore have bounding boxes in the Top view in the Canvas.

There are many times you'll want to break this rule for creative purposes, but if you don't need to change the orientation of layers in a set, or of a set itself, it will make the camera animation much easier to execute if your sets face the same direction along the Z-axis.

Rule 3: Keep the anchor point for each set group located within the bounding box for the group.

The anchor point is located where the three colored axis handles intersect. In **FIGURE 13.6**, you can see it is inside of the bounding box for each of the selected groups.

Since the anchor point for a layer, and therefore a group, is located by default in the center of the layer, you may think to yourself, why would I have to worry about this? Well, here's the issue: if you move the camera, then add a layer (such as an image, a video clip, or some text) to the Active Camera view, the object gets added right at the focal plane of the camera (as we discussed in detail in Part 2). This is very handy for quickly building sets in other parts of 3D space, but when you do so, *the anchor point for the group containing those layers remains at 0,0,0, the center of the virtual world.*

So what? Well, if you attempt to rotate or scale the group, it will rotate or scale around its anchor point, which could be very far from the layers in the group, thus creating quite unexpected results. And, more pertinent to this discussion, there is an incredibly useful behavior for animating the camera that just won't work correctly if the anchor point of the group is located somewhere away from the group.

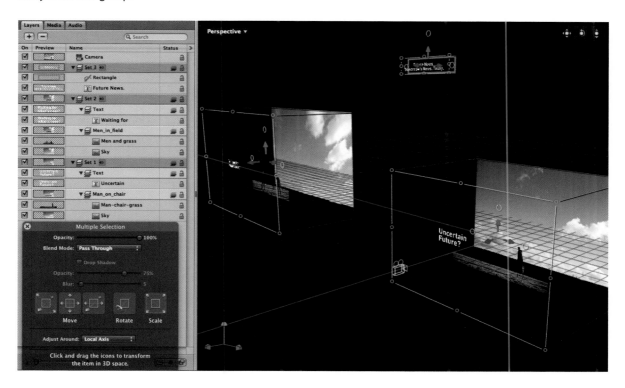

FIGURE 13.6: In Perspective view, you can see that the anchor point (where the three arrows are) for each group is located inside the group's bounding box.

To summarize: In order to make the process of animating the camera to move from set to set go as smoothly as possible, you need to do the following:

1. Build your first set at the center of the virtual world (at 0, 0, 0).

2. Have all your sets face the same direction.

3. If needed, move the anchor point for each group inside the group.

If you follow these three rules as you start to work with cameras, you'll understand the implications when you intentionally break them later on.

With our project properly prepared, we can now get to the good stuff—putting the camera into motion.

Animating the Camera: Keyframes or Behaviors?

Motion uses two distinct approaches to animation: keyframing and behaviors. With traditional keyframing, you set specific values at specific points in time and then determine how Motion changes, or *interpolates*, the value between any two keyframes. Behaviors are *procedural* animations, which means you apply them, make a few setting changes perhaps, and away they go; their own internal mathematics take over.

You can use either of these approaches, or a combination of both, to animate anything from a bouncing ball to the blur of a background to the speed of a video clip. Which one you use is really a matter of your specific goals: generally speaking, behaviors are very fast, and keyframing gives you more precise control. Behaviors allow you to create animation that would be time-consuming or in some cases downright impossible with keyframes (such as simulation behaviors); keyframes let you create very precise animation, particularly when it comes to coordinating the timing of the animation of multiple objects.

When it comes to animating cameras, you have the same two options: keyframing or behaviors. In this chapter, we'll explore using keyframes; in the next, we'll work with behaviors.

Camera Animation with Keyframes

When you create animation with keyframes in Motion, you have two options: you can set the keyframes manually, or you can use the Record button to record the keyframes automatically. We'll use both approaches together.

The goal for this project is to start with the camera facing Set 1, move it to view Set 2, then finally move it to view Set 3. To start, you should be in Active Camera view, and you should see the first set as shown in Figure 13.4. Double-click any 3D View tool to reset the camera just in case.

Now, you'll need to consider the timing of the animation. The full project is 10 seconds long, which you can determine by looking at the Duration field at the bottom right of the Canvas (see **FIGURE 13.7**).

FIGURE 13.7: The Duration field indicates the project is 10 seconds long. Click the clock icon to toggle the view between SMPTE timecode and frames.

Let's have the camera view Set 1 for 3 seconds, then move it to Set 2 over the course of one-half of a second (or 15 frames), where it will then remain for 3 seconds before taking 15 frames to move to Set 3, where it will remain until the end of the project.

Adding Keyframes

Since the camera will stay still for the first 3 seconds of the project, you'll need keyframes at the beginning and end of this time span. To add the keyframes, follow these steps:

1. Move the playhead to the start of the project. Click the **Record** button at the bottom of the Canvas to turn on recording.

   You want to set a keyframe at the first frame. But when recording is turned on, keyframes get recorded only when you *change* a parameter value. Since we don't need to change anything here, how do we set a keyframe?

   One option would be to move the camera just a little and move it back. That action would set a keyframe, but you might not move the camera back to exactly where it was, so it's not a very precise method.

   Another option is to set our first keyframe manually. Whether recording is turned on or not, you can always set keyframes manually in either the Inspector or the Keyframe Editor.

2. With the camera selected, select the Properties tab of the Inspector, click the Animation menu for Position (the small dash to the right of the word Position), and choose **Add Keyframe** (**FIGURE 13.8**).

FIGURE 13.8: Setting the first keyframe manually. Note that the camera is selected in the Layers tab. Note also that the value fields in the Properties tab are all red, indicating that recording is turned on.

Solid diamonds appear in the Animation menu for Position X, Y, and Z, indicating there is now a keyframe for all three of these parameters at the current playhead location (**FIGURE 13.9**).

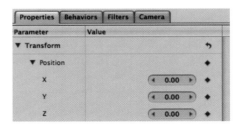

FIGURE 13.9: Solid diamonds indicate a keyframe at the current playhead location.

3. It's a good practice to set keyframes for both the camera's position and its rotation (also called its orientation) in case you decide to rotate it later. Go ahead and set a keyframe for the Rotation values as well using the same method. Or, you can press and hold the **Option** key while clicking the dash. It may not seem like much, but when you are adding a lot of keyframes, you'll be glad you know this shortcut.

4. OK, our first keyframe is set. Now move the playhead forward 3 seconds. By the way, you don't need to click in the Current Time field; you can just type +3. (plus 3 period) and press **Return** to move the playhead. (This trick won't work if the Timeline is open. Instead, the selected layer will move over 3 seconds, so be careful!).

   Notice in the Inspector that the diamonds in the Animation menu are now hollow: This indicates that there is at least one keyframe somewhere for the parameter, but there isn't one at the current playhead location (**FIGURE 13.10**).

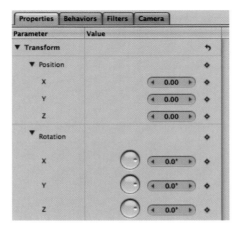

FIGURE 13.10: Hollow diamonds tell us there is at least one keyframe somewhere in time for these parameters, but not where the playhead is right now (at 3:00).

5. Because you want the camera to remain still from the beginning of the project to this point, facing Set 1, you can manually set position and rotation keyframes here just as we did at the beginning of the project.

6. Now type **+15** and press **Enter** to move forward 15 frames. This frame is where you want the camera to arrive at Set 2.

   Since recording is turned on, as soon as you change the camera's position and/or rotation, keyframes will be set automatically. In fact, if you change *any* parameter of *any* layer, keyframes will be set, which can be dangerous. So before you do anything, let's make a quick change to how Motion sets keyframes.

7. Choose **Mark > Recording Options**. Select the "Record keyframes on animated parameters only" checkbox (see **FIGURE 13.11**).

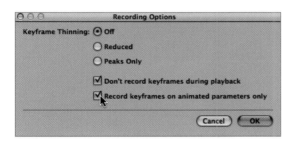

FIGURE 13.11: The Recording Options window. Selecting the bottom checkbox can keep you out of trouble.

   Now if you change the camera's position or rotation, keyframes will still be recorded, since these parameters already have a keyframe. But you won't accidentally set keyframes if you decide, for example, to tweak the layout of the layers in one of the sets.

8. Click **OK** to close the Recording Options window.

Moving the Camera with the Frame Objects Command

Now, back to business: you want to move the camera to the Set 2 group in order to set the next keyframe. But how do you know where to move the camera, and what do we use to move it? There are many different ways to move and rotate the camera: by using the HUD, the 3D View tools, the Inspector, or even the on-screen controls (if you aren't in an active camera view). You can split the Canvas into two separate viewports so that you can see the camera's point of view in one viewport while you manipulate the camera in the other viewport.

However, you aren't going to do any of that here. Instead, you'll take advantage of an incredibly handy command called Frame Objects.

1. First, in the Layers tab, select the Set 2 group.

2. Now, in the Camera menu, choose **Frame Objects**—or better yet, just press **F** (**FIGURE 13.12**).

FIGURE 13.12: The innocuous-looking yet super-powerful Frame Objects command.

The camera suddenly shoots over to Set 2. You can see the bounding box for the group just touches the edge of the Canvas; in other words, the camera has perfectly framed the selected object (**FIGURE 13.13**).

Frame Objects is a great tool to quickly move the camera to a specific layer or group of layers. And, if recording is turned on, keyframes will be set at the playhead. One thing to note: the camera will not change its orientation when it moves to frame the objects. In other words, it will not rotate, even if the objects it is framing are rotated at an angle. Thus the reason for my second rule in preparing your project: if you orient all your layers to face the same direction, you can use the Frame Objects command to very quickly move the camera to an object and set keyframes, and you'll be sure to be facing the layers correctly.

However, we still have some work to do: there's a lot of empty black space around our second set. This is because the layers in this group have been spread out in Z-space, and the bounding box of a group expands to contain all of the layers inside it.

Video: Animation with Keyframes

To see a video demonstration of the steps in this chapter, please visit the book's companion Web site.

FIGURE 13.13: The result of the Frame Objects command. With the Set 2 group selected, the camera moves so that the bounding box of the selected object(s) (a group in this case) touches the edge of the Canvas.

3. So, click-drag the Pan and Dolly controls in the 3D View tools to move the camera forward and properly frame the group (**FIGURE 13.14**).

FIGURE 13.14: Adjusting the final framing for Set 2 with the Pan and Dolly controls in the 3D View tools.

Don't use the middle Orbit control because right now you don't want to change the rotation of the camera. Although there are many different ways to move the camera, the nice thing about the 3D View tools is that the camera doesn't need to be selected in order to use them.

4. Finally, keyframes didn't get set for the rotation of the camera because you changed only its position. So select the camera, and in the Properties tab of the Inspector, Option-click the Rotation animation menu to set keyframes for Rotation X, Y, and Z (**FIGURE 13.15**).

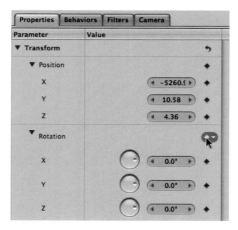

FIGURE 13.15: Manually setting Rotation keyframes for the camera at 3:15. Note that the non-zero position values indicates the camera has left its comfortable home base at 0,0,0. Dorothy, we aren't in Kansas anymore!

Lather, Rinse, Repeat

Creating the rest of the animation involves repeating the same process, so I won't belabor it. Here's what to do:

1. Type +3. (plus 3 period) to move the playhead forward 3 seconds, to 6:15.

2. In the Properties tab, Option-click Position and Rotation for the camera to set manual keyframes. (Remember, we want the camera to remain still and facing Set 2 for these 3 seconds.)

3. Move the playhead forward 15 frames, to 7:00.

4. In the Layers tab, select the Set 3 group and press **F** to frame it.

5. If needed, use the 3D View tools to reframe the set in the Canvas (**FIGURE 13.16**).

6. Add a manual keyframe for rotation.

FIGURE 13.16: Framing Set 3. It shouldn't need any adjustment; just press F to move the camera to it.

That's it! Play back the project to check out the animation.

Polishing the Animation

It's likely that you'll see some strange behavior while the camera is on the second set: Rather than staying still, the camera dollies back and then shoots back in. To see what's going on, make sure the camera is selected, then follow these steps.

1. Press **F6** to open the Timing pane, and select the **Keyframe Editor** (**FIGURE 13.17**).

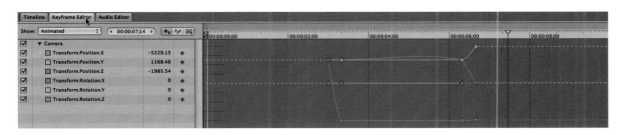

FIGURE 13.17: The Keyframe Editor, showing the keyframes you have set for the camera.

Note how the blue Transform.Position.Z line, rather than staying nice and flat, rises a little between 3:15 and 6:15? You don't want this parameter to change values between these two keyframes, so you'll need to change its interpolation.

2. Option-click the checkbox next to the Transform.Position.Z parameter to solo it in the Keyframe Editor. This action gets rid of all the other curves so you can focus in on just this one parameter.

3. Then, right-click or Control-click the third keyframe and choose **Interpolation > Constant** (**FIGURE 13.18**).

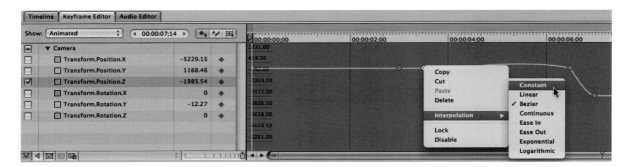

FIGURE 13.18: Changing keyframe interpolation. Note how only the Position Z parameter is visible.

Constant interpolation means the value won't change between the two keyframes. Linear would work here as well. Now play the project.

Taking It Up a Notch

It plays correctly now, but the animation is a bit dull: When the camera isn't racing from one set to the next, it's sitting dead still. It would be more interesting to have it rotate slightly while looking at a scene, thereby revealing the depth of the different layers, wouldn't it?

We can accomplish this quite easily. The key is to make sure we are parked directly on a keyframe before rotating the camera.

1. With the camera selected and the Properties tab visible, press **Home** to move the playhead to the beginning of the project.

2. In the Properties tab, check to make sure you see solid diamonds, which will confirm that you are, in fact, parked on a keyframe.

3. In the Inspector, drag left in the Rotate Y value field to rotate the camera just slightly to the left. In the Canvas, you'll likely expose the edge of the sky.

4. Open the Set 1 group, select the Sky layer, and increase its scale to fill the Canvas. You may need to do the same with the Man-chair-grass layer (**FIGURE 13.19**).

FIGURE 13.19: Scaling up the sky to fill the Canvas; rotating the camera can reveal the edge of your sets, so keep your eyes peeled.

The project now begins with the camera rotated slightly to the left on its Y-axis.

5. Close the Set 1 group, select the camera, and press **Shift+K** to move to the next keyframe, at 3:00. (By the way, this is the same keyboard shortcut as Final Cut Pro; moving backward is Option+K, also the same.)

6. Use the Inspector to rotate the camera slightly to the right on the Y-axis. The camera will now rotate, or "sweep" over Set 1 before moving on to Set 2.

7. To finish, you just repeat the same process for Sets 2 and 3: Press **Shift+K** to jump to the next keyframe, adjust the starting camera rotation, move to the next keyframe, adjust the ending camera rotation. Adjust the scale of any layers in the set that no longer fill the Canvas.

You can use the 3D View tools or the HUD instead of the Inspector if you want to slightly pan, orbit, and/or dolly the camera, but if you want to precisely change just one axis of position or rotation, the Inspector is your best bet.

For Set 3, you'll need to add ending keyframes for position and rotation. Rather than adding them at the very end of the project, add them at 9 seconds so the camera will sit still on the phrase for the last second. Make the ending text phrase start off-center, then rotate it to perfectly face the camera.

To tweak the camera rotation, you might want to change the keyframe interpolation to linear so you won't see a slight delay as the camera starts up its rotation (**FIGURE 13.20**).

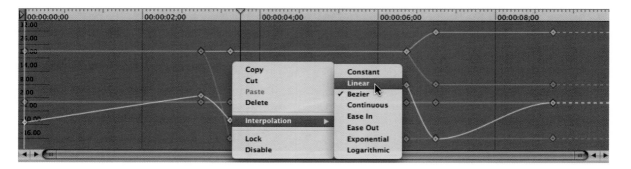

FIGURE 13.20: Changing keyframe interpolation for the Transform.Rotation.Y parameter for the curve as the camera sweeps across Set 2. As the camera moves between sets, leave the interpolation set to Bezier for smooth acceleration and deceleration.

That's the basics of animating the camera with keyframes. By using keyframe recording and the Frame Objects command, you can very quickly rough in your animation, then clean it up by changing the keyframe interpolation, adjusting camera angles at keyframes, and scaling layers.

As we have now demonstrated, you can animate the camera in a very specific manner using keyframes. There's much more to using keyframes than we have been able to cover here, but hopefully this will get you started.

As you'll see in the next chapter, behaviors offer an alternative approach to animating the camera, and they allow for a variety of interesting and creative options.

Chapter 14

Animating Cameras in Motion's 3D Space Using Behaviors

MARK SPENCER

In Chapter 13, I discussed three "rules" for preparing your 3D project that will go a long way in making the camera animation process go smoothly:

1. Build your first set at the center of the virtual world (at 0,0,0).

2. Have all your sets face the same direction.

3. If needed, move the anchor point for each group inside the group.

As discussed, Motion uses two distinct approaches to animation: keyframing and behaviors. With traditional keyframing, you set specific values at specific points in time and then determine how Motion changes, or *interpolates*, the value between any two keyframes. Behaviors are *procedural* animations, which means you apply them, make a few setting changes perhaps, and away they go—their own internal mathematics take over.

Behaviors allow you to create animation that would be time-consuming or in some cases downright impossible with keyframes (such as Simulation behaviors). Let's see how they work for animating a camera.

You'll create the same animation from Chapter 13, but this time without a single keyframe. You can then be the judge as to which approach you prefer.

Project Files

The project files and the content used in this chapter are available for download. If you'd like to follow along, please visit the book's companion Web site.

Preparing the Project: Using Markers and Clearing Keyframes

Before we get rid of the keyframes we applied in the last chapter, let's add some markers to the Timeline—they will help us in the steps ahead.

1. If the Timing pane isn't open, press **F6** to open it. Select the Timeline tab.

2. Press **Home**, then press **Shift+K** to jump to the keyframe at 3:00. (The keyboard shortcut will work only if the camera is selected.)

3. Press **Shift+M** to add a project marker. Repeat for the rest of the keyframes (**FIGURE 14.1**).

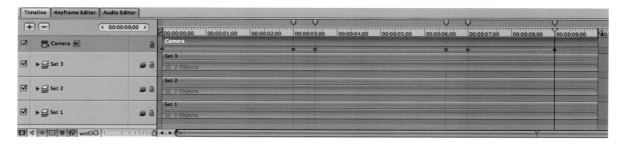

FIGURE 14.1: Creating markers to identify the location of the camera moves.

4. Select the Properties tab of the Inspector and click the hooked arrow, which will reset all the camera's Transform parameters (**FIGURE 14.2**).

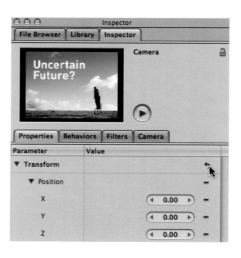

FIGURE 14.2: Removing all keyframes with one click by resetting the Camera properties. Note the dashes in the Animation menus for the Position parameters, indicating there are no longer any keyframes present.

5. Press **Home** to return the playhead to the beginning of the project. Leave the Timeline open. The project is back to where we started at the beginning of this article: there is no camera animation, and the camera is at 0,0,0, facing Set 1.

The Camera Behaviors

Before we animate the camera with behaviors, let's check them out. Go to the Library, select the Behaviors category, then select the Camera folder. Inside, you'll find four different camera behaviors. If you select one, you'll see a little animated preview of what it does in the Preview window (**FIGURE 14.3**).

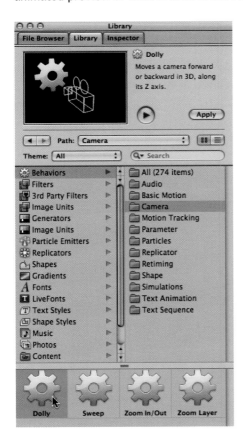

FIGURE 14.3: The four Camera behaviors in the Library—Dolly, Sweep, Zoom In/Out, and Zoom Layer.

You'll use two of these behaviors for this project: Sweep and Zoom Layer. First, drag the Zoom Layer behavior from the Library to the Camera in the Layers tab. In the Timeline, trim it to fit between the first two markers. You can either drag the ends, holding the Shift key to snap them to the markers, or move the playhead to each marker, pressing **I** to trim the In point of the behavior and **O** to trim the Out point. Rename the behavior **Zoom Set 2** (**FIGURE 14.4**).

FIGURE 14.4: The Zoom Layer behavior in the Timeline, neatly trimmed and renamed.

If you play back the project now, you'll be disappointed because nothing happens. The Zoom Layer behavior is supposed to move the camera to a layer (or a group), but before it can work, you need to tell it what layer (or group) to move to.

Select the Zoom Layer behavior. If the HUD isn't visible, press **F7**. Now drag the Set 2 group from the Layers tab into the well in the HUD (**FIGURE 14.5**).

FIGURE 14.5 Giving the Zoom Layer behavior the information it needs.

Now when you play the project, the camera zips from Set 1 to Set 2, starting right at that first marker. No keyframes used. Cool! But we still need to make a couple of adjustments (after all, that's what motion graphics is all about).

Fine-Tuning a Behavior

First, rather than taking the full 15 frames between the two markers, the camera finishes its move in only half that time. This is due to the Transition parameter, which as you can see in the HUD in Figure 14.5, is set to 50% by default. Change it to **100%,** so the move takes the full length of the behavior to complete.

By the way, the reason for the default value of 50% is to allow the camera to zoom in or out on the layer once it has arrived. You adjust the zoom amount using the Zoom slider in the HUD (thus the Zoom Layer behavior's somewhat odd name). Although this can be an interesting effect, we won't use it here.

Second, the animation is rather abrupt. This is because the default Speed (as you can see in the HUD in Figure 14.5) is Constant. Click the pop-up menu in the HUD and change it to **Ease Both**, which will create a smooth acceleration and deceleration effect (**FIGURE 14.6**).

FIGURE 14.6: The HUD with our two adjustments: Transition has been changed from 50% to 100% so the camera finishes its move at the end of the behavior, and the Speed has been changed to Ease Both for a smooth start and stop motion.

Finally, if you select the behavior and press **Shift+O** to move the playhead to its Out point, you'll see that the framing of the scene isn't so hot: the text is almost off the screen, clearly outside of title safe (**FIGURE 14.7**).

FIGURE 14.7: The result of the Zoom Layer behavior, before tweaking.

This is because the Zoom Layer behavior moves the camera's anchor point, which is located at the center of the camera's focal plane, to touch the anchor point of the group. Depending on the location of the anchor point of the group, this fact may result in a framing that doesn't work for you. That is why one of my project preparation rules is to make sure each group's anchor point is located within the group.

Adjust Zoom Layer Framing

To fix the framing, you can't change the position of the group—the camera would just move with the group—but you *can* change the group's anchor point. It's easiest to use the Inspector to do so: If you use the Anchor Point tool in the Canvas, you'll need to use two viewports, but with the Inspector, you can keep the single Active Camera view.

Therefore, in the Layers tab, select the Set 2 group, and in the Properties tab of the Inspector, drag the Anchor Point X, Y, and Z controls to change the camera framing to taste (**FIGURE 14.8**).

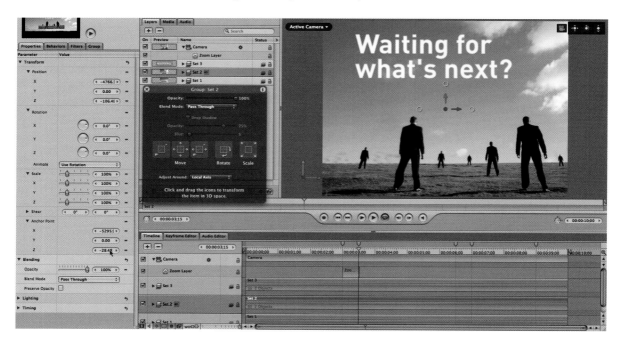

FIGURE 14.8: Reframing the scene by changing the Anchor Point in the Inspector. Note the playhead location on the last frame (the Out point) of the Zoom Layer behavior in the Timeline, which allows us to see the scene at the point the camera has stopped moving.

Lather, Rinse, Repeat

With the behavior and the group tweaked, it's a simple matter to do the same for the move from Set 2 to Set 3:

1. Select the behavior once again, and press **Command+D** to duplicate it.

2. Rename the copy **Zoom Set 3**.

3. Slide the effect down between the third and fourth markers in the Timeline (holding down Shift to snap to the markers).

4. Drag the Set 3 group into the well in the HUD.

5. Press **Shift+O** to move the playhead to the end of the behavior

6. In the Inspector, use the Anchor Point X, Y, and Z parameter to adjust the framing as necessary.

If you play back the project, you should now see a quick but smooth 15-frame transition from set to set.

Using the Sweep Behavior

Now, just like with the keyframing example in Chapter 13, you want the camera to move while it is looking at each set, not just when it's transitioning from one set to the next. For this you'll use the Sweep behavior.

1. In the Layers tab, select the camera.

2. In the toolbar, click the **Add Behavior** icon and choose **Camera > Sweep**. Change the name of the behavior to **Sweep Set 1**.

3. Trim it to end at the first marker.

4. In the HUD, set the Start to about **-5** degrees and the End to about **+5** degrees (**FIGURE 14.9**). By the way, to make small adjustments in the HUD, hold down the Option key and click on one side of a slider.

5. Play the project to see the result.

Video: Animation with Behaviors

To see a video demonstration of the steps in this chapter, please visit the book's companion Web site.

FIGURE 14.9: The first Sweep behavior, renamed and trimmed in the Timeline and tweaked in the HUD.

The camera now sweeps gently around the first set, causing the text and the man in the foreground to shift in relation to the sky, revealing the 3D nature of the scene. Then it shoots over to Set 2.

Setting the Start and End parameters for the Sweep behavior is like setting keyframes for the camera's rotation. Note that you can choose which axis the camera rotates around in the HUD. If you want to rotate around more than one axis at a time, just add another Sweep behavior, or duplicate the current one.

Sweeping the Set 2 and Set 3 Groups

To sweep the Set 2 and Set 3 groups, you can just use copies of the first Sweep behavior, with one important consideration. Follow these steps:

1. In the Layers tab or the Timeline, select the Sweep Set 1 behavior, press **Command+D** to duplicate it, and name the copy **Sweep Set 2**.

2. In the Timeline, drag the Sweep Set 2 behavior to between the second and third markers, holding down the Shift key to snap to the markers.

3. Now this is the part you need to think about: You left the first set with the camera already rotated +5 degrees. If you use the same Start value (-5 degrees) as the first Sweep behavior, that amount will be added to the current rotation of +5 degrees, so the camera will actually start out looking at the scene straight on (+5 + -5 = 0). So if you want to start out rotated +5 degrees (in the opposite direction from the first behavior for some variety), you'd actually need to set a Start value of 0 (+5 + 0 = +5). Make sense? Great! Go ahead and set the start value to **0**.

4. Set the end value to **-10** degrees so the total rotation is 10 degrees, the same as the Sweep Set 1 behavior (**FIGURE 14.10**).

FIGURE 14.10: The second Sweep behavior, completed.

NOTE: The general rule of thumb is this: To avoid any jumps in camera movement, make sure all Sweep behaviors after the first one have a Start value of 0.

5. For the final sweep over the Set 3 group, duplicate the Sweep Set 2 behavior, rename it **Sweep Set 3**, move it to start at the fourth marker, and then trim it to end at the last marker. In the HUD, leave the Start at **0** degrees and set the End to **+5** degrees.

6. Play back the project. You should now have a camera animation very similar to the first exercise, created without using a single keyframe.

As demonstrated in this and the previous chapter, you can animate the camera in a very specific manner using either keyframes or behaviors. So which is better? Both methods usually require various adjustments, so there's no clear winner. Plus, there's much more to using either keyframes or behaviors than we have been able to cover here, so the jury is really out until you have had a chance to work with both in depth. I love the speed, predictability, and simplicity of behaviors, but sometimes I find keyframes are the only way to do something I have in mind.

Finally, just a reminder that you really don't have to make a choice. You can always freely mix and match behaviors and keyframes to get the result you want—Motion will add the effects of each together. The key is to not just fall back on what you already know how to do: Always push yourself to try a new approach.

Video: Creating Paths in Motion

Visit the companion Web site to see a video about using the Path tool in Motion to create all kinds of straight and curved lines.

Audio Profile

RYAN KENDRICK
Owner, Digital Bohemia, **www.digitalbohemia.com**

 Ryan Kendrick shoots and edits documentaries on up-and-coming bands. In this interview, available on the companion Web site, discover his approach to editing these projects.

Part 4

Soundtrack Pro

The next step in completing your project is sound editing and mixing, which is what this section is all about. The next three chapters mirror the editing workflow.

First, Mary Plummer describes the process of prepping your audio and making simple repairs. What I find most helpful about her chapter is the workflow she presents at the beginning, laying out what needs to be done to the audio first.

Second, Stephen Kanter tells how to mix your projects to make them sound their best. Mixing, at its core, is the process of making the most important audio loud and the least important audio soft. In theory, it sounds simple. In practice, well, let's just say that practice makes perfect.

Finally, Stephen returns with an excellent approach to media management in Soundtrack Pro. Just as Final Cut Pro creates media files, so does Soundtrack. This chapter explains what you need to know, where media files are stored, and what you need to do to keep them under control.

Chapter 15

Clean Up Your Audio

MARY PLUMMER

Why do so many video editors dread audio work? Perhaps it's the fear of the unknown. Maybe it's a psychological avoidance of things that aren't visual and fun. It's possible someone else has always handled the dreaded "A" word. Whatever the reason, there is good news! Audio for video can be both visual and fun, thanks to Soundtrack Pro.

Where Do You Start?

Working with your audio is like going to the dentist. Sometimes audio just needs a little cleaning. Sometimes there are audio cavities or decay that require more invasive procedures. Sometimes you need a whole new set of teeth or, in production terms, dialog replacement or a re-shoot. For this article we'll focus on routine cleaning.

The first step is to assess the audio. You don't need fancy equipment, just a set of ears and some objective thinking. How does it sound? Is it great? Is it good enough to edit picture? Is it a disaster? Bad audio is like a cold: No project is immune, regardless of the budget. I've been a freelance editor over 17 years and I've dealt with nearly every audio snafu known to production, including low levels, feedback, power line hum, college radio stations contaminating the signal, excess noise, audio drop out, squeaky dolly wheels, squeaky voices, overdrive, airport traffic, clipping, bleeding sound, and dead microphones. If it's a big-budget project, they can easily afford a reshoot or dialogue replacement. For all other projects that are on a smaller scale, you have to work with what you've got.

Understanding Audio Priorities

Assuming you don't have to re-shoot, what's next? Audio priorities are simple and vary slightly depending on the type of project. For example, a documentary using hidden cameras and microphones will likely have more noise and need more work. However, on the upside, audiences are forgiving because they understand it's a covert recording. Ironically, if the recording is too good the piece loses its authentic feel. Commercials and narrative projects, on the other hand, are expected to have great audio, so audiences are much less forgiving of errors. In fact, weak audio is the most obvious indicator of amateur status for student and independent films. If the audio is great, they'll be judged on other more important criteria like story and acting.

TIP: Prioritize audio cleanup. Start with adjusting overall levels, then work your way to the effects and sweetening.

So, what are the priorities? Let's focus on cleanup priorities for dialog.

1. **Audibility.** Can you hear the dialog? Is it low? Try raising the overall level of the audio file or track. If it is too loud, turn it down.

2. **Clarity of spoken words.** There are two types of clarity that need to be assessed and possibly cleaned up. Most of your cleanup will fall into this category.

   - **Clarity of content.** Can you hear and understand the individual words? Often a word or two is garbled, slurred, left out, out of place or otherwise indiscernible. If so, you'll need to find a donor word—preferably a match—and perform a dialogue transplant.

   - **Clarity of sound.** Are certain words or phrases hard to hear due to levels? Is there noise, hum, distortion, clicks and pops, or something else contaminating the sound? If so, you'll need to use filters or other processes to clean it up for better clarity.

3. **Consistency.** Are the dialog levels consistent throughout the piece? Is the background ambience, room tone, or noise consistent or does it cut in and out with each edit?

4. **Sound enhancement in the mix.** This is like icing the audio cake. Once the sound has been edited, clarified, and made consistent, you can move on to making it better using filters or equalization (EQ). Sometimes the goal is to make the sound worse, such as filtering a voice to sound like a telephone, small radio, or robot.

5. **Stretch timing (if voiceover or narration).** This is where you tweak the timing of phrases to better fit the edited picture. This can be done at any time within the audio editing process. Soundtrack Pro includes a handy waveform stretching tool.

Now that you know the priorities and where to start, let's focus on the most common cleanup task—clarity. First, you need to know where to work.

Timeline Vs. Waveform Editing

Editing audio clips in a Soundtrack Pro Multitrack project is very similar to editing audio in Final Cut Pro. If you know how to cut, copy, paste, move, blade, keyframe levels, and delete clips in the Timeline of Final Cut Pro, you can do virtually the same things in a Soundtrack Pro Multitrack project's Timeline. In fact, many of the keyboard shortcuts are the same.

Keyboard Shortcuts: FCP Window Wonders

SHORTCUT	FUNCTION
Return	Jumps playhead to beginning of Timeline
Shift+Return	Starts playback from beginning of project
Control+A; Control+S; Control+D	Shows (or hides) the Left, Lower, or Right panes
M	Creates a marker
Shift+M or Option+M	Jumps playhead to next or previous marker, respectively
Option+[Up/Down arrow]	Move playhead one video frame left or right
Option+X	Deletes a workspace (In/Out point in Timeline)
F1	Displays default Soundtrack window layout
Shift+Z	Scales project to fit in Timeline
Shift+Cmd+plus/minus	Increases/decreases track height in multitrack
Double-click volume slider	Resets volume to 0.00 dB
Double-click pan slider	Resets pan to center

Like Final Cut Pro, when you edit clips in the Soundtrack Pro timeline you are performing non-destructive editing of clips. You can also apply audio level and panning keyframes (automation) to tracks. A difference between the programs is that Final Cut Pro only lets you place filters on either individual clips or nested sequences, while Soundtrack Pro allows you to apply filters to the overall project, a bus (collection of tracks), an individual track, or, using the Waveform editor, a single clip.

The Waveform Editor is an extremely effective tool and offers nearly unlimited power to fix, enhance, change, improve, or manipulate audio files. If that wasn't enough, you can choose to wield that power to destructively or non-destructively change your audio files.

EDITOR'S NOTE: Destructive editing permanently changes the audio of the source file. Non-destructive editing changes a copy of the source file, without altering the original audio file.

Cleaning up audio in the waveform editor can be a small job or a big one, depending on the project. It is often the case that independent projects, documentaries, or corporate videos can take a lot more time because you may be working with inexperienced directors, poor equipment, and non-professional talent, all of which can affect audibility, clarity and consistency.

NOTE: Non-professional doesn't mean they are rude, show up late, or that they aren't professionals in their occupation. They could be an athlete, a bride or groom, a school principal, CEO, or even Governor (assuming he or she is not an actor). The non-professional status refers to their speaking voices and lack of vocal training. Non-professional speakers tend to wreak audio clarity havoc with uhhs, umms, errs, flubs, and staggered pauses, not to mention the ability to leap many decibels in a single sentence.

Editing the Waveform Content

Editing audio in the waveform editor is just like it sounds—you are editing the actual waveform within a clip, rather than tiling together pieces of clips that were sliced with the blade tool.

To open a clip as an audio file project, simply double-click the clip (**FIGURE 15.1**) and choose **Create audio file project** from the Preference dialog (**FIGURE 15.2**).

FIGURE 15.1 Double-click a clip in the Soundtrack Pro timeline to open it as an Audio File project.

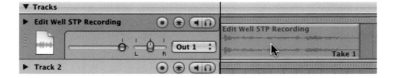

FIGURE 15.2 To edit a clip non-destructively, choose **Create audio file project**.

In Soundtrack Pro 2, you can edit a clip either in the File Editor in the lower pane of the multiclip window or using the Waveform editor. Whichever you use, the process is the same.

NOTE: When you create an audio file project from a clip in the timeline, the entire audio file is included in the project, not just the portion in the timeline. Loading the entire clip is the same as showing additional media (handles) outside of your In and Out points in Final Cut Pro.

TIP: You can quickly zoom in or out of the timeline or waveform by pressing the up and down arrows. Press Shift+Z to scale the entire waveform to fit in the window.

Once the waveform editor is open, you can edit words just as you would in a word processor (**FIGURE 15.3**). It's really that easy. Select any portion of the waveform down to the smallest space and cut, copy, paste, silence, or delete. Keep in mind that deleting a selection in the waveform editor works like a ripple delete in Final Cut Pro—it not only removes the selection but also moves over everything to the right of the deletion. This is great for removing gaps, uhhs, and excess words in voiceover and narration audio, but is *not* recommended if you are working with synced dialogue because, since the picture isn't affected by the edit, your audio and video will move out of sync.

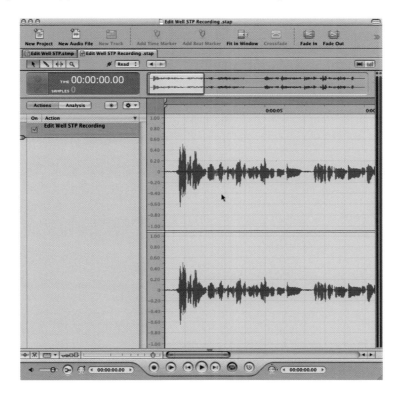

FIGURE 15.3 The waveform is displayed as two tracks for stereo and a single track for mono clips. Press Shift+Z to scale the entire waveform to fit in the window.

To delete a gap, word, or phrase in the waveform editor:

1. Click-drag the pointer to make a selection (**FIGURE 15.4**)

FIGURE 15.4 To make a deletion in the waveform editor, first select the portion of the waveform you wish to delete.

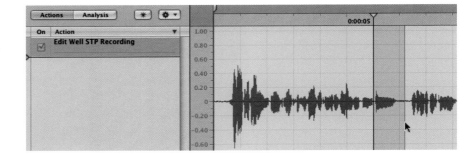

2. Press **Delete** (**FIGURE 15.5**).

FIGURE 15.5 Simply press Delete and you're done, the gap is closed automatically.

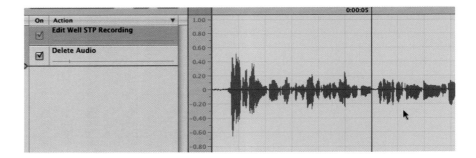

Replacing a word with a different take is another simple and common task.

1. Locate the "good" take that you want to use. This could be in a different audio file or audio file project.

2. Drag a selection around the words you'd like to copy, but don't actually copy.

NOTE: You can adjust a selection inward or outward to the nearest zero crossing. In general, adjusting inward works best because it tightens your selection slightly inward rather than making it slightly wider.

3. Choose **Edit > Adjust Selection to Zero Crossing > Inward**, or press **Shift+I** (**FIGURE 15.6**).

   This tightens the selection In and Out points at the sample level so they start and end at the zero crossing.

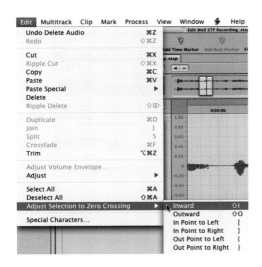

FIGURE 15.6 When replacing a word, you must first adjust selections to the zero crossings. To start, choose **Edit > Adjust Selection to Zero Crossing > Inward**.

Adjust Selections To the Zero Crossings to Avoid Pops

Before you copy, it's important to adjust your selection to the zero crossing. The zero crossing is the dark horizontal line in the middle of the waveform, which represents the point where the audio has absolutely no volume (**FIGURE 15.7**).

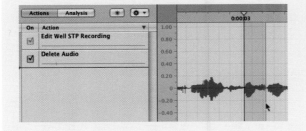

FIGURE 15.7
To make clean edits, adjust the In and Out points of your selection to match the zero crossing.

This audio secret is well known among audio engineers and dialog editors, but less commonly known among video editors. Have you ever sliced up audio with the Razor Blade or Add Edit functions in Final Cut Pro and heard the cut when you played it back? There's a little pop sound because you aren't cutting with precision. It's like doing knee surgery with a machete. You cut the knee all right, but your precision will be questionable and the whole procedure far too messy.

Editing audio waveforms at the zero crossing is cutting at the sample level at the exact point where the waveform crosses the center (zero).

4. Choose **Edit > Copy** or press **Cmd+C**.

5. On the original audio file project, select the word or words that you wish to replace. This technique is actually called Paste Over in Soundtrack Pro (**FIGURE 15.8**).

FIGURE 15.8 Select the word or words that you wish to replace.

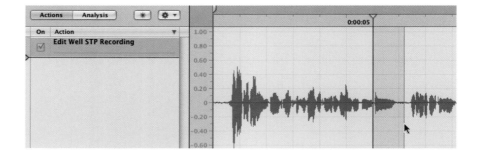

6. Press **Command+I** to adjust the selection to the zero crossing points.

7. Choose **Edit > Paste** or press **Command+V**.

Voila! Just like using a word processor (**FIGURE 15.9**).

FIGURE 15.9 By matching the In and Out to the zero crossing, you create an inaudible edit which perfectly replaces one word with another.

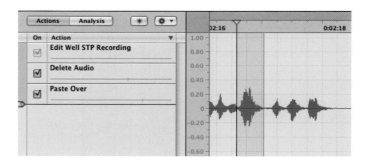

NOTE: If the selection that you copy and paste is longer or shorter than the selection that was replaced, the waveform to the right of the edit will automatically move right or left to accommodate the difference in length.

External Interfaces for Soundtrack Pro

Soundtrack Pro lets you record single takes or multiple takes, which are incredibly useful for voiceover and narration recordings. The trick is connecting your trusty XLR microphone to your computer so that you can record. If you're using an external mixer controlled by Soundtrack Pro's Control Surfaces feature, you can plug your microphones directly into the mixing board and you're ready to go. Otherwise, you'll need some kind of audio interface. Some interfaces require additional software to use them, so you'll need to do your homework before purchasing.

In the past few years, with the advent of more digital audio software such as Soundtrack and GarageBand, newer devices have appeared. Since I haven't tried all of these devices, I can't fairly recommend a best choice. Generally, I prefer a FireWire interface for speed and ease of connection; the USB interfaces tend to have more latency in the signal. The interface I've been using in my studio is the Edirol FA-101, which uses FireWire to connect to the computer, and is capable of 24-bit/96 kHz, 10 channels in and out. It also addresses almost every type of audio connection, including XLR. Edirol also makes a smaller, six-channel FireWire interface, the FA 66.

Editing Waveform Levels for Clarity of Sound

Once the content of the dialog, voiceover, or narration has been cleaned up for clarity of content, you can move on to tweaking the levels.

TIP: Tweak levels of individual words in the waveform editor to make the file more consistent before mixing. Automating levels in the mixing process is great for overall levels, but it's difficult to move levels up and down for specific words or partial words. If you fine-tune levels first in the waveform editor, then you can focus on the overall sound during the mix.

As I mentioned earlier, working with non-professional talent often leads to fluctuating volume levels within a sentence, or sometimes within a word. Professionals may fluctuate their voice levels for inflection as part of a performance. The non-professional does it because of nerves, lack of experience, or poor breath control.

NOTE: It is common for non-professional talent to take a big breath and start talking very loudly, then gradually fall quieter until they run out of air and take another breath. Then they are loud again. Fortunately, it's easy to fix in the waveform editor; tedious, but easy.

You can use the waveform editor to raise or lower the amplitude (loudness) of any selection, thus allowing you to tweak the most difficult dialogue.

1. In the waveform editor, select a word or phrase that is much louder, or quieter, than the rest of the sentence (**FIGURE 15.10**).

FIGURE 15.10 To change the amplitude of a selection, first select the word or phrase in the waveform monitor.

2. Adjust the selection to the zero crossing.

TIP: Take the guesswork out of level changes and adjust the amplitude using decibels instead of a normalized scale.

3. Control-click the scale on the left edge of the waveform editor and choose **Decibels** from the pop-up menu (**FIGURE 15.11**).

FIGURE 15.11 Control-click the scale to switch between measuring audio as normalized levels (linear) and decibels (logarithmic).

Now you can see precisely how loud the waveform really is and adjust accordingly. Not only that, you can see the difference in decibels between words (**FIGURE 15.12**).

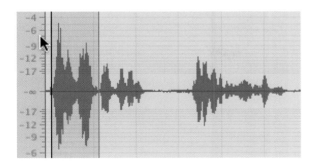

FIGURE 15.12 Look at the decibel scale to see how much you'd like to raise or lower the amplitude of the selection.

4. Choose **Process > Adjust Amplitude**, or press **Shift+Command+L**.

   The Adjust Amplitude control dialog opens.

5. Type the number of decibels you'd like to raise or lower the selection. In this case I tried **-6** to lower the amplitude by 6 dB (**FIGURE 15.13**).

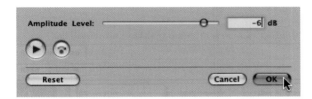

FIGURE 15.13 Adjust the decibels of your selection.

The entire audio selection raises or lowers its volume relatively by the amount you specified in the dialog; in this case, -6 dB. (**FIGURE 15.14**)

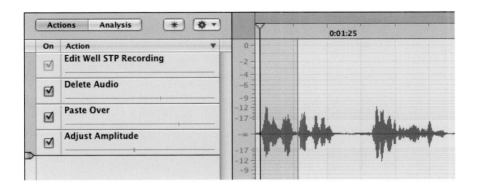

FIGURE 15.14 Compare the audio here (after the level adjustment) to the audio in Figure 15.12. This audio has dropped in level, making it blend more smoothly with the rest of the clip.

TIP: Once you have adjusted the levels of individual words for consistency, you can normalize the entire waveform. This technique is not recommended for dialogue, but works well for voiceover or narration.

That's it. Now you have your own bag of tricks that you can use as a video editor to clean up audio in Soundtrack Pro's waveform editor. Keep in mind that you can send an audio clip from the Final Cut Pro Browse or Timeline to the waveform editor as well. Hopefully this will take some of the guesswork out of your audio workflow, and arm you with a few powerful tools to make the audio cleanup process less painful.

Video Tutorial: Repair Audio with Soundtrack Pro 2

 Do you have an audio clip that needs some help? Please visit the companion Web site to learn four techniques you can use to:

- Improve low audio levels

- Replace umms and ahhs with ambient noise

- Remove power line hum

- Reduce background noise

Audio Profile

JAMES WALSH
Owner, JPI Creative Group, **www.jpicreativegroup.com**

 Jim Walsh has been an editor for over 24 years, starting long before computer-based systems were invented. In this conversation, available on the companion Web site, he discusses the evolution of this industry and shares tips for other editors.

Chapter 16

Sound Advice: Mixing

STEPHEN KANTER

The sound mix starts with the picture edit in Final Cut Pro. Even before the final audio mix, gain levels must be adjusted so that all the different types of audio clips—SOT (sound on tape), sound effects, music—can be heard clearly by the editor, as well as by any producers, directors, or clients that visit the edit bay to review a cut. By toggling on clip overlays, you can adjust the pink overlay representing gain level, with or without keyframes, directly in the Final Cut Timeline (**FIGURE 16.1**). Although most adjustments to place sounds in a 3D space occur in the final mix, not during the rough cut in FCP, you can also load a clip into the Viewer to adjust and keyframe the pan as well (**FIGURE 16.2**).

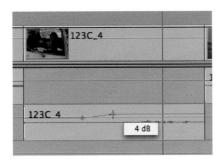

FIGURE 16.1 Using keyframes to adjust gain in the FCP Timeline.

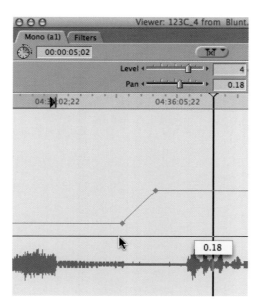

FIGURE 16.2 Using keyframes to adjust pan in the FCP Viewer.

To make adjustments to gain or pan you can either set levels and keyframes manually or adjust them in real time by enabling **Record Audio Keyframes** in Final Cut Pro to record automation keyframes as you play your Timeline. Whichever way you choose to adjust gain or pan, the good news with Final Cut Studio 2 is that all of that information is now preserved when you use **File > Export > Audio to OMF** to create an audio project ProTools can open, or send the sequence to Soundtrack Pro for finishing.

Here's how to send a sequence to Soundtrack Pro:

1. Open a Final Cut Pro project.

2. In the Browser, select a sequence you wish to send to Soundtrack Pro.

Audio Profile

TED LANGDELL

Ted Langdell Creative Broadcast Services, **www.tedlangdell.com**

 Like many editors, Ted Langdell is a visual storyteller. What makes Ted's job more difficult is that he practices his craft far away from major media centers. Visit the companion Web site to hear about the challenges he faces working on projects from large to small.

3. Do one of the following:

   • Choose **File > Send To > Soundtrack Pro Multitrack Project**.

   • In the Browser, Control-click the sequence icon and choose **Send To > Soundtrack Pro Multitrack Project** from the shortcut menu (**FIGURE 16.3**).

4. In the Save dialog, name your new project and click **Save**.

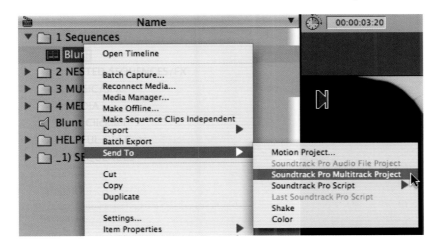

FIGURE 16.3 Sending a sequence to a Soundtrack Pro multitrack project from the Browser.

Soundtrack Pro automatically opens, transforming your sequence into a Soundtrack Pro multitrack project, ready for sound design and mixing. All gain and pan information added in Final Cut Pro, including keyframes, remain attached to each clip. In this way, sending the sequence to Soundtrack Pro allows a sound mixer to literally "finish" the mixing process where the picture editor left off. As we will see, if the mixer is the Final Cut Pro editor, the switch is made easier because the two applications share many of the same functions and even the same keyboard shortcuts. In this way, the tight Final Cut Studio integration makes moving from one application to another seamless.

Taking the Pane Out of Mixing

The first stage of mixing usually involves balancing the levels between tracks, starting with dialogue or narration, and then balancing music and effects relative to that.

When you first open a Soundtrack Pro project, all four panes of the interface are open (**FIGURE 16.4**).

Each pane contains useful tabs offering a variety of options, but if you are using only one monitor, it may be necessary to close some of the panes so you can focus solely on mixing functions.

Track headers   Project pane   Meters tab

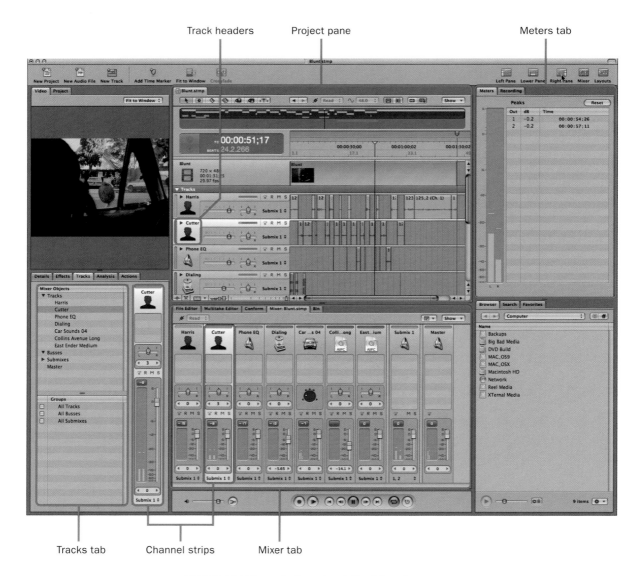

Tracks tab   Channel strips   Mixer tab

FIGURE 16.4 The main Soundtrack Pro 2 interface.

The right pane contains the Meters tab, and while it may seem counterintuitive to close this tab while mixing, you can gain valuable screen real estate if you do. You can see more clips at once in the Timeline and more channel strips in the Mixer, with negligible loss of monitoring capability, as there are audio meters in each of the other panes. The Timeline track headers in the Project pane each contain their own meters and track controls. In the Mixer tab, each Timeline track has a corresponding channel strip with dB scaled meters and track controls. All the track controls, such as gain faders, pan sliders, and toggles for recording, mute, and solo, mirror those in the track headers, although they are in left-to-right order instead of top-to-bottom (**FIGURE 16.5**). Clicking a button or adjusting a fader or panner in either pane does the same thing. To focus on adjusting one track at a time with greater precision, click the Tracks tab in the left pane to access a longer channel strip, which allows for finer adjustments and the most precise audio meters on this side of the right pane.

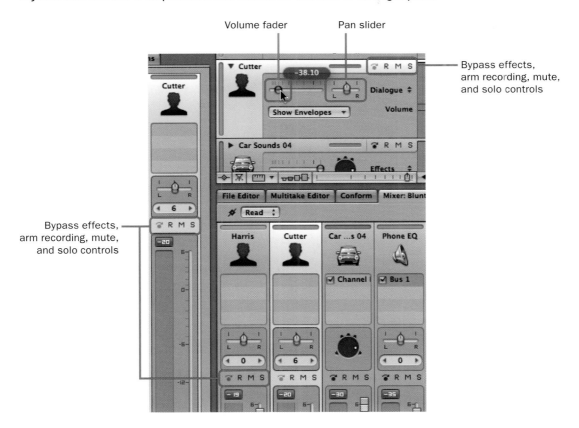

FIGURE 16.5 Volume adjustments can be made in the Mixer, the Tracks tab, or the track itself.

EDITORS NOTE: If you wish, you can also drag the Meters tab from the right pane to the left pane, similar to reorganizing tabs in DVD Studio Pro.

Since you can only adjust one control strip at a time, unless you have an external control surface, you can even close the lower pane to see more Timeline tracks, and use the Tracks tab to select and adjust one track at a time. When displaying the Mixer in the lower pane, you can't set the height of the channel strips as high as in the Tracks tab. However, you could accidentally set the height so low the full controls won't even display (**FIGURE 16.6**).

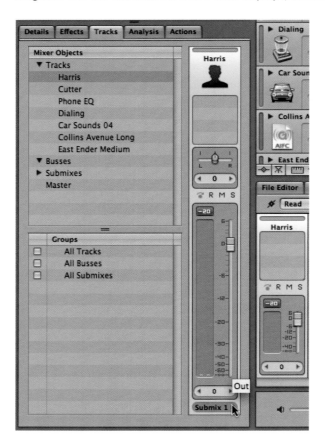

FIGURE 16.6 A closer look at the Tracks tab in the left pane showing the enlarged track controls for gain, pan, sends, and effects, along with a listing of all tracks and groups.

At certain monitor resolutions and window layouts, controls such as the Submix pop-up menu, as well as the playhead location and selection length value sliders, will not even display in the lower pane. To see these controls, it may be necessary to close other panes and/or dynamically resize the lower pane.

The channel strip in the Tracks tab suffers no such limitation at any height. More height equals more fine control when mixing in real time, as each movement of your mouse on your desktop results in a smaller movement of the gain fader in the interface.

You will no doubt use each pane in the mixing process, just not usually all at once. Of course, if you have two monitors and aren't hurting for screen real estate, you can tear off the Mixer tab and display it full screen in your second monitor, while displaying the Project pane full size in the first monitor.

May I Have the Envelope, Please?

In Soundtrack Pro, you can mix sound just like in Final Cut Pro, using the mouse to adjust horizontal lines representing gain and pan. These lines are called envelopes in Soundtrack Pro, and the keyframes you add to them are called envelope points. Instead of adding them to an overlay, as in Final Cut, you add and adjust envelope points using what could be described as an envelope "underlay." This underlay runs the entire length of each track, so you can adjust volume, pan, and other envelopes for entire tracks, not just a clip at a time like in FCP.

Here's how it works:

1. In the Project pane, click the Envelopes disclosure triangle to display envelopes (the purple bars) for Volume and Pan.

2. In the track header, adjust envelopes for the entire track using the volume fader and pan slider. (You can also do this using the channel strips in the Mixer or Tracks tab.)

    In the Timeline, add envelope points by double-clicking the envelope line, then dragging the points up or down, as you would keyframes in Final Cut Pro (**FIGURE 16.7**).

1. Show/Hide all Envelopes

2. Track header slider and panner

3. Choose individual envelopes to display or hide

4. Use channel strip sliders and panners

5. Choose next track to mix in Tracks tab channel strip

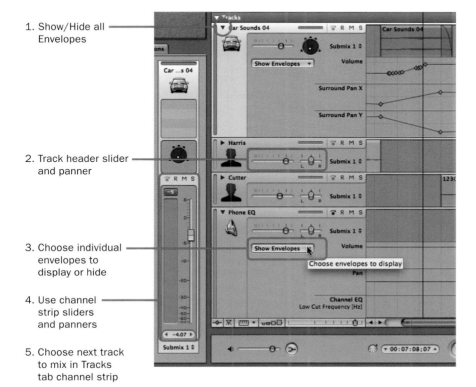

FIGURE 16.7 Setting gain and pan settings using envelopes.

3. From the Show Envelopes pop-up menu, choose which envelopes to display in the Timeline.

4. In the Tracks tab, choose another track to work with from the Mixer Objects pane, and use the fader and panner in the channel strip to adjust levels.

Recording Automation in the Mixer

Just as you would in Final Cut Pro's Mixer tool, you enable automation in the Mixer in Soundtrack Pro by making a selection in the Automation pop-up menu (**FIGURE 16.8**). However, STP gives you three keyframe options, rather than just one as in Final Cut. The three options are:

Read: Reads envelope points only, but does not record over existing levels during playback.

Latch: Records new envelope points based on fader or panner movements, then maintains the current level when user releases the fader or slider.

Touch: Like Latch, records new envelope points during playback, but when you let go of the fader or slider, automation returns to Read mode. Unless you "touch" a fader or slider, it does not record new automation.

FIGURE 16.8 Choose Latch or Touch to record automation during playback.

To record automation for Volume and Pan, follow these steps:

1. In the Mixer tab, choose an automation mode from the Automation pop-up menu. By default, this menu is set to Read, which is the same as turning keyframe recording off. My recommendation is to use Touch, as it is the safest way to preserve any keyframes you have already recorded.

2. Position the playhead at the beginning of the project.

3. Play the project. As you drag the faders and panners in any pane for any track, envelope points are recorded.

4. If you make a mistake or wish to refine your first mixing attempt, either press **Command+Z** to undo and try again from scratch, or reposition the playhead and play over the existing automation while adjusting the fader or pan slider. Remember that in Latch mode, existing envelope points will be erased in favor of the "latched" audio level even after you release the graphic or external slider. To "punch in" and record a new mix for a small

region, use Touch mode. When you release the mouse, envelope point recording will stop, and STP will simply read any envelope points it encounters until playback is stopped or you select a fader or slider again.

For another example of recording keyframes, see the sidebar "Recording Automation for Effects."

Recording Automation for Effects

With keyframe recording enabled, you can also automate effects parameters. To do so, select the Effects tab in the left pane, twirl down the triangle next to the effect you wish to automate, and select the checkbox for any parameter you wish to automate in the Auto column. The automation envelopes will be displayed in the purple area below the track (**FIGURE 16.9**).

As you play the project, any slider adjustments are recorded.

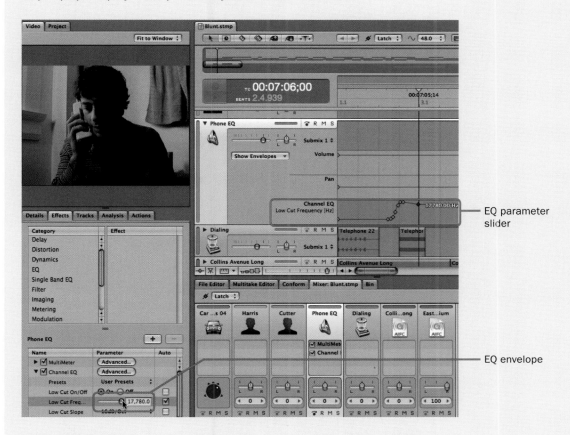

FIGURE 16.9 Adjusting a slider for an effect parameter with its Auto checkbox enabled will allow you to record automation in real time, just as with gain or pan.

Using Busses and Submixes

Busses and submixes will be unfamiliar to many picture editors, but audio pros have been using them for a long time. Sending multiple tracks to a bus or submix is much like nesting multiple tracks in Final Cut Pro. Solo and mute controls, as well as any fader or panner adjustments, affect all tracks that are routed to the same bus or submix.

Take the Last Bus to Submixville

One analogy for an audio bus is a real bus. Just as a bus collects a variety of people from many different locations and delivers them all to a single point, an audio bus collects signals from multiple sources and delivers them to a single submix. A submix (explained in greater detail in the next section), combines several signals, generally all related, into one fader for easier control. The route an audio signal might follow is in the same order, from left to right, that the tracks, busses, and submixes are arranged in the Mixer itself. One or more tracks might be sent to a bus, and each bus must be routed to a submix before finally passing through the master fader.

In the following example, a track that contains only the parts of a telephone conversation that are heard through the telephone earpiece is sent to a bus with an applied EQ effect, before finally passing to Submix 1 (**FIGURE 16.10**).

FIGURE 16.10 In this figure, the Phone track is sent to Bus 1, which has an applied effect, and Bus 1 then passes the signal to Submix 1, which routes to outputs 1, 2.

Audio Profile

RON KANTER
Video/Film Associates, **www.newcops.com**

 What's it like to work on a documentary for PBS that's taken over five years to produce? Or shoot documentaries in New Guinea, where camera batteries are charged using solar power? Visit the companion Web site to find out.

Busses are commonly used to add digital signal processing effects. By sending one or multiple tracks to the same bus, you can adjust the parameters and balance the amount of "wet" processing effects added to the "dry" signal from the sent track(s).

To send a track (or tracks) to a bus, follow these steps:

1. In Soundtrack Pro, choose **Multitrack > Add Bus**.

2. Control-click a track in the Timeline, or in the Mixer or Tracks tab, and choose **Add Send** from the shortcut menu (**FIGURE 16.11**).

FIGURE 16.11 Control-click to choose Add Send from the shortcut menu.

3. In the effects slot at the top of the channel strip in the Mixer or Tracks tab, Control-click the word "Send" and choose **Reconnect Send > To Bus 1** from the shortcut menu (**FIGURE 16.12**).

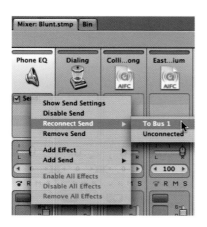

FIGURE 16.12 Control-click to choose a bus (destination) from the shortcut menu.

4. In the channel strip, Control-click Bus 1 and choose **Add Effect > EQ > Channel EQ** (or any other effect) (**FIGURE 16.13**).

FIGURE 16.13 Control-click the effects well near the top of the bus to choose an effect from the shortcut menu.

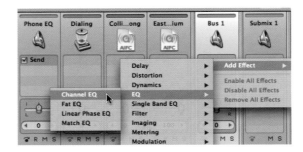

5. In the Effects tab, double-click the name of the effect to display its interface, then adjust the effect. You can also click **Show Presets** to display all presets, and then click **Apply Preset** when you find one you like (**FIGURE 16.14**).

FIGURE 16.14 Adding an effect to a bus affects all tracks sent to that bus.

Any adjustments made to the effect will apply to the bus and any tracks sent to it. In this case, the Phone EQ track is sent to the Bus affected by the Phone Filter Notch preset of the Channel EQ effect, which is applied (and adjusted) equally to all clips on the track.

Pre- or Post-Fader Sends

By default, sends are pre-fader, which means that the signal is sent to the bus at full volume, ignoring the level of the track fader. You can change the send to a post-fader send, and the track signal will be adjusted by the track fader before passing along to the bus.

To change a send to post-fader:

1. In the Effects tab, click the disclosure triangle for the send to reveal the parameters.

2. Click the On radio button for Post-Fader.

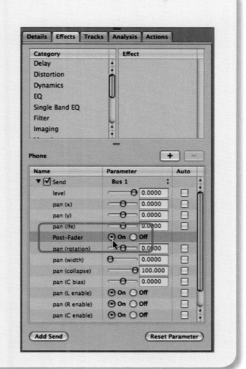

Video Tutorial: Soundtrack Pro Filters

To learn about using the Limiter, Fat EQ, and Channel EQ audio filters, as well as how to produce a telephone effect, visit the companion Web site.

Using Submixes

A submix is simply a type of bus. All tracks and busses must pass through a submix on their way to the Master fader. Each submix can be routed to different output channels, so you can route all the dialogue or narration to one submix, the effects to another submix, and the music to a third submix. Routing all the effects tracks and music tracks to separate submixes means you can both adjust effects and music relative to the dialogue tracks and output separate files for dialogue, music, and effects. This is a common practice when outputting a final mix for foreign distribution.

To create and route submixes do the following:

1. Choose **Multitrack > Add Submix**.

2. In the track header or channel strip, single-click the name or double-click the icon to change the name or icon for a submix (see **FIGURE 16.15**).

FIGURE 16.15 Double-click the icon in the track header or channel strip to change the icon.

3. From the Submix pop-up menu at the bottom of each channel strip, choose the appropriate submix to route the track to (**FIGURE 16.16**).

Post-fader levels can be raised or lowered for multiple tracks using the submix channel strip or track envelopes. Each submix passes to the Master fader, where you adjust the final combined mix levels.

Audio Profile

CHRIS ROBERTS
Apple Certified Trainer and Editor

Chris Roberts is based in Birmingham, England, and trains Final Cut Studio users all across the UK. Visit the companion Web site to hear his views on Final Cut Pro's role in editing in the UK and the future of production in England.

FIGURE 16.16 Click the Submix pop-up menu to route a track to a submix.

Final Export

Upon export, while you generally export the master mix, you also have the option to export separate mixes for each bus and submix.

To export files for each submix and bus, follow these steps:

1. Choose **File > Export**.

2. In the Export dialog, choose **All Tracks, Busses, and Submixes** from the Exported Items pop-up menu (**FIGURE 16.17**).

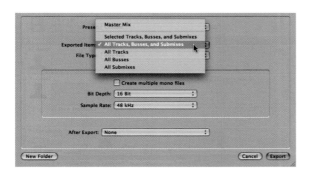

FIGURE 16.17 Choose All Tracks, Busses, and Submixes from the Exported Items pop-up menu.

3. In the Save As field, enter a name for your mix.

4. Choose settings for Bit Depth and Sample Rate; generally 16 Bit and 48 kHz are good choices.

5. Click **Export**.

When the export is complete, you will have one file for each of your tracks, plus separate stereo files for each bus and submix (see **FIGURE 16.18**).

FIGURE 16.18 In addition to exporting a file for each track's content, each bus and submix is exported as a separate file as well. This makes it easy to export music and effects files for foreign distribution.

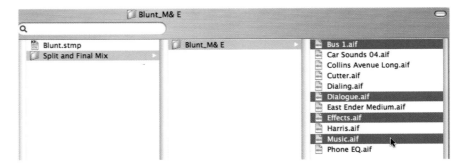

To export a master mix, follow these steps:

1. Choose **File > Export**.

2. In the Export dialog, choose **Master Mix** from the Exported Items pop-up menu.

3. Choose settings for Bit Depth and Sample Rate.

4. Enter a name for the mix and click **Export**.

5. The mix of all tracks, busses, and submixes is exported according to your specifications.

6. Import the resulting AIFF file into Final Cut and add it to your project. Then, turn off all other audio tracks in Final Cut so only your mix is played.

Feel free to experiment as you develop the finished sound for your projects. The features in Soundtrack Pro 2 give you all the tools you need to create a well-designed and well-mixed soundscape.

Chapter 17

Media Management in Soundtrack Pro 2

STEPHEN KANTER

O ne of the great advantages of using Final Cut Studio is the tight integration between Final Cut Pro and the companion applications such as Soundtrack Pro. Through the sharing of media and XML metadata, Final Cut Studio allows a workflow that is so seamless it's hard to tell where one application ends and another begins. However, when the intent is to archive a Final Cut Pro project or bring it to an online session, particular care must be paid to the handling of Soundtrack Pro audio file projects. I'll offer some suggestions to properly manage these projects and avoid common pitfalls.

Anatomy of a Soundtrack Pro Audio File Project

Unlike Final Cut Pro projects, which are independent of their media, Soundtrack Pro audio file projects are a hybrid of both media and project. The Soundtrack Pro audio file project file, or STAP for short, is actually a project bundle or package, and it contains various types of media. To some extent the user can determine how much and what kind of media the STAP contains by making choices at the point of project creation and again when the project is first saved. If you plan on moving a Final Cut Pro project containing embedded STAP files to another system, you need to send and save the STAP files in a particular way to ensure success.

To send a clip to a Soundtrack Pro audio file project, follow these steps:

1. In a Final Cut Pro project, select a clip in the Timeline and do one of the following:

   - From the File menu, choose **Send To > Soundtrack Pro Audio File Project**.

   - Right-click the audio clip in the Timeline and choose **Send To > Soundtrack Pro Audio File Project** from the shortcut menu (**FIGURE 17.1**).

FIGURE 17.1 Sending an audio clip to a Soundtrack Pro audio file project by right-clicking or Control-clicking the clip.

2. In the Save dialog, enter a unique name for the audio file project and click **Save**. Final Cut Pro sequences often contain multiple affiliates from the same master clip, so you must save each sent clip with a unique name if you want to be able to distinguish one audio file project from another in the reconnection process.

3. Select the "Send only referenced media" checkbox. This will also help with media management, especially if you send two or more affiliate clips of the same master clip (**FIGURE 17.2**).

FIGURE 17.2 To ensure efficient media management, always select the "Send only referenced media" checkbox. Reduce the length of the handles to reduce the size of the STAP file.

4. Choose a destination for the audio file project. Since it contains media, a folder on your scratch disk or media drive is preferable to the system drive. It is strongly recommended that you save all audio file projects to their own folder, separate from Soundtrack Pro multi-track projects or captured media.

5. Click **Save**.

When you send a clip to Soundtrack Pro, a QuickTime reference movie of the clip and a copy of your audio file, plus any handles, is saved inside the audio file project package. This QuickTime reference movie is what allows you to view the video in Soundtrack Pro while editing the audio non-destructively.

EDITOR'S NOTE: If you only need to listen to the audio, and your video files need a lot of time to render, deselect the Include Video check boxes. This will send the audio without including the video.

To show the contents of an audio file project package, do the following:

1. In the Finder, navigate to the Soundtrack Pro audio file project.

2. Right-click the file and choose **Show Package Contents** from the shortcut menu (**FIGURE 17.3**).

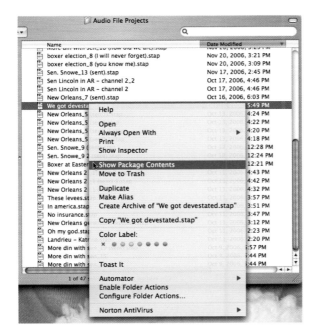

FIGURE 17.3 Right-click a file and choose **Show Package Contents**.

The package will open in a new Finder window. It contains the QuickTime reference movie, a file to help it integrate with a Soundtrack Pro multi-track project, and a file called render.mov (see **FIGURE 17.4**).

FIGURE 17.4 An audio file project package.

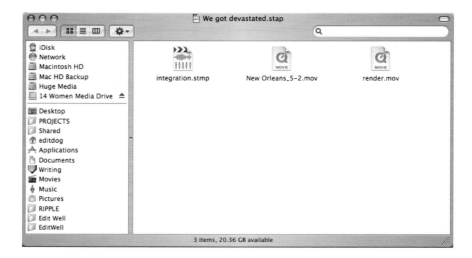

When you begin editing the file in Soundtrack Pro, the processes, effects, and EQ you add, such as normalization, noise reduction, and filters, are saved as actions in the Action tab (**FIGURE 17.5**).

FIGURE 17.5 Actions applied to an audio file project are listed in the Actions tab.

Files representing these actions are placed inside the project package, alongside the reference movie, while a Metadata file keeps track of change history so you can reorder, disable, or re-enable actions at will. When you save the audio file project, the combined result of all your actions is rendered into the render.mov file, and it is this file that the clip in the Final Cut Pro sequence references. Every time you save in Soundtrack Pro, the render.mov file is updated, and Final Cut reconnects to and plays the updated audio in the sequence (**FIGURE 17.6**).

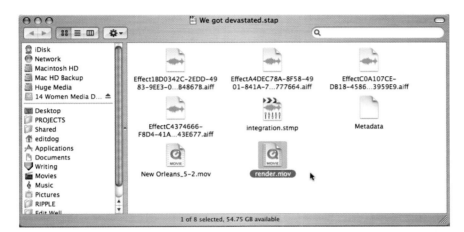

FIGURE 17.6 All actions are rendered into the final render.mov file when you save the STAP. This file is what the clip in FCP references and plays.

When you save the project for the first time, you will be presented with a crucial choice in the Save Audio File Project Preference dialog (**FIGURE 17.7**).

NOTE: Choose Include Source Audio if you use the Media Manager to archive the Final Cut Pro project or take the project offline and recapture to an online resolution.

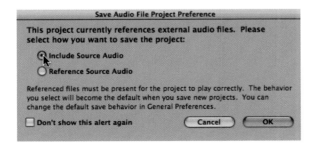

FIGURE 17.7 The Save Audio File Project Preference dialog.

If you are cutting an uncompressed or native resolution project and do not plan to recapture media or move the project to another system, choose **Reference Source Audio**. However, if you plan to archive the project or create an offline sequence for recapture using Media Manager, you must choose to include the source audio.

Referenced vs. Included Audio

Two audio file project packages are pictured here. The first contains referenced source audio; the other contains included source audio.

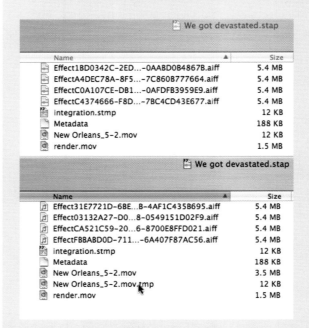

Notice that the first package contains a small 12 KB reference movie that points to the original media file in the FCP capture scratch. The second, with an included source audio package, contains a 3.5 MB self-contained movie.

So, unlike in the top project, the audio in the second package will still play if it is moved to a different system or in a case where the original FCP media is deleted or lost. The drawback is that the self-contained movie takes up more space inside the project package, which is why it is wise to send only the referenced media, plus handles, instead of the whole media file. The advantage is that the package is now a self-contained unit that can be archived or moved to another system and reconnected to a Soundtrack Pro multi-track project or FCP project at a future date.

Managing Media Instead of Mangling It

When you use Media Manager in Final Cut Pro to create an offline sequence for recapture, only media from tape sources is taken offline. Audio from other sources, including audio file projects, remains online and connected in your Browser and sequence (**FIGURE 17.8**).

FIGURE 17.8 A Final Cut Pro sequence created with the Make Offline operation in Media Manager. Audio from non-tape-based sources, such as audio file projects, remains online.

Of course, if you delete the low-res media or take the project to another facility, all the STAP-linked clips will go offline again, unless you bring all the audio file projects with you and they include the source audio.

To prepare a sequence containing STAP clips for an online session, do the following:

1. If possible, add a color label to every clip you sent to Soundtrack Pro, which will make it easier to reconnect the clips later.

2. Use Media Manager to create an offline version of your FCP sequence. Choose clip names from the "Base media file names on" pop-up menu (**FIGURE 17.9**).

EDITOR'S NOTE: If you are new to Media Manager, be sure to read the manual before using it. It is very easy to make permanent, and unwanted, mistakes by trying to guess how this function works.

FIGURE 17.9 Selecting clip names means that Media Manager will rename the new clips it creates based upon their file names in the Browser.

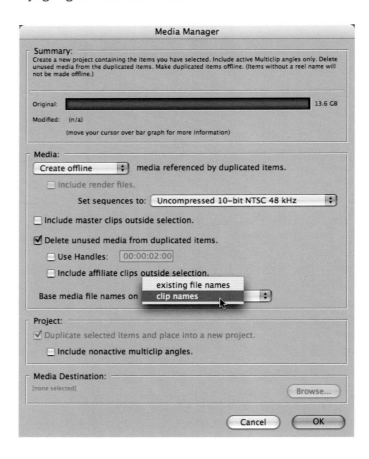

3. In the Finder, copy the folder containing your STAP files to an external hard drive, along with the online project file created by Media Manager and any assets you cannot recapture from tape—like fonts, graphics, audio files, and nonstandard plug-ins.

4. Bring the drive to the online session. Copy the project file to the desktop, and the STAP folder and all other media files to the device used for capture scratch.

5. Proceed to the steps for reconnecting the STAP clips in the next section.

When archiving or consolidating a Final Cut Pro sequence with Media Manager, it is just as important to have saved all STAP files to a common folder with source media included. This may seem redundant, since the whole point of using Copy or Move in Media Manager is that it will consolidate all the necessary media inside a common folder. The problem is, every STAP clip in the FCP sequence references a file inside its project package called render.mov, and while FCP will increment the render.mov files it extracts from each package, it doesn't do a good job reconnecting the STAP clips to their respective files. Even worse, the media managed render movies are all unplayable (**FIGURE 17.10**).

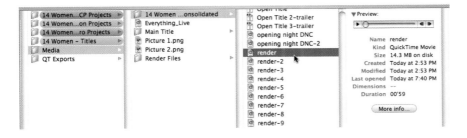

FIGURE 17.10 All STAP clips in a Final Cut Pro sequence reference a file called render.mov. Note in the preview column for the selected file the mini-Quick-Time controller has no control for volume; this is because none of the render files will actually play.

The lesson, learned from painful experience, is that Media Manager does not yet play nice with STAP media, which is why it is vital to save all STAP projects you create into a common folder.

Reconnecting Media

When it comes time to open a Final Cut Pro project file created by Media Manager, whether you used the Make Offline command or the Copy or Move commands, you will likely encounter numerous errors, such as the one shown in **FIGURE 17.11**.

FIGURE 17.11 A common error message when FCP tries to reconnect to media-managed STAP files.

My advice is to manually reconnect any offline STAP clips once the project loads into FCP.

WARNING: You may have to wait a long time for FCP to search in vain and give you the above error message for *every* **STAP** clip in your sequence, so be patient, and just click Cancel every time you are prompted.

When a consolidated FCP project loads, it will look something like **FIGURE 17.12**.

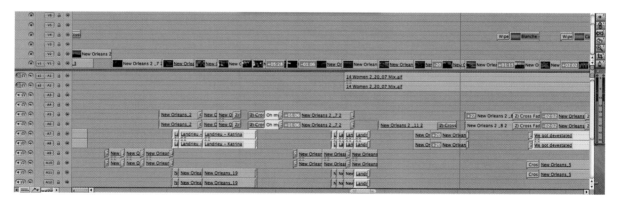

FIGURE 17.12 A sequence created by Media Manager's Copy command. A sequence created using Make Offline will have all clips offline. In both cases, labeling STAP clips ahead of time with color labels makes them easy to spot.

Offline projects intended for recapture will have all clips offline. If you labeled the STAP clips with a color label ahead of time, they will be easy to spot in the sea of white offline clips. If you didn't label the STAP clips, recapture the sequence using Batch Capture first, then proceed to the next step.

To manually reconnect STAP files, follow these steps:

1. In the Timeline, right-click or Control-click an offline STAP clip and choose **Reconnect Media** from the shortcut menu (**FIGURE 17.13**).

FIGURE 17.13 Reconnecting clips using a shortcut menu. You can also select a clip and choose **File > Reconnect Media.**

2. In the Reconnect Files dialog, click **Locate**. The file listed in the Files to Locate pane may or may not be helpful, so make sure you can see the name of the clip that you are trying to reconnect in the Browser or Timeline (**FIGURE 17.14**).

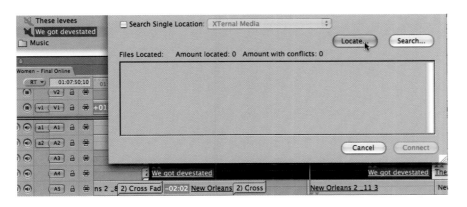

FIGURE 17.14 You must manually reconnect to the STAP file using Locate.

3. Navigate to the folder containing your STAP files, select the STAP file that matches your clip name, and click **Choose**.

   The file will be listed in the Files Located pane.

4. Click **Connect** to connect to the file.

5. Repeat steps 1 through 4 for every STAP clip in the sequence.

You must reconnect each STAP clip one at a time. Reconnecting multiple clips will not work, because you do *not* want to reconnect to the media-managed render files in the consolidated Media folder. Even though all the STAP files are in one folder, the filename FCP is looking for is *not* the STAP filename, it's *render.mov*. Only by directing FCP to each STAP file one at a time can it reconnect to the correct render.mov file inside each project package.

If you take steps to name and save each clip you send from Final Cut Pro as a unique Soundtrack Pro audio file project inside a common folder, you will find it relatively easy to reconnect any sent clip to its STAP file.

Whether you're taking the STAP folder to an online session or saving it as part of an archived (i.e. media-managed) project, you will find that you are able to manage the media better manually than if you let the computer do it (at least until the kinks are worked out).

Video Tutorial: Editing Spectrums in Soundtrack Pro

 One of the exciting new features inside Soundtrack Pro 2 is the ability to edit audio by frequency, not just waveform. In this tutorial available at the companion Web site, you'll learn how this feature works.

Audio Profile

STERLING NOREN

Senior Editor, Wide World HD Productions, **www.wideworldhd.com**

Sterling Noren is senior editor and owner of Wide World HD Productions. Sterling is a documentary editor, specializing in shooting and editing programs shot in exotic locations around the world. In this audio profile on the companion Web site, Sterling talks about his editing techniques and the power of letting his dreams shape his editing career.

Part 5

Color

Possibly no recent software release has caused as much simultaneous excitement and confusion as when Color was released as part of Final Cut Studio 2.

Its interface is totally unlike any of the other Studio applications. Its hardware requirements are equally outlandish. But, oh, the results it can achieve if you know what you are doing.

And no one knows Color better than Alexis Van Hurkman. In addition to writing two books on the topic, Alexis earns his living as an award-winning colorist. In the two chapters in this section, Alexis looks at the hardware requirements to run Color and how to prepare your Final Cut Pro projects for Color.

Then, he explains how to improve the contrast and exposure of your images, and concludes by showing how to color correct your images using Color.

It is an amazing tour-de-force that will help you jump-start your success with this amazing application.

Chapter 18

Setting Up Your Color System

ALEXIS VAN HURKMAN

Before you start using Color for serious work, you'll want to consider whether or not your current system is going to meet this software's unique demands. Is your computer fast enough? Do your graphics card and computer displays need updating? And what about your hard drive storage? These are all important questions.

What Is "Real Time" Anyway?

As you contemplate how much of an investment you want to make in your system, you need to understand what Apple means when they talk about real-time effects particular to Color. All adjustments that you make in Color update the image and the video scopes in real time (or, if you have a control surface, you can even use its controls to make adjustments during playback). However, the more rooms you enable in Color (in Color, using more "rooms" applies more effects to any given shot), the more processor intensive the shot becomes.

When making grading decisions, it's vital to see the full-resolution image as you work, and so Color has been designed to sacrifice frame rate, when necessary, to maintain high image quality as you make adjustments and play shots and sequences back in the application. When correcting standard definition video on a fast enough system, you have to do some serious color correction to experience a reduction in frame rate. However, high definition video exposes the outer boundaries of your system's performance much more quickly, especially once you start combining multiple effects on the same shot.

For example, I'm currently using an 8-core Mac Pro with an ATI X1900 card and a Kona LHe video capture and output card. My storage is a 10-drive array using a port-multiplied eSATA interface and enclosures. In a purely unscientific test of color correcting 1080p, 23.98 fps video encoded using the Uncompressed 10-bit 4:2:2 codec (setting Color's Internal Pixel Format to 12-bit), my system exhibited the following performance:

- 16 fps, using a single primary

- 14 fps, using a primary and two secondaries (one vignette, one HSL qualifier)

- 10 fps, adding Color FX on top of it all with blur and vignette

Now, this system is not the end-all, be-all. For example, anecdotal feedback on the message boards indicates that performance could be improved by upgrading the drive storage to a striped pair of Xserve RAIDs. But it serves to illustrate the kind of high definition performance you might expect from a reasonably equipped Mac Pro system.

The Need for Speed—Get a Fast Computer

Before you start going nuts with Color, it's important to consider the capabilities of your computer. Those of you who are upgrading your Final Cut Studio bundle on older machines may discover that, while perfectly adequate for many of the other applications in the Studio, your current setup lacks the horsepower to support Color's demands for real-time effects processing.

The good news is that if you've been waiting for an excuse to upgrade your old Power Mac G4 Quicksilver to a shiny new Intel-based Mac Pro, this is it. Although Color will run capably on PCIe-based G5 computers with suitable graphics cards, it runs much more efficiently on Apple's newer Intel-based Mac Pros. I've used Color on both a quad-core G5 and the newest 8-core Mac Pro, and although the G5 does nicely for standard definition projects, the Intel-based Mac Pro is clearly the better machine for working in high definition (as far as RAM goes, I always recommend at least 4 GB).

EDITOR'S NOTE: Currently, although no single application can address more than 4 GB of RAM, additional RAM can be useful when running concurrent applications. This frequently happens when you send a project to Color, since Final Cut Pro remains running in the background.

But What About My MacBook Pro?

Technically, Color will run on a current-generation 17-inch MacBook or on an Intel-based iMac. This can be a good way to practice with the application, or to use it in educational situations, but it's not a practical way to work. Since Color doesn't support monitoring via FireWire, there is no way you can evaluate an image for broadcast, and even a calibrated computer display will give you only an approximation of the image. Furthermore, the interface does become rather cramped at lower resolutions. Lastly, the lack of memory and the lower performance of the on-board graphics processors built into these systems relative to a desktop means your performance will be far less than that available to a desktop system.

Get a Fast Graphics Card

The model of computer you're using is only part of the story. Like Motion, Color is a GPU-based (graphics processing unit) application. This means that all the effects you apply to your projects in Color are performed by your computer's graphics card, rather then the CPU (central processing unit). This doesn't mean that having a newer computer isn't important. The latest and greatest Mac Pro tower computers have faster overall PCIe and memory bus architectures then the G5 Power Macs, all of which translates into more data being moved from hard drive to graphics card to video card, which translates into more real-time performance. Apple's quad-core systems run Color just fine, though I think the 2.66 GHz model is the best bang for the buck. On the other hand, if you find yourself lusting over an 8-core Mac Pro, know that you'll be using those extra cores more with Compressor and Shake than you will with Color.

Because of Color's reliance on GPU processing, you'll absolutely want a high-end video card. The ATI X1900 is an excellent choice, due to its high price-to-performance ratio and support for all the Internal Pixel Format bit depths that are selectable in Color. You should note that Color does not support computers with more than one graphics card, so those of you desiring three or more computer displays connected to your machines all at once will have to settle for two if you want to use Color.

Displays and Monitoring

As far as displays go, Color has been designed to present its interface on two displays, with the majority of the correction controls on the main display, and an image preview and three video scopes on a second display. If necessary, you can also run Color in single-display mode, in which case a narrower scopes window with a smaller image preview and only two scopes sits to the left of a shrunken version of the interface (**FIGURE 18.1**). Personally, I think two 23-inch Cinema HD monitors are the best way to present the Color interface, and they will also provide plenty of room for working with the other applications in the suite when you're not using Color.

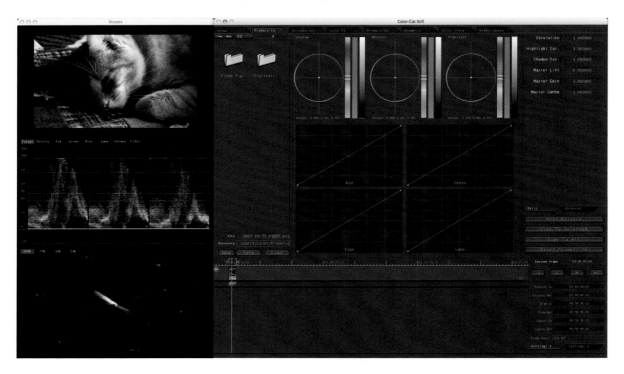

FIGURE 18.1 The Color interface, with the Primary room selected.

To view your video on a broadcast monitor (and as I've said in many past columns, you *will* want to use a broadcast monitor), you'll also need an approved PCIe-based third-party video interface. These include AJA's Kona and Blackmagic's DeckLink line of cards. Unfortunately, FireWire interfaces are not supported for monitoring as they are with Final Cut Pro or Motion. Although this limitation is acceptable for professional users who really ought to be monitoring using Y'PbPr, SDI, or HD-SDI, one hopes that Apple will add this functionality for the low-end crowd in future versions.

Get a Fast Hard Drive Storage System

When putting together a system, there's one other issue you need to take into consideration. Color's real-time performance depends as much on the speed of your hard drive storage as it does on CPU and GPU performance. It doesn't matter how fast the rest of your computer is if your storage system can't feed it data fast enough. In general, you'll want *at least* 50 MB/second performance for good standard definition performance, and 320 MB/second for optimal uncompressed high definition and 2K performance.

EDITOR'S NOTE: For comparison purposes, a single FireWire 400 drive delivers 20 to 25 MB/second of data. A single FireWire 800 drive delivers 45 to 50 MB/second of data. And a single SATA drive delivers about 75 to 90 MB/second of data. All these numbers assume the drive is less than 50 percent full.

This means that for standard definition, you may find that a striped array of three internal hard drives in your Mac Pro is perfectly sufficient. However, many high-end users typically rely on one or more Fibre Channel-based Xserve RAIDs to obtain the performance they need to work with uncompressed HD and 2K media.

Another possibility for those on a budget may be to investigate high-performance eSATA-based storage solutions. In particular, a variety of port-multiplying eSATA interface cards allow you to stripe drive arrays of 5, 10, and even 20 hard drives together in order to deliver high-speed throughput. There are many eSATA interface cards available, with varying performance and capability, and you should do your homework before going that route.

However, you should be aware that the more drives you use in a simple RAID 0 drive array, the greater risk you place on your media. All it takes is one drive failure in a RAID 0 array to lose all of the data that's been striped across all the drives. To minimize risk, many users set up Xserve RAID and eSATA drives as RAID 5 arrays. With RAID 5, one of a group of drives is used to store redundant information such that it is possible to restore an entire RAID volume in the event any single drive goes bad, simply by replacing it and setting the array to rebuild itself. RAID 5 configurations are not typically as fast as RAID 0 configurations with the same number of hard drive mechanisms, but shops that are working on schedule-critical programs may require this kind of rapid-recovery insurance. Not all eSATA interface cards support RAID 5, so if this is something you require, you'll want to do some homework.

Control Surfaces—Are They Necessary?

Unlike Final Cut Pro, Color supports a variety of control surfaces available from Tangent Designs and JL Cooper that are dedicated to grading. These typically consist of a set of three trackballs (sometimes called "joyballs") that control the shadow, midtone, and highlight color balance controls. Three accompanying rings adjust the black point, midtone, and white point contrast controls, and additional knobs, buttons, and transport controls let you adjust other parameters in Color's interface (**FIGURE 18.2**) using the JL Cooper MCS-Spectrum color correction control surface).

FIGURE 18.2 The JL Cooper MCS-Spectrum color correction control surface.

The advantage of a control surface is that you can adjust multiple aspects of the video simultaneously. Once you've gotten used to it, the increase in productivity is significant, not only in terms of speed, but also in terms of the sophistication with which you can make corrections for parameters that interact with one another. If your business is doing paid work for clients, you owe it to yourself and their schedules to get a control surface. On the other hand, these control surfaces can be somewhat pricey. If you're working on your own projects, and speed is not an issue, then learn the keyboard shortcuts and modifiers that Color offers, and you can do perfectly well without a control surface.

For the best experience in Color, you need to make sure that your system is up to the task. Although this excludes the cheapest systems that Apple offers from professional use, the cost of putting together a capable system is certainly far lower than it has been in the past, and it is quite accessible to the midrange user.

Setting Color's Scratch Disks

When you start using Color, the first screen will ask you to add scratch disks. To set the scratch disks, follow these steps:

1. Click the Browse button in either the opening dialog or the Setup room.

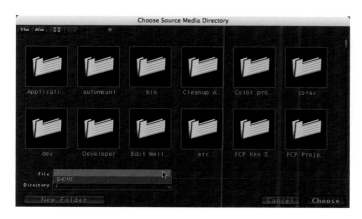

2. In the navigation dialog, click the "up directory path" button in the upper-left corner (drive icon with red arrow up) until you're all the way at the top of your drive hierarchy.

3. Scroll down the list of folders until you find **Volumes**, then double-click it.

    You should now see all the hard drive volumes that are currently mounted on your computer presented as individual folders (or items if you're in list view).

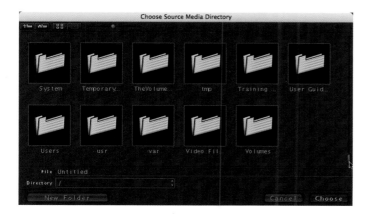

4. From the list of available drive volumes, double-click the one you want to use to open it.

5. Create a new folder to store your media, and double-click it to open it as well.

6. Click **Choose**.

Repeat this process to create a new folder to store render files.

Steps 4 through 6 are essential because, unlike other Mac OS X apps, the Choose button only sees the current directory path, which ends with the directory that's currently open. Directories that are selected but not open are not considered to be part of the current path. This isn't the way the file dialogs work in any of the other Final Cut Pro Studio applications. But the Volumes directory is in fact a standard bit of OS X-ness that's good to know about, especially for applications like Color and Shake, which treat the file browsing experience in a much more Unix-like fashion.

One other note: Color really likes big screens. Apple lists the minimum resolution for Color as 1680 x 1050, and they mean it. Color will run on a smaller monitor, but trying to use it on a 1280 x 768 monitor is an exercise in futility.

Chapter 19

Roundtripping with Color

ALEXIS VAN HURKMAN

As you no doubt already know, Color is a dedicated video color correction and film grading application that has been designed to fit into the finishing stage of your postproduction workflow. How seamless this workflow actually is depends on the attention you pay to the preparation and organization of your projects and sequences in Final Cut Pro, as well as the settings you choose in Color.

Now, let's look at the basics of the Final Cut Pro-to-Color roundtrip. You'll discover how to prepare your media and Final Cut Pro sequence to make this journey a success, learn some basic corrections, and finish the process by rendering your Color project and sending it back to Final Cut Pro.

Buy a Roundtrip Ticket to Color

Color has been designed to fit between the editing and output stages of your postproduction workflow (**FIGURE 19.1**) and to maximize your program's image quality before sending it out into the world. Color is used *only* for color correction, so Color and Final Cut Pro have a truly symbiotic relationship—you cannot capture video using Color, you do not typically edit your program within Color, and Color is incapable of either outputting to tape or rendering self-contained QuickTime movies. Instead, Final Cut Pro is relied upon to perform those functions.

FIGURE 19.1 The Final Cut Pro-to-Color workflow.

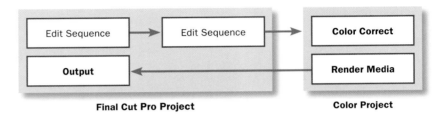

Although Color supports many workflows for projects from a variety of different sources, I'll focus on the most widely followed path—moving a program from Final Cut Pro to Color and back again. The Final Cut Pro-to-Color roundtrip goes like this:

1. Edit your program in Final Cut Pro.

2. Prep your media and edited sequence for working in Color.

3. Send your sequence to Color.

4. Color correct the sequence.

5. Render your Color project.

6. Send the Color project back to Final Cut Pro.

Now, let's take a look at steps 2 through 6 in a little more detail.

Preparing Your Media for Finishing

As with any finishing workflow, it's essential to use media that has been captured in Final Cut Pro at the highest possible quality. If you're following an offline/online workflow where you captured the source media at low quality in order to save hard drive space, you'll need to recapture that media at its highest original quality. This is not to say that you need to recapture everything at 10-bit Uncompressed 4:2:2 if it was originally shot using a compressed format.

For example, if you're working on a program that was shot on NTSC DV tape but that was originally captured and edited with the Offline RT format, you need only recapture the source media at its original resolution and format using the DV/DVCPRO–NTSC codec. When working in Color, image data—whether compressed or uncompressed—is converted to an uncompressed format at the beginning of the image-processing pipeline, which means all image processing in Color is performed on uncompressed data. During rendering, the uncompressed graded image is written to disk using the mastering codec you specify in the QuickTime Export Codecs pop-up menu. In essence, Color upconverts your program at the same time it renders your color corrections, in order to preserve maximum image quality.

Picking the Right Codec to Master

It's always desirable, after color correcting, to master to a higher-quality codec, ProRes or Uncompressed, preferably at 10-bit/4:2:2 chroma subsampling. This is true even if your footage started as DV or HDV. This will preserve the high-quality color correction image data processed by Color (recompressing it to a highly compressed format needlessly double-compresses the data) and also preserve the quality of any gradient or feathered-edge effects you created such as sky ramps, vignette effects, and so on. Dropping down to 8-bit may introduce unwanted banding, especially if your footage is really clean with little image noise to naturally dither such effects.

On the other hand, if you're working with media that is already in an analog or digital mastering format, such as Betacam SP, Digital Betacam, or D-5, you'll want to capture it using either 10-bit Uncompressed 4:2:2 (if you want it to remain uncompressed) or using the new ProRes 422 (for standard definition) or the higher data-rate ProRes 422 HQ (appropriate for high definition) codecs. Apple's ProRes 422 is a new high-quality compressed codec that's suitable for mastering 10-bit, 4:2:2 chroma subsampled image data in an extremely space-efficient manner.

Preparing Your Final Cut Pro Project File

Once you've made sure that your media is at its highest quality, it's a good idea to do some housecleaning to your edited sequence before you send it to Color. There are a variety of effects and media types that aren't supported in Color, and although these effects are generally ignored, preserved, and sent back to Final Cut Pro after you've finished your work in Color, a bit of Timeline reorganization will help you to keep track of things. In general, I would first recommend making a duplicate of your edited sequence as a precaution to make sure you can always go back to your original edit if necessary. Then, make the following organizational changes:

1. It's best to move all noncomposited clips to track V1 (**FIGURE 19.2**). Many editors use superimposed series of clips not to create layered effects, but to edit a scene together. Although this works well within Final Cut Pro, color correcting a program in Color that has numerous clips spread across several video tracks can be a pain in the neck. It's much easier to manage grades across multiple shots when they're all on the same video track.

FIGURE 19.2 When sending to Color, collapse all clips to be color corrected from a multi-track layout (top) to a single layer (bottom). Move clips that don't need color correction to a different track from video clips.

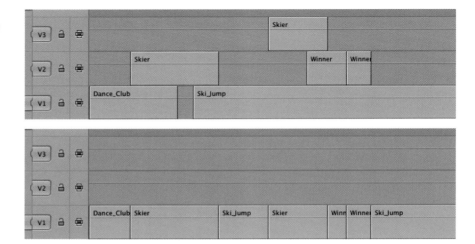

On the other hand, if there are superimposed clips that are part of a compositing or transparency operation, leave them be. Color doesn't support transfer modes or opacity effects, but these effects will nonetheless be preserved and will reappear when the project has been sent back to Final Cut Pro. In the meantime, you can grade the top- and bottom-most superimposed clips as necessary in Color.

2. Move all unsupported clips to a superimposed video track. Color does not support long-duration still image files, Final Cut Pro freeze-frames, generators, LiveType projects, or Motion projects. When you send your project to Color, these types of clips will either not appear, or they will appear as disconnected media. However, all of these clips will be preserved internally, and when the project is sent back to Final Cut Pro, all of these clips will once again show up on the Timeline, exactly where they were.

    If you have these types of clips in your project, and you don't need to grade them along with the rest of the shots in Color, you can simply ignore them. For example, you typically won't color correct clips such as titles, lower thirds, or other graphics that you've created specifically for the program.

NOTE: A handy trick is to put all your unsupported clips on one track, then disable them by choosing Hide Track from Color's Timeline shortcut menu.

On the other hand, if you have freeze-frames or composited effects that you need to grade in Color, here's a good workflow to follow:

- Move the unsupported clip to track V2.

- Render it as a self-contained QuickTime clip using either the 10-bit Uncompressed 4:2:2 or ProRes 422 codecs.

- Edit the QuickTime movie you rendered back into your sequence on track V1.

You can disable the original, superimposed clip in track V2, but leaving it there makes it easier to locate and rework should you decide you ever need to make a change to the effect. Now that the effect has been turned into a QuickTime movie, it can be graded in Color just like any other clip.

3. As mentioned in the Release Notes, Color does not support variable speed effects. However, linear speed effects, such as simple 50% or 200% speed changes, will play and render just fine. What may be a better plan is that variable and linear speed effects can be rendered at much higher quality using the new capability of Motion 3 to render adaptive speed effects— in effect generating new in-between frames to create extremely smooth slow-motion effects. Given this, you may also want to send any clips with variable and linear speed effects to Motion to perform higher-quality speed analysis, and then place rendered, self-contained QuickTime versions of these clips into your Timeline as outlined in step 2, above.

4. Color does not support either FXScript or FxPlug filters from Final Cut Pro. Similarly to all other unsupported effects, these filters will be preserved and sent back to Final Cut Pro once you're finished in Color. However, if you've done any color correction or effects in Final Cut Pro that you want to redo in Color, it's probably best to eliminate these filters to prevent them from reappearing in your project after you've applied these corrections in Color.

On the other hand, it's often useful to refer to such offline corrections and effects as you work in Color. One useful tip is to render a self-contained version of the entire sequence using a compressed codec, and then superimpose this "reference copy" of the program in an unused video track of the sequence so that it lines up with the original edits. Now, when you send the sequence to Color, you can disable this superimposed reference movie track to work on the original shots, and enable it whenever you want to take a quick look at the offline effects that were previously created. After you send the project back to Final Cut Pro, you can easily delete the superimposed movie.

5. Lastly, if your sequence's Timeline options are set to drop frame timecode, you'll want to turn off the Drop Frame checkbox. Color doesn't support drop frame timecode, but turning off this checkbox eliminates any problems this might create.

Using Send to Color after the Project's Prepped

You can only use the Send to Color command on sequences selected in the Browser (**FIGURE 19.3**). Once used, the Send to Color command in Final Cut Pro works somewhat differently than the "Send to" commands for Motion, Soundtrack, or Shake. Instead of replacing the media that's been sent from your Final Cut Pro project with a new clip that serves as the receptacle for the output from the remote application, the Send to Color command simply sends the sequence data, with links to the original source media, to Color. This does not change the sequence that you send, and nothing new is added to your Final Cut Pro project at that time.

FIGURE 19.3 The Send to Color command.

Once the Send to Color command has been used, you are asked to provide a name and location for the Color project file that's about to be created (**FIGURE 19.4**). Upon clicking OK, Color automatically launches, and your sequence appears in the Color Timeline (**FIGURE 19.5**). Now you're ready to work.

FIGURE 19.4 Choosing a name for the Color project file you're creating.

FIGURE 19.5 The shots in the Color Timeline after sending your Final Cut Pro sequence to Color.

Render Before You Return

We'll save the actual process of color grading a sequence for future articles. Once you've finished grading your program in Color, it is necessary to render *a new set of media files* from within Color before you send the program back to Final Cut Pro. Color renders a new color corrected media file for each and every shot in your edited program that's been corrected, and it is this new media that the clips within the sequence you send back to Final Cut Pro will be linked to.

When you're ready to render your program, follow these steps:

1. In the Prjct Settings tab (that is, Project without the vowels), choose the codec you want to use to master the program in from the QuickTime Export Codecs pop-up menu (**FIGURE 19.6**)

FIGURE 19.6 Select the render codec from this pop-up menu.

In general, you always want to master the program at the highest possible quality. Even if the source media was a compressed format (Color applies all its corrections to an uncompressed version of the image data), it's best to avoid recompressing the result to maintain this quality. If you have the hard drive space and you're an absolute stickler, use 10-bit Uncompressed 4:2:2. Otherwise, you will obtain excellent results using the ProRes 422 codec for standard definition mastering, or the ProRes 422 (HQ) codec for high definition mastering.

2. Choose the grade you want to render for each shot. Each shot in Color can be switched among four grades by pressing Control-1 through Control-4, allowing you to try alternate looks and change your mind later. When you add shots to the Render Queue (**FIGURE 19.7**), Color adds the currently selected grade for each shot to the queue, so be sure that you've selected the right one.

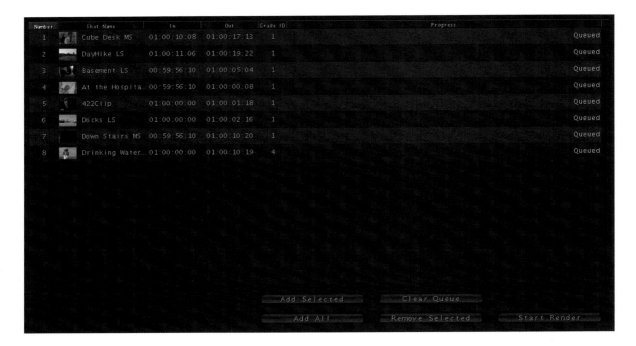

Number		Shot Name	In	Out	Grade ID	Progress
1		Cube Desk MS	01:00:10:08	01:00:17:13	1	Queued
2		DayHike LS	01:00:11:06	01:00:19:22	1	Queued
3		Basement LS	00:59:56:10	01:00:05:04	1	Queued
4		At the Hospita..	00:59:56:10	01:00:00:08	1	Queued
5		422Clip	01:00:00:00	01:00:01:18	1	Queued
6		Docks LS	01:00:00:00	01:00:02:16	1	Queued
7		Down Stairs MS	00:59:56:10	01:00:10:20	1	Queued
8		Drinking Water...	01:00:00:00	01:00:10:19	4	Queued

Add Selected   Clear Queue

Add All   Remove Selected   Start Render

FIGURE 19.7 This dialog allows you to add shots to the Render Queue.

3. After steps 1 and 2, you're ready to open the Render Queue, and add all of the shots that need to be rendered. You add shots to the Queue by clicking one of the following icons:

   Add Selected adds only the shots you select in the Timeline to the Render Queue. This is useful if you're working on a multiday project, and you want to render each day's work when you finish.

   Add All automatically adds every single shot in the Timeline. You should note that Add All also adds shots that you haven't graded. Ungraded shots will be re-rendered using the currently selected output codec.

4. Once you've set up the list of shots to be rendered, click **Begin Render**.

   A render bar displays for each shot in the shot list; as each shot is finished, its render bar in the Timeline turns green.

Sending Your Project Back to Final Cut Pro

After you've rendered every shot in the program, choose **File > Send To > Final Cut Pro** to send the Color sequence that references the corrected set of media files you rendered back to Final Cut Pro. Final Cut Pro opens, and the color corrected program appears within the Final Cut Pro project from which it came as an entirely new sequence, sitting alongside the original edited sequence.

At this point, you can make any remaining adjustments to the Final Cut Pro effects that remain in the project, render if necessary, and then output the sequence in the usual ways.

Changing Grades After You've Rendered

In a perfect world, you make your corrections, render your project, send it back to Final Cut Pro, output it, and are done. In the real world, there's always going to be something you need to tweak.

Because of the unique roundtrip workflow employed by Color, you need to be careful about how you make changes. If, after you've rendered the shots in Color and sent the project back to Final Cut Pro, you discover shots or scenes that you need to regrade, you should open the Color project, make your changes, and then re-render the shots that you regraded. Once you've re-rendered the shots that you changed, then you can open the project.

This is important: Shots are rendered in Color with the grade number included in their name. If you change the grade used by a clip and then re-render, you'll need to resend the Color project to Final Cut Pro in order to make sure the clips are linked properly. However, if you simply updated the same grades, then the sequence that you previously sent to Final Cut Pro should automatically pick up the new media.

As you can see, a bit of preparation can go a long way in preventing small issues from derailing your roundtrip experience. With the right preparation, however, the trip from Final Cut Pro to Color and back again is a fairly straightforward procedure, and the added capabilities that Color provides make it well worth the visit.

Chapter 20

Using Curve Controls in the Primary In Room

ALEXIS VAN HURKMAN

F or those of you who have been doing color correction in Final Cut Pro using the Color Corrector 3-way filter, you'll see a resemblance between many of its controls and those found in Color (**FIGURE 20.1**). For example, the Color Balance controls and contrast sliders in the Primary In room work more or less the same way as their Final Cut Pro counterparts, and the HSL (Hue, Saturation, and Lightness) qualifiers in the Secondaries room are nearly the same as the Limit Effect controls, albeit with a fancier, more industry-standard name.

However, many other controls are available only within Color. Principal among these are the curves controls found in the Primary In and Primary Out rooms (**FIGURE 20.2**). The curves controls let you make specific adjustments to individual color channels by adding control points to bend a diagonal line. There's one curve control for each color channel (red, green, and blue) and a fourth that controls luma (which controls the lightness of the image).

Those of you who work with Photoshop and other image editing applications are probably already familiar with curves; in fact, the more vocal souls among you may have already been asking for them in Final Cut Pro. Meanwhile, video colorists who've been working in other applications specific to color correction and film grading may be asking "why should I use curves when I'm already used to the other primary controls?"

One of my favorite features in Color is the Luma curve (the fourth one at the bottom right). The Luma curve simultaneously adjusts the red, green, and blue components of the image, with the result being a change to the overall lightness of the image. In this article, we'll focus on how you can use the Luma curve control to make some incredibly specific contrast adjustments that would be difficult to perform with the regular contrast sliders.

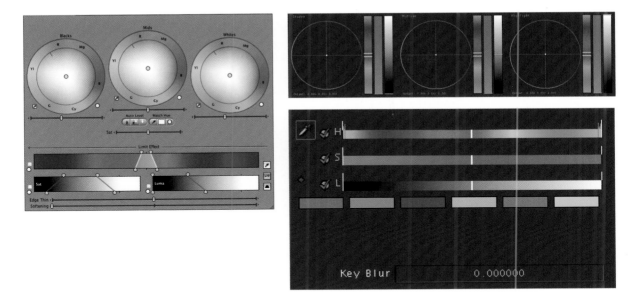

FIGURE 20.1 The Final Cut Pro Color Corrector 3-way filter (left) compared to the 3-way color control and contrast sliders in the Primary In room (right above), and the HSL qualifier controls found in the Secondaries room (right below).

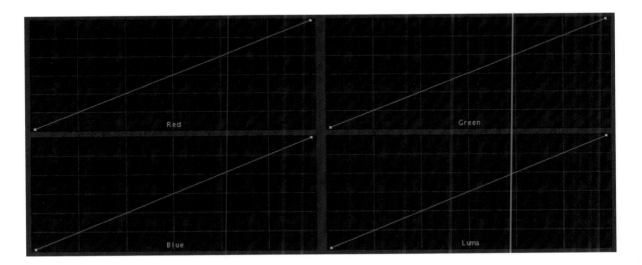

FIGURE 20.2 The curves controls found in the Primary In and Primary Out rooms. Clockwise from the top left, these control the Red, Green, Luma, and Blue channels.

How Can Some Wiggly Line Adjust My Image?

Before diving into the practical examples, let's step back for a theoretical overview of how, exactly, curves affect the image. Curve controls are essentially two-dimensional graphs. In **FIGURE 20.3**, the color curve control graph has two dimensions; one is the source axis (the X-axis), and the other is the adjustment axis (the Y-axis).

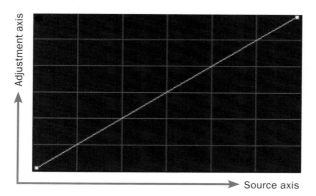

FIGURE 20.3 The curve control at its most neutral position, where the white line shows all source values equal to the adjustment values.

You may consider the white line of the curve itself to represent the actual values in the image. The leftmost part of the curve represents the darkest pixels in the image; the rightmost part of the curve represents the lightest pixels in the image.

When this white line is a straight diagonal from left to right (its default position), the source axis equals the adjustment axis, and the result is that *no change* is made to the image. The grid in the background of the control helps you verify this, since at its most neutral position the line of the curve control intersects each horizontal and vertical pair of grid lines through the middle diagonal, as you can see in Figure 20.3.

Curves get interesting when you add a control point with which to make adjustments. **FIGURE 20.4** shows a control point dragged up, increasing the values along the middle section of the curve.

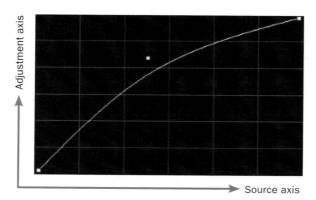

FIGURE 20.4 A curve control with one control point making an adjustment. The curve representing the color or luma values in the image is moved up along the adjustment axis.

In this case, you can see that the values along the middle of the image (the midtones) are raised. The curve is higher along the adjustment axis than the source axis, so the midtone image values in that channel are consequently raised. If this was the Luma curve, you'd be brightening the midtones of the image. If you instead dragged this control point down in the Luma curve, then the same parts of the image would instead be lowered, darkening the image.

By default, each curve begins with two control points that pin the left and right of the curve to the bottom and top corners. These can also be adjusted to manipulate the darkest and lightest values in that channel, but most of the time you'll be adding one or more control points along the middle of the curve to make your adjustments.

With that explanation in mind, let's take a look at how this works in a practical sense.

Set the Overall Contrast

Let's begin by importing a project into Color and clicking the Primary In tab at the top of the Color window to open the Primary In room. We'll demonstrate with a shot of the London Bridge (**FIGURE 20.5**). It's a late afternoon shot, and the shadows of the towers face the viewer, obscuring valuable detail. Furthermore, the director wants to match this establishing shot to a scene shot earlier in the day, so it would be good to reduce the depth of those shadows for simple continuity. Additionally, the sky is looking a bit flat, so we'll see if we can't bring some more detail out of those clouds.

If it's necessary to expand the overall contrast ratio of the image (to adjust the white and black points of the image to maximize the available contrast), it's best to do this first. It's best to make changes to an image's overall contrast by adjusting the primary contrast sliders to the right of each of the Color Balance controls (**FIGURE 20.6**).

Since the Luma curve control is pinned at both the highest and lowest parts of the curve control graph, you cannot raise the brightest highlights or lower the deepest shadows using just curves. For this reason, you might consider the Luma curve to be an extremely detailed midtones control.

In the London Bridge shot, the white, sunlit highlights in the clouds would look better boosted up to just under 100 percent, maximizing the contrast ratio of the image and giving us more range to work with in the curves control. To do this, simply click anywhere within the Highlight contrast slider and drag up or down to make the adjustment. In **FIGURE 20.7**, we can see the results of boosting the highlights using the Highlight contrast slider in the Luma graph of the Waveform Monitor.

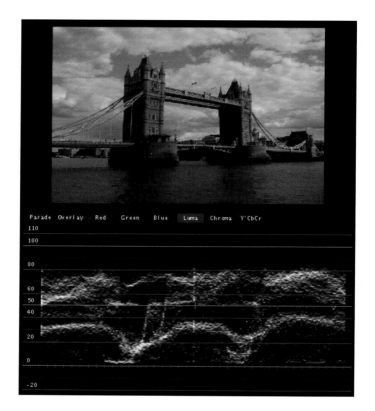

FIGURE 20.5
The original, unaltered shot.

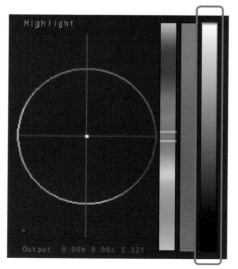

FIGURE 20.6 Adjusting the Highlight contrast slider.

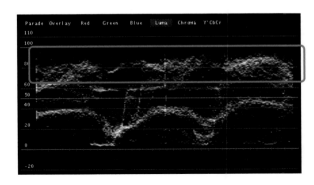

FIGURE 20.7 Moving the Highlight contrast slider up adjusts the white point of the image, seen at the top of the Waveform's Luma graph.

Once this is done, we can now move on to the adjustments we want to make using the Luma curve. The first order of business is to reduce the depth of the shadows on the bridge. The tricky part of this is that we don't want to lose all of our deep blacks in the shot; that would make the image look flat and lifeless. Instead, we want to preserve the very deepest shadows in the image, but lighten those shadows on the towers of the bridge. This can be done by adding two control points to adjust the Luma curve.

However, where to add the control points? One thing you should notice is that there's a rough correspondence between the height of portions of the graph in the Waveform Monitor and the height of the control points you add to a curve control. Since we know we're making adjustments to the shadows, we want to add control points near the bottom of the curve roughly corresponding to the bottom two dips in the graph that match the position of the shadows on the tower (**FIGURE 20.8**).

NOTE: The horizontal position of features on the Waveform Monitor graphs correspond to the horizontal position of features in the image.

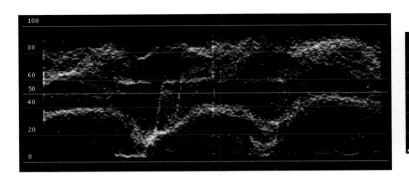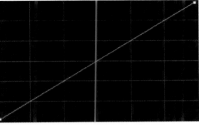

FIGURE 20.8 The height of features in the Waveform graph can be used to estimate where, on a curve control, to add control points to adjust those features.

To preserve the darkest shadows in the image, we click once on the white line to add a control point at the bottom-left side of the curve control, and drag it down to reduce the levels. Then we add a second control point to the right of the first one, corresponding to the height of the tower shadows in the waveform graph, and drag the second point up to lighten that portion of the image. The final Luma curve adjustment can be seen in **FIGURE 20.9**, with the final result in both the image and Waveform graph in **FIGURE 20.10**.

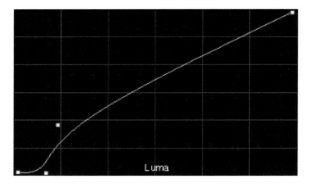

FIGURE 20.9 Two control points added to the bottom-left of the Luma curve darken the deepest shadows and brighten the lighter shadows on the bridge towers.

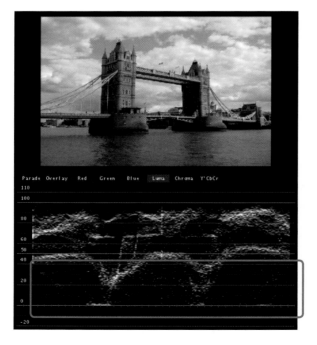

FIGURE 20.10 The portion of the Luma graph corresponding to the control points that were added to the Luma curve, with the resulting change to the image.

Now the bridge shadows are suitably lightened, but the result has been a lightening throughout the midtones of the image, which is not what we wanted. To correct this, we need to add another control point at the upper-right part of the curve and drag it down to bring the midtones and highlights back down. The change to the curves is shown in **FIGURE 20.11**, the change to the image in **FIGURE 20.12**.

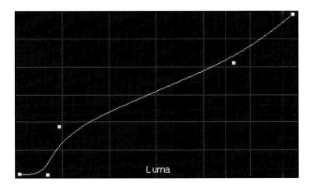

FIGURE 20.11 A third control point has been added to lower the midtones and highlights that were brightened by the previous adjustment.

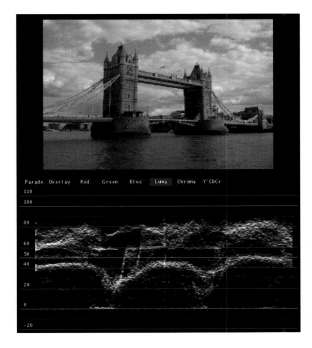

FIGURE 20.12 The resulting change to the image.

Adjusting Curves in Color

To add control points to any curve in Color, simply click anywhere along the white line that makes up the curve. Curves in Color are manipulated with B-splines, rather then the Bézier splines that other applications employ. This means that the control points are not actually attached to the curve; instead they influence the shape of the curve like a magnet.

To adjust the curve, simply drag the control point in any direction. To remove a control point, drag it out of the curve control rectangle and let go of the mouse button. To reset the entire curve to its default neutral state, click the small round reset button at the upper-left corner of any curve control.

You should be noticing that these curve adjustments are pretty subtle. With the Color curve controls, a little bit goes a long way.

Adding Even More Detailed Adjustments to the Curve

Now that the shadows and midtones of the image have been adjusted, it's time to do something to pep up those clouds. One of my favorite tricks with curves is to make extremely selective stretches to the contrast in the highlights in order to bring out more cloud detail. The effect can add quite a bit of drama to an otherwise dreary gray day. To do so, we add one more control point to the right of the one we added previously (**FIGURE 20.13**), affecting the very top of the highlights that correspond to the lighter portions of the clouds. Dragging this control point up selectively stretches the contrast in the clouds, while leaving the rest of the image relatively untouched. The result is more dramatic looking clouds with lots more visible detail, as you can see in **FIGURE 20.14**.

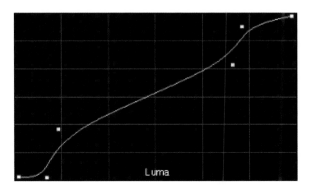

FIGURE 20.13 Adding another control point to the highlights at the upper right of the curve and dragging it up to selectively brighten the highlights in the clouds.

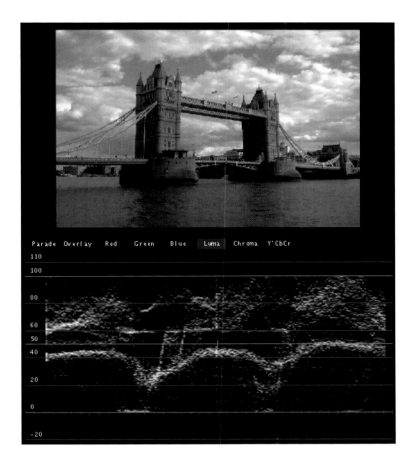

FIGURE 20.14 The resulting image and waveform graph.

At this point, I'm satisfied with the image. The overall contrast ratio is nice and wide, with deep blacks and bright highlights; the time of day matches the other scene; and there's lots of pleasing detail throughout the frame. Let's take a look at the before (**FIGURE 20.15**) and after (**FIGURE 20.16**) to get a better sense of what's happened to the image.

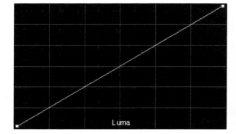

FIGURE 20.15 Before

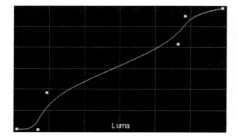

FIGURE 20.16 After

Chapter 21

Adjusting Red, Green, and Blue Channel Curves

ALEXIS VAN HURKMAN

The red, green, and blue color adjustment curves in Color are located underneath the color balance controls in the Primary In and Out rooms, as shown in **FIGURE 21.1**.

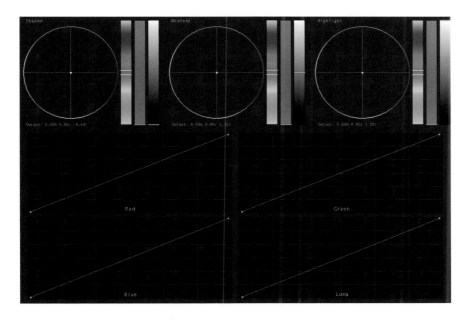

FIGURE 21.1 The color curves are located underneath the color balance controls in the Primary In and Out rooms.

Each color curve controls the amount of one primary color component of the image. Adding control points to a curve lets you raise or lower the level of the red, green, and blue color channels to different values at different areas of image tonality. In other words, you can raise the amount of red at the top of the midtones while simultaneously lowering the amount of red at the bottom of the midtones, as shown in **FIGURE 21.2**.

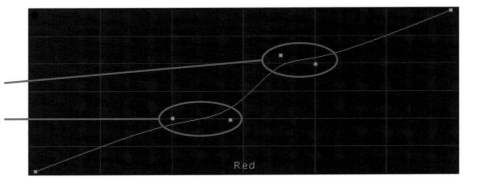

FIGURE 21.2 Adjusting the red channel within two different areas of image tonality.

Adjusts Upper Midtones

Adjusts Lower Midtones

This will be explained in greater detail later on. For now, let's begin with a simple example of curves in action. **FIGURE 21.3** shows the relatively neutral image of the London Bridge.

NOTE: In all examples in this chapter, the video scope graphs are shown with the Broadcast Safe controls turned off, in order to let you compare the tops and bottoms of the Parade scope graphs without clipping at 0 and 100 percent.

To add more red to this image using the curves, simply click the middle of the Red curve to add a single control point, and then drag it up to raise the amount of red, as shown in **FIGURE 21.4**.

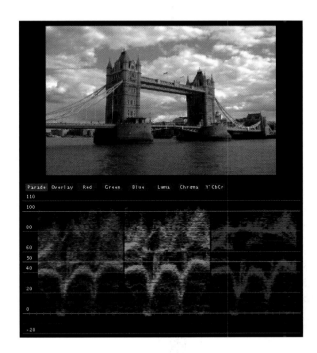

FIGURE 21.3 A neutral image with balanced graphs in the Parade scope.

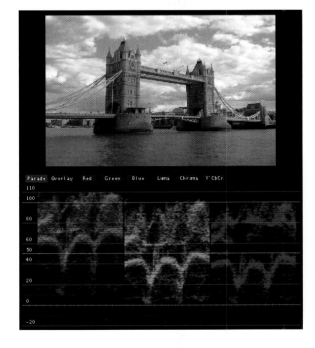

FIGURE 21.4 Add a control point to the Red curve to raise the red channel of the image.

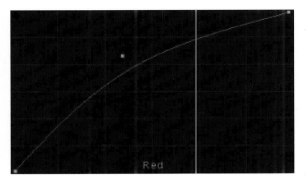

As you can see in Figure 21.4, dragging up the control point boosts the amount of red throughout the midtones of the image. Making an adjustment with only one control point results in a fairly extreme overall adjustment to the image, since it pulls nearly every part of the curve upwards. This creates a warm color cast over the entire scene.

You should note that the initial two control points that the curve starts out with at the bottom left and upper right (shown in Figure 21.4) partially pin the darkest and lightest parts of the red channel in place. With ordinary adjustments of modest scale, this default position helps to preserve the neutrality of the darkest shadows and the brightest whites in the image. **FIGURE 21.5** compares the unadjusted and adjusted red graphs of the Parade scope from the previous image. If you look closely at the top and bottom, you can see that the midtones of the red channel have been stretched by a greater amount than the shadows and highlights of the red channel.

FIGURE 21.5 Comparing the unadjusted red channel at the left to the curve-adjusted red channel at the right.

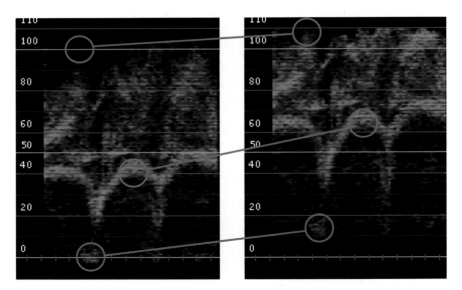

However, the beauty of the curves interface is that it lets you apply multiple adjustments throughout the tonal range of an image from the shadows to the highlights, depending on how many control points you add to the curve, and where you place them. **FIGURE 21.6** shows a rough breakdown of which parts of the default slope of the curves interface correspond to which tonal areas of the image. Bear in mind that since the practical definition of shadows, midtones, and highlights overlaps considerably, this is only an approximation.

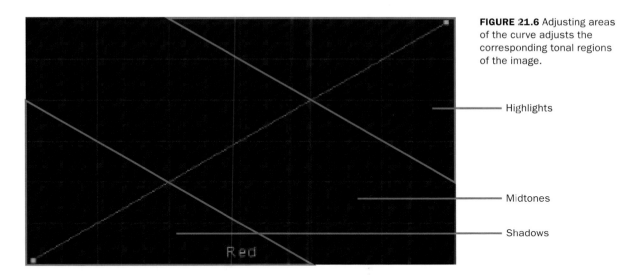

FIGURE 21.6 Adjusting areas of the curve adjusts the corresponding tonal regions of the image.

Highlights

Midtones

Shadows

In **FIGURE 21.7**, we've added a second control point to the middle of the Red curve to more finely control the effect. The control point to the left continues to boost the red channel, but now it's specific to the lower portion of the midtones and shadows. Meanwhile, the second control point to the right pins the Red curve at a more neutral diagonal in the highlights. The curve from one control point to the other is kept very smooth, resulting in a very gradual transition from one region's adjustment to the next.

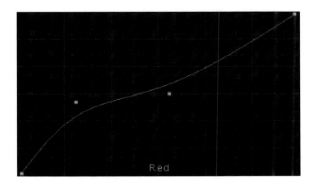

FIGURE 21.7 Boosting red in the shadows while keeping it neutral in the highlights.

The result is that the bridge, the city, and the water that comprise the midtones have the red cast we've introduced, but the sky and clouds in the highlights remain neutral, as you can see in **FIGURE 21.8**.

FIGURE 21.8 The image with a two-point curve adjustment to the red channel. The shadows and midtones are affected, but the highlights remain neutral.

This is the power of curves. They give you specific, customizable control over the color in different tonal regions of an image that can sometimes border on secondary color correction.

Making Controlled Corrections Using the Parade Scope

If you want to use curves as a corrective tool to neutralize color casts, one of the best ways to spot which curves need to be adjusted to make the necessary correction is to use the Parade scope. As you've already seen in the previous example, the graphs for each of the three color channels in the Parade scope correspond perfectly to the three available color curve controls. Since color casts generally reveal themselves in the Parade scope as an elevated or depressed graph corresponding to the channel at fault, you have an instant guide to show you which curve you need to adjust, and by how much.

FIGURE 21.9 shows an image with a green channel that is obviously too high relative to the rest of the picture, and it's throwing off the highlights of the shot.

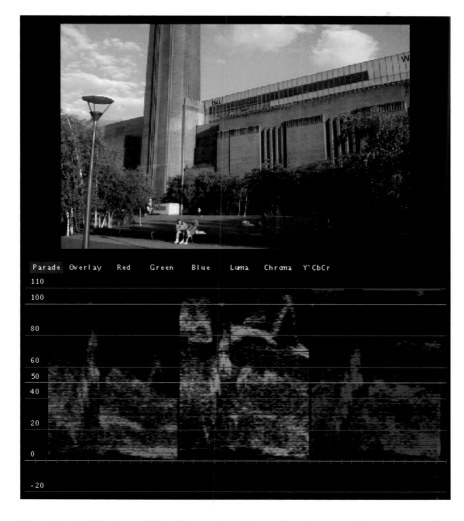

FIGURE 21.9 The green channel is too high, introducing a color cast throughout the image.

If you look at the tops of the three colors in the Parade scope that correspond to the highlights, you can see that the green channel exhibits a higher graph, contributing to the overly cyan look of the sky and clouds. Since you can measure how much higher the top left portion of the green graph is than the top left portion of the red graph, you have an idea of how much of an adjustment you have to make.

Dragging down the upper-right control point that's already at the top of the Green curve control causes a corresponding drop at the top of the green graph of the Parade scope. Dragging it down until the top of the green channel lines up with the top of the red channel in the Parade scope corrects the highlights (see callout A in **FIGURE 21.10**). Clicking the middle of the Green curve control to add another control point and then dragging it down lowers the amount of green in the upper area of the midtones (see callout B in Figure 21.10), revealing an instant improvement to the color of the sky in Figure 21.10.

FIGURE 21.10 Lowering the green channel to correct the sky has muted the plants at the bottom.

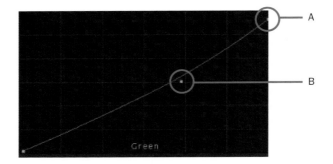

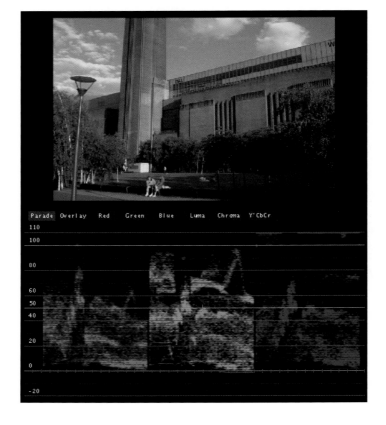

Unfortunately, the same correction that gives the sky a nicer blue shade has the side effect of desaturating the foliage of the plants. However, this is easily fixed by adding a second control point to the Green curve to boost the bottom half of the curve (see callout A in **FIGURE 21.11**). I've also taken the liberty of adding a third control point to the bottom shadow portion of the Green curve to desaturate and deepen the shadows (see callout B in Figure 21.11). The result is visibly healthier plant life with good color contrast.

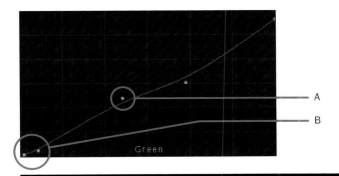

FIGURE 21.11 Boosting the green channel improves the color of the foliage. However, the midtones of the blue channel are still a little high.

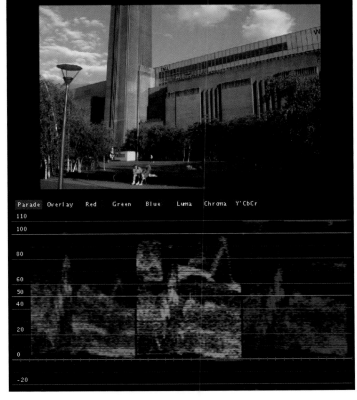

With these other corrections made, it becomes apparent, both visually and by looking at the top of the midtones of the blue Parade scope graph (see the callout in Figure 21.11), that the blue channel is inappropriately high. Looking at the Parade scope graph, it makes sense that the top of the blue graph should be higher than the tops of the red and green graphs, since the brighter sky is blue, but the midtones are proportionally higher as well, which is affecting the building and plants. The solution, shown by callout A in **FIGURE 21.12**, is to click the upper-middle of the Blue curve to add a control point to the Blue curve, and then gently lower it.

FIGURE 21.12 Lowering the blue channel just a bit improves the color of the building and intensifies the green of the trees and grass.

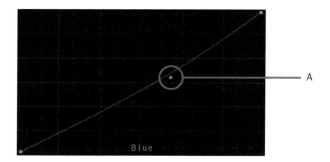

As you can see, there is a fairly direct correspondence between the values displayed in the three graphs of the Parade scope and the three color curve controls. **FIGURE 21.13** shows the before and after of all the adjustments made to the image up to this point.

FIGURE 21.13 Before and after the correction.

Which are Faster, Color Balance Controls or Curves?

Unlike the color balance controls, which simultaneously adjust the mix of red, green, and blue in the image, each of the color curves adjusts just one color component at a time. This means that sometimes you have to adjust two curves to make the same kind of correction that you could achieve with a single adjustment of the appropriate color balance control.

For example, in **FIGURE 21.14**, the Parade scope indicates a color cast in the shadows of the image, via a blue channel that's too high and a red channel that's too low.

FIGURE 21.14 A color cast in the shadows stemming from red, green, and blue channels at different levels.

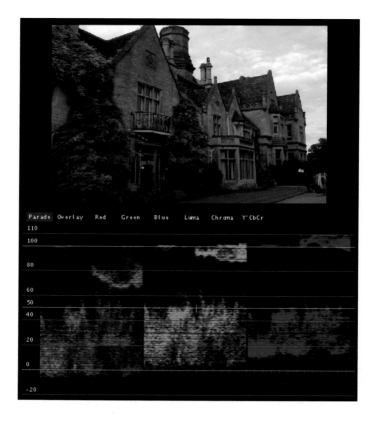

To correct the color cast using the curves controls, you'd have to make two adjustments: raise the bottom control point of the Red curve (callout A in **FIGURE 21.15**) and crush the shadows of the Blue curve (callout B in Figure 21.15). However, to make the same adjustment using the color balance controls, you would only need to drag the Shadow control up towards orange (callout C in Figure 21.15). Both adjustments result in the same correction.

A

C

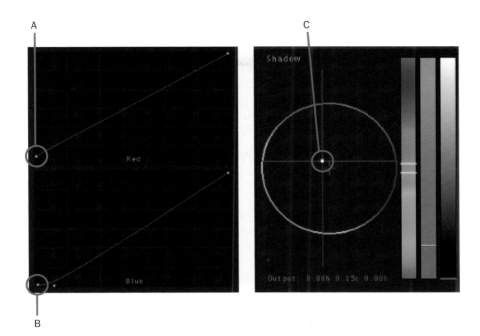

FIGURE 21.15 Two ways of making the correction to the shadows of the image produces the same results.

B

Which way is better? Well, that's really a matter of personal preference. The real answer is whichever way lets you work faster. In a client-driven color correction session, time is money, and the faster you work, the happier your client will be.

Both controls have their place, and my recommendation is that if you're coming to Color from a Photoshop background, take some time to get up to speed with the color balance controls; you may be surprised at how quickly they work. And for colorists from a video background who haven't used curves that much before, take the time to learn how to make curve adjustments efficiently, as it may open up some quick fixes and custom looks that you may have wrestled with before.

Creating Color Undertones Using Curves

Lastly, one of the more creative uses of the color curve controls is to add tinted undertones to a specific tonal region of the image. This is the way to create the "green shadows" look seen in various film scenes and commercials, although you can use this technique to add any color tint to any area of the image.

The trick is to use a group of control points to add a tightly controlled boost or drop in a particular color channel of the image. For a more sophisticated look, try keeping the darker shadows in the image untinted, so that there's some contrast between the tinted and untinted regions of shadow. For example, **FIG-URE 21.16** shows a neutral interior scene.

FIGURE 21.16 A neutral scene.

In **FIGURE 21.17**, you can see a fairly narrow boost to the green channel created with four control points. Notice in particular the pair of control points at the right. Whenever you want to create a sharper curve in order to make an adjustment that's not so gradual, bring a pair of control points closer together. In this example, the result is to flatten out the curve to a neutral diagonal from the lower midtones all the way through the highlights.

NOTE: A curve is at its neutral position when it crosses the middle intersecting gridlines.

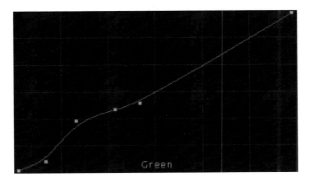

FIGURE 21.17 Making a selective boost in a portion of the shadows of the green channel. (For a reminder of which parts of the curve correspond to which tonal areas of the image, see Figure 21.6.)

The result of this selective boost is shown in **FIGURE 21.18**: green undertones throughout the image that contrast well with the natural color and lighting from the original scene.

FIGURE 21.18 Note the green tones in the shadows created by the curve drawn in Figure 21.17.

If you examine some of the premade looks provided in the Color FX bin of the Color FX room, specifically the Movie_Look_Green color effect, you'll see that the same method is employed there, along with some other selective adjustments to other tonal regions of the red and blue channels, using curve nodes applied to individual image channels.

As you can see, color curves are extremely powerful tools that can be used for a number of corrective and creative tasks. Although they may seem a bit daunting at first, as with all things, the more time you put into practicing to create different effects, the faster you'll be in using them.

Chapter 22

Making Color Adjustments in the Primary In Room

ALEXIS VAN HURKMAN

The various "rooms" of the Color interface are ordered according to a traditional colorist's workflow. Basic corrections to the overall shot are usually performed using the Primary In controls, found in the Primary In tab, located at the top of Color's interface (**FIGURE 22.1**). Next, the controls in the Secondaries room are used to make more targeted adjustments to specific features within the shot. After that, the Color FX room provides additional ways to create custom effects and more extreme stylizations, building upon the Primary and Secondary corrections you've already made. Lastly, the Primary Out room provides additional controls for fine-tuning the overall shot, allowing you to adjust the output of all work done in the first three rooms.

With one minor exception, the Primary In and Primary Out rooms have the same controls. Interestingly, the Secondaries room also uses many of the controls found in the Primary In room. The bottom line is that once you learn how to use the controls in the Primary In room, you end up learning how to work within many other areas of Color's functionality. For that reason, it's worth spending some time to learn how these controls work.

FIGURE 22.1 Access the Primary In room by clicking the Primary In tab at the top of Color's interface.

Using the Auto Balance Control

Before we dive into how to make corrections the "long way," it's worth taking a quick look at one of the few automated tools that Color provides—the Auto Balance control. The Auto Balance control, found under the Basic tab at the right of the Primary In room (**FIGURE 22.2**), provides a fast, "one-click" correction that simultaneously adjusts the color and contrast of an image.

FIGURE 22.2 The Auto Balance control.

When you click Auto Balance, Color "auto-magically" samples *the frame at the position of the playhead* to determine the darkest five percent of the image, the lightest five percent of the image, and the most neutral midtone pixels that fall between the two. These three sets of values are used to figure out how to adjust the shadows, midtones, and highlights of the image in order to maximize the image contrast, stretching it to fit from 0 to 100, and correcting whatever color casts appear throughout.

To use the Auto Balance button, follow these simple steps:

1. Move the playhead in the Timeline to a frame of the current shot that's representative of the image. If you're correcting a shot with variable exposure, try to pick a reasonably well-exposed frame with visible areas of desaturated white, gray, and/or black.

2. Click the Auto Balance button.

That's pretty much it. Color takes a second to think, and then the correction is made. Unlike Final Cut Pro, in which the Automatic Color Balance and Contrast buttons make adjustments to the main controls of the Color Corrector 3-way filter, the automatic adjustments in Color populate the Lift, Gain, and Gamma parameters found in the Advanced tab (**FIGURE 22.3**). The graphical color balance controls and contrast sliders are left alone for you to make further adjustments.

This may at first seem deliberately obtuse, but trust me, it's a good thing. The Auto Balance button is meant to give you a head start for your grade, but invariably you're going to make further manual tweaks as you work on your shot. Doing so with a fresh set of controls is a good way to keep *your* adjustments separate from those made by the Auto Balance control. If at any point you want to reset your manual adjustment, you won't also reset the original automatic adjustment.

FIGURE 22.3 The Lift, Gain, and Gamma parameters in the Advanced tab are automatically adjusted after clicking the Auto Balance button.

How well does it work? Well, results vary depending on the shot you're trying to correct. I've found that the effectiveness of the Auto Balance button depends in large part on the type of image you're correcting. Shots requiring smaller contrast adjustments, and with clearly visible areas of desaturated white, black, or gray, tend to give better results than clips that are under- or overexposed, or with regions that are off-white, such as a pale yellow wall.

In general, I recommend trying it out, and if it provides a good starting point for your work, then great, you're ahead of the game! If you don't like the results, you can always click Reset Primary In, located under the Auto Balance button.

Making Contrast Adjustments

Color provides separate controls for contrast and color adjustment. I begin with the manual contrast controls because, in general, these are the first adjustments you'll make when you start work on a shot.

There are three sets of controls in the Color interface that provide control over contrast (**FIGURE 22.4**): the Shadow, Midtone, and Highlight contrast sliders; the Lift, Gain, and Gamma parameters in the Basic tab; and the Luma curve control.

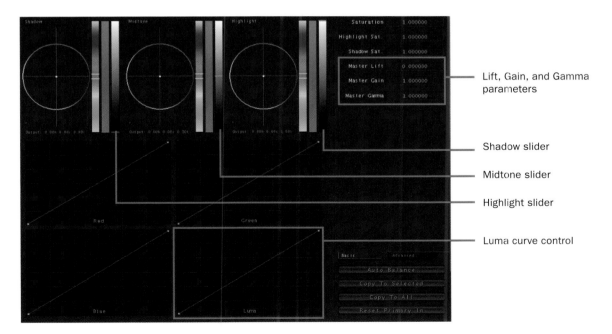

Lift, Gain, and Gamma parameters

Shadow slider

Midtone slider

Highlight slider

Luma curve control

FIGURE 22.4 Contrast controls in the Primary In room.

All of these controls affect image contrast, which I like to define as the distribution of tonality from the darkest to the lightest pixels in an image. The Luma curve control provides another method of adjusting the contrast of your image. The curve interface allows for extremely detailed contrast adjustments, but we'll focus on using the primary contrast sliders and the Lift, Gain, and Gamma parameters.

The three primary contrast sliders appear as vertical gradients in the Color interface. Clicking within one of these sliders and dragging up or down lets you adjust the region of image tonality affected by that slider. For example, the Shadow slider lets you adjust the black point of the image, darkening or lightening the shadow region of the image by raising or lowering the darkest pixels, and scaling everything between the shadows and highlights. Similarly, the Highlight slider lets you adjust the white point of the image, darkening or lightening the lightest pixels of the image, and scaling everything between the highlights and shadows.

In **FIGURE 22.5**, the image contains overexposed highlights, as well as shadows that are somewhat light relative to absolute black. This can be seen by examining the very top and bottom of the graph in the Waveform Monitor while it's set to Luma, the Waveform Monitor's mode for evaluating the luma-only component of the image. (In this example, Broadcast Safe is turned off so you can see the overexposed portion of the image.)

To adjust the image so that the shadows are darker, you can click anywhere within the gradient of the vertical Shadow slider, to the right of the shadow color balance control, and drag down to lower the bottom of the graph in the Waveform Monitor until it just touches 0 percent. You can also "crush" the shadows a bit by lowering the Blacks slider (see **FIGURE 22.4** to locate the Blacks slider) even more so that even more of the shadows are flattened down to 0 percent, in order to create even denser portions of black in the shadows. Doing so sacrifices a bit of shadow detail, but if we're careful and don't overdo it, this isn't necessarily a problem. If it looks good in your broadcast monitor, then it's the right thing to do.

Now it's time to turn your attention to the highlights. All luma above 100 percent is considered "superwhite," and is not legal for broadcast. (Send a broadcaster a video master with superwhite, and more likely than not it'll be returned to you with a stern note to fix it.) By default, Color "clips," or eliminates, all superwhite values *above* 100 percent *to be* 100 percent using the built-in Broadcast Safe settings, found in the Project Settings tab of the Setup room. However, clipping the superwhite values in the image will eliminate valuable detail in the highlights, flattening out these areas unnecessarily. Dragging down the Highlight slider brings image detail over 100 that would otherwise be clipped back into the allowable 0 to 100 percent range.

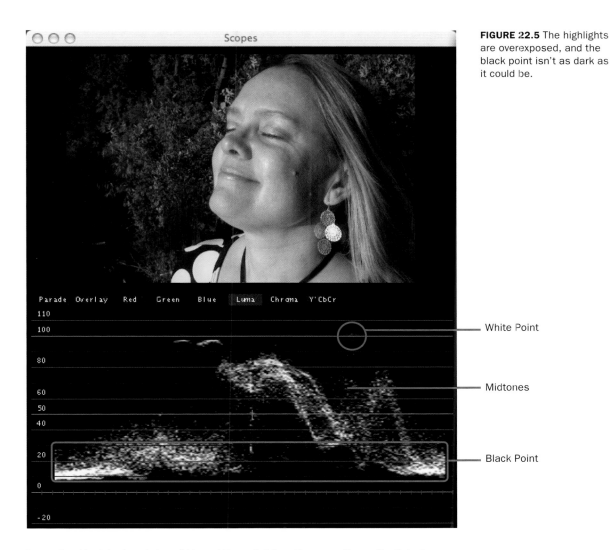

FIGURE 22.5 The highlights are overexposed, and the black point isn't as dark as it could be.

Lowering the black point and the white point has the overall result of darkening the entire image, which is not exactly what we want, so dragging up within the Midtone slider lets you raise the average midtones of the image that fall between the shadows and highlights, to brighten the image. Doing so invariably requires readjustments to the Shadow and Highlight sliders, and you'll move from one slider to the other, raising the midtones and then lowering the shadows and highlights until you're satisfied with the overall image.

You'll notice by now that I'm not showing you screenshots of these slider adjustments, and that's because the sliders aren't really that visual—the small blue indicator is not a handle, and the amount you can adjust each slider is not limited by the slider's height. However, if you look at the bottom of each of the three groups of color and contrast controls, you'll see a small set of three values labeled "Output," shown in **FIGURE 22.6**. These show you the (H)ue and (S)aturation of any color control adjustments you've made, and the (L)ightness of your contrast adjustment. In the example in Figure 22. 6, since we've not made any color adjustments yet, we see only that the Shadow contrast slider has been set to a value of –.11.

FIGURE 22.6 The Output values show you a numeric representation of your contrast and color adjustments.

After all of these adjustments are made, **FIGURE 22.7** shows the resulting image and Luma graph.

Why Are There Additional Lift, Gain, and Gamma Parameters in the Basic Tab?

The Lift, Gain, and Gamma parameters are an additional set of contrast controls that let you make one more set of adjustments, without modifying the adjustments you've made to the contrast sliders described previously. However, there is one key difference between these controls. The Lift parameter performs a different type of adjustment than the default behavior of the Shadow contrast slider. Whereas the Shadow contrast slider (with Limit Shadow Adjustments turned on in the User Preferences tab, the default in Color 1.0.1) lets you adjust the black point of the image while leaving the white point pinned at 100, the Lift parameter actually lifts the *entire* signal up, lightening the shadows, midtones, and highlights by the same amount.

NOTE: The contrast rings on a connected control surface, if you have one, adjust the Shadow, Midtone, and Highlight contrast sliders, not the Lift, Gain, and Gamma parameters.

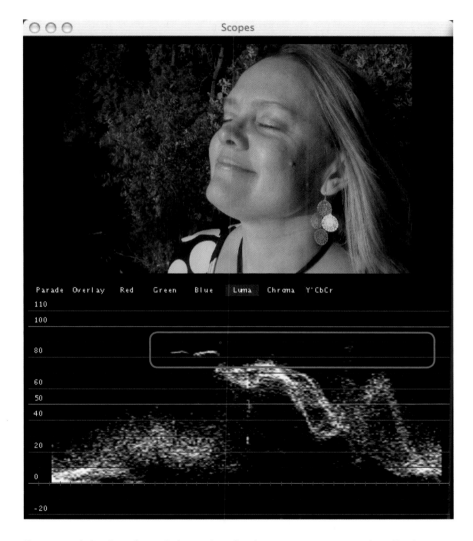

I've turned the Broadcast Safe settings back on, so you can see the clipping that's occurring at 0 percent in the Waveform Monitor. You may also notice that I've flattened the contrast in the highlights of the image by significantly lowering the highlights of the image and simultaneously raising the midtones. I've done this in order to minimize the shiny highlights on the woman's face. Shine on a face is sometimes considered undesirable, depending on the program, and reducing the amount that the highlights stand out from the average brightness of the face is almost like applying digital powder. If the image is looking a bit flat at the moment, don't worry, it'll look better after we start adjusting the color of the image.

Color Balance Controls

Once the contrast has been adjusted, it's time to start working on the color of the image. You have three sets of controls for color, two of which are visible in **FIGURE 22.8**. The color balance controls let you simultaneously adjust all three of an image's color channels at once, in specific regions of image tonality. For example, in order to rebalance a color cast (or tint) in the highlights, you'd use the Highlight color balance control. If your color cast was in the shadows, you'd use the Shadow color balance control instead. The tonal regions that are affected by each of the three color balance controls overlap broadly, but generally speaking you want to try and identify which part of the image has the color cast (is it the shadows, the midtones, or the highlights?), and then use the color balance control that corresponds to that region of image tonality.

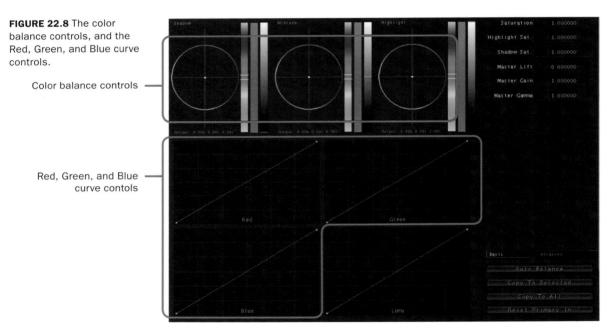

FIGURE 22.8 The color balance controls, and the Red, Green, and Blue curve controls.

Color balance controls —

Red, Green, and Blue — curve contols

You can also use the Red, Green, and Blue curve controls, which are used for extremely detailed adjustments to each individual color channel of the image. (See Chapter 21 for more details). In general, you may find that the color balance controls are the fastest way of making corrections to the garden variety color casts that come from color temperatures in lighting that are incompatible with the white balance of the camera or the film stock being used.

However, there's no reason you can't use the color balance and curve controls together. I frequently use the color balance controls for simple color temperature corrections, and then use the curve controls to make more specific, nitpicky adjustments. There's no right or wrong way to work; it's all a matter of preference.

Speaking of preference, the third set of color controls in the Primary In room are those found in the Advanced tab shown in **FIGURE 22.3**. Some colorists like to type in the specifications to make fine-tuning adjustments, but I personally prefer the color balance controls and color curves for their graphical interface. Also, if you have used the Auto Balance controls, those parameters will already be populated with values that you may or may not want to adjust further.

Let's get back to our image. Just from looking at it in **FIGURE 22.9**, we can see that there's a blue cast to the image that's probably the result of an incorrectly white-balanced video camera. However, if we switch the Waveform Monitor to a Parade scope analysis (click the Parade button at the top of the video scope), we can see exactly where within the image the color cast lies.

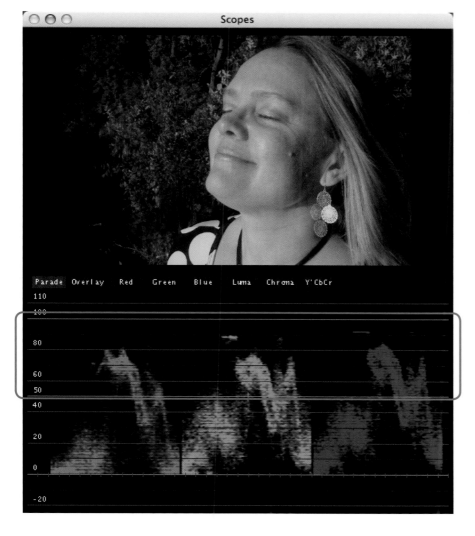

FIGURE 22.9 The top of the blue waveform is too strong for this image, relative to the red and green channels displayed in the Parade scope. This indicates a color cast in the highlights.

The Parade scope shows graphs of the red, green, and blue channels in the image next to one another, so you can see how they're balanced. Areas of the image with no saturation, like white, gray, and black areas, should have corresponding waveforms in the Parade scope that line up. In particular, the tops and bottoms of the graphs are good places to look for color casts, since the brightest highlights and darkest shadows of any image are typically supposed to be desaturated. In this image, the top of the blue channel is really high, even though the image itself consists of the greens of the background foliage and the reds of the woman's face. This shows how much of a color cast there is right off the bat.

To make an adjustment using any color balance control, you simply click anywhere within the color wheel and drag in the direction you want to manipulate the color. As you drag your mouse, crosshairs with a white dot at the center show you how much of an adjustment you're making, and the Output values below it show you the hue and saturation of your adjustment. The two sliders immediately to the right of each color balance slider let you make individual hue and saturation adjustments to the color balance control's correction (**FIGURE 22.10**).

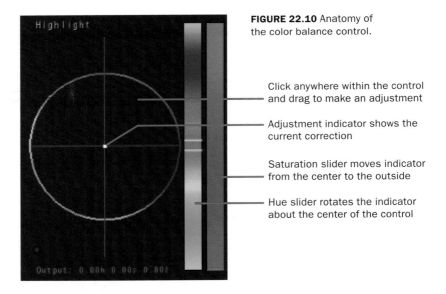

FIGURE 22.10 Anatomy of the color balance control.

Click anywhere within the control and drag to make an adjustment

Adjustment indicator shows the current correction

Saturation slider moves indicator from the center to the outside

Hue slider rotates the indicator about the center of the control

Now that we know what color we want to neutralize (blue), and where the adjustment needs to take place (in the highlights), we can go ahead and make the necessary adjustment using the Highlight color control.

The Relationship Between Color and Contrast

There is an interplay between contrast adjustments and color adjustments. However, because of the different ways in which video is processed in Final Cut Pro and Color, the relationship is different in each application.

In Final Cut Pro, images are processed in the Y'CbCr color space. The practical result of this is that adjustments you make using the contrast sliders have no effect on the measured color of the image, and adjustments made to the color balance controls have no effect on the contrast. However, whenever you "expand" contrast by lowering the black point and raising the white point beyond the image's original luma values, you may notice that the apparent saturation, or intensity, of the color throughout the image diminishes. The saturation isn't really lowering numerically—you can see this in the Vectorscope's unchanging graph— but lightening the image significantly can make the color seem less vivid. As a result, expanding contrast in Final Cut Pro's Color Corrector 3-way filter is often accompanied by raising the saturation slider.

In Color, images are processed in the RGB color space. As a result, adjustments to color and contrast have an interactive effect on one another, and changes made to one often alter the other. For example, in Color, expanding the contrast actually *increases* saturation, an increase which can be measured with the Vectorscope. Furthermore, adjustments that you make using the color balance controls alter the contrast, lightening or darkening the image depending on the adjustment you're making.

Neither method of image processing is right or wrong. However, both result in a distinctly different *feel* to similar sets of color balance and contrast controls in each application. For this reason, if you're used to Final Cut Pro's Color Corrector 3-way filter, Color might take a little getting used to, and vice versa.

In **FIGURE 22.11**, a small adjustment to drag the Highlight color balance control to the right, towards a green/yellow split, neutralizes the blue color cast we're trying to eliminate by combining it with its complementary (or opposite) color value, while at the same time strengthening the golden yellow in the highlights of her hair. A second adjustment to drag the Midtone color balance control up towards an orange/red split enhances the color in her face, while further reducing the cyan-ish tint that remains in the midtones (orange is the complementary, or opposite, color of cyan).

FIGURE 22.11 Dragging within the Highlight and Midtone color balance controls to adjust the image. Notice the crosshairs, which show how much of an adjustment is being made within each control, and the corresponding values that appear in the Output values at the bottom.

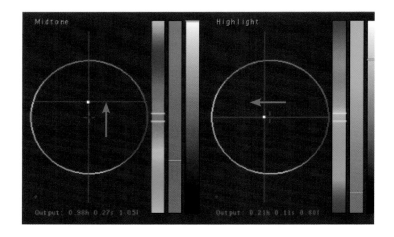

The final result of these adjustments can be seen in **FIGURE 22.12**. The prominent reddish/orange of the woman's face in front of the predominantly green background provides excellent *color contrast*, which gives depth to the image and compensates for the lack of vivid highlights in bringing the foreground image to the viewer's attention.

FIGURE 22.12 The now color-balanced and red-boosted image.

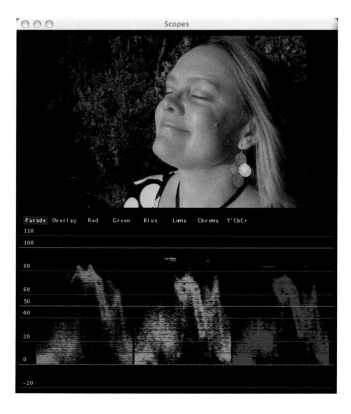

Saturation Controls

Now that we've adjusted the contrast and color balance of the image, it's time to turn our attention to the last major aspect of the image that remains untouched, the *saturation* or intensity of the color.

Unlike Final Cut Pro's Color Corrector 3-way filter, which has a single slider that controls the overall saturation of the image, Color provides three controls in the Basic tab of the Primary In room for controlling saturation, as shown in **FIGURE 22.13**. The Saturation parameter at the top controls the overall saturation of the entire image. A value of 1 results in no adjustment to image saturation. Higher values result in more intense color (the maximum value is 4); lower values diminish color intensity. A value of 0 results in a grayscale-only image (which reveals the luma-only component of the image).

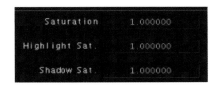

FIGURE 22.13 Color has individual saturation adjustments for overall Saturation, Highlight Saturation, and Shadow Saturation.

NOTE: These are completely different controls from the saturation sliders found next to the color balance controls, which affect only the intensity of the color balance adjustment being made, not the overall image saturation.

Separate Highlight Saturation and Shadow Saturation controls are valuable for preventing unwanted oversaturation in the shadows and highlights of the image, which can give your images a "cheap plastic" look. In general, both deep shadows and bright highlights tend to be desaturated when properly exposed and captured by professional film and video cameras. For this reason, large boosts to overall saturation can be prevented from bleeding into your shadows and highlights with a reduction to highlight and shadow saturation.

In our image, we might suppose that the client is happy with the overall color balance of the image but wants a more "muted" look, with less intense color. This is easily accomplished by lowering the Saturation, as seen in **FIGURE 22.14**. This can be done by middle-clicking and dragging in the Saturation parameter field using a three-button mouse (if you're using Apple's Mighty Mouse, you can program the scroll ball to be mouse button 3 in the System Preferences). This works with any parameter in Color. Dragging to the left lowers the value; dragging to the right raises the value.

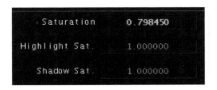

FIGURE 22.14 Lowering overall image saturation.

The result of this adjustment, along with a before-and-after comparison of what we've accomplished in this shot, can be seen in **FIGURE 22.15**.

FIGURE 22.15 Before and after—the final corrected image with reduced saturation.

So there you have it. This is but one possible treatment of the example clip. There are many other directions in which we could have taken this initial primary correction, depending on our creative goals, and of course the client's preference. In addition, the shot might well benefit from additional adjustments in the Secondaries and Color FX rooms—Color gives us plenty of room for further development! However, if you master the ability to manipulate color and contrast using the color balance, contrast, and saturation controls, you'll be well positioned to be able to use these other rooms effectively.

Secondary Color Corrections Using Vignettes

There are times when vignettes can be incredibly fast and intuitive to use when making color corrections. Alexis shows you how in this online article available at the book's companion Web site.

Audio Profile

EVAN RICHARDS
Videographer, Madison Savoyards

 Evan Richards has become the official videographer for the Madison, Wisconsin Savoyards. Visit the companion Web site and listen as he describes what it takes to create videos of theatrical productions.

Part 6

Additional Tools

So far, we've covered Final Cut Pro, Soundtrack Pro, Motion, and Color. But there are a total of seven different applications in Final Cut Studio 2, so we address the rest here.

First, we look at LiveType, a text animation package that has a lot of powerful features lurking just below the surface, as the first chapter in this section illustrates. Then, Mike Krause shows you how the easy roundtripping between LiveType and Final Cut Pro lets you create animated graphics files quickly and easily.

With all the hype surrounding digital downloads on the Internet, it is easy to lose sight of the fact that *billions* of DVDs are sold every year. The next chapter, written by the DVD expert Bruce Nazarian, illustrates easy, yet sophisticated techniques you can use to author your DVDs using DVD Studio Pro.

Finally, while not officially a part of Final Cut Studio 2, Final Cut Server is Apple's most recent release for the professional video market. In our concluding chapter, Matt Geller looks at the initial release of this powerful software to see what it can do and what it can't.

The video tutorials in this section can be found on the companion Web site and two of them show techniques you can try in Compressor.

Chapter 23

Hidden Secrets in LiveType

LARRY JORDAN

O K. I confess. I really like LiveType. Motion is a great program, but LiveType is like an old friend. I'm going to show you some LiveType tricks you may not have discovered for yourself. Because even with old friends, it's nice to have new things to talk about.

You Can Work in HD

LiveType supports a variety of video formats. Its default setting is broadcast NTSC. However, you can easily change this by choosing **Edit > Project Properties** and choosing a different video format from the Presets pop-up menu (**FIGURE 23.1**).

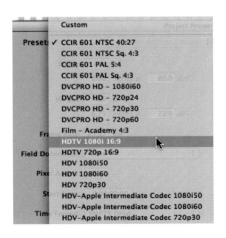

FIGURE 23.1 You configure video formats in LiveType using the Presets pop-up menu. If your HD format isn't listed, use HDTV 1080i for 1080 projects or HDTV 720p for 720 projects.

There are three HD categories: DVCPRO HD, HDV, and HDTV. Pick the video format and image size that matches your sequence. If you are working with ProRes 422, or your video format isn't part of the list, use the HDTV category and match the image size of your project. Final Cut will render the LiveType project to match your sequence as necessary.

NOTE: To create a 16:9 DV project, select NTSC DV 3:2 and change the Pixel Aspect to 1.20.

You Can Put Text on a Curve

When you enter text into LiveType, the letters are automatically placed into a track in the Timeline, represented by a blue line in the Canvas. The LiveType manual doesn't really give this blue line a name—I've always called it a "baseline," meaning the line upon which the letters of a font rest. So, you can call it a track, the blue line, or the baseline. Whatever you call it, it doesn't have to be straight.

The nice thing is, getting the baseline to curve is easy:

1. In the Timeline, select the clip containing the text you want to curve.

2. Control-click (or right-click) the blue dot at the beginning or end of the baseline and choose **Curve In or Out** from the shortcut menu, depending upon which end you select (**FIGURE 23.2**).

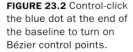

FIGURE 23.2 Control-click the blue dot at the end of the baseline to turn on Bézier control points.

3. About a half-inch in from the endpoint dot you click, if you look really carefully, you'll see a blue dot a little bit wider than the blue baseline. (With its typical graphical restraint, Apple has made this dot darn near invisible.) Grab this larger blue dot and drag it. As you do, the baseline starts to curve (**FIGURE 23.3**).

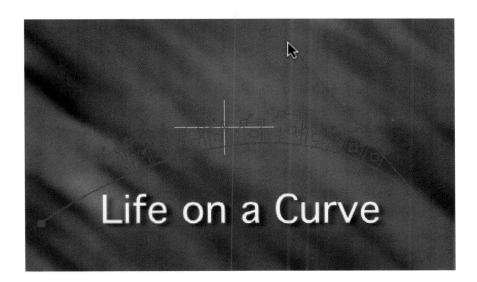

4. Do the same with the blue dot at the other end of the baseline (**FIGURE 23.4**). Drag the blue control dots until your text is curved to your satisfaction.

NOTE: If you plan to automate your text, and you want it to revolve around this curved baseline, choose Link Endpoints from the shortcut menu. This option forces the text to jump from one end of the line to the other during movement.

You Can Import a Photoshop Image

One of the limitations of LiveType is that it doesn't create images. However, since we can create virtually anything inside Photoshop, this isn't a big limitation. Here's how to get a Photoshop image into LiveType:

1. Create your image in Photoshop. If you want your Photoshop gamma (that is, the mid-tone grays) to match video gamma, use the sRGB color profile.

NOTE: Multilayer Photoshop graphics are imported as a single layer. However, you can create a two-layer graphic in Photoshop and set the background layer to invisible so the only image you see when importing into LiveType is the image on layer 2 with its alpha channel intact.

2. In LiveType, choose **File > Place** (**Command+I**). This places your graphic on one of the foreground tracks; that is, one of the tracks above the heavy gray line in the Timeline.

3. If you want your image to be placed in the background, choose **File > Place Background Movie**. This places whatever file you select, and it doesn't have to be a movie, below the heavy gray line separating the foreground (above) from the background (below).

NOTE: The advantage to placing movies in the background is that you can control whether background images are exported with a simple preference setting. This makes it easy to use a movie to help place the position of a lower-third super without exporting the movie as part of the final project (FIGURE 23.5). To set this, choose Edit > Project Properties.

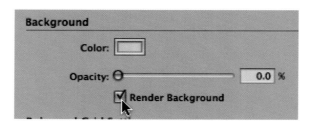

FIGURE 23.5 If you select the Render Background option, every clip below the heavy gray line in the Timeline will be exported. If you don't select this option, every clip below the line will be ignored.

4. From the Media Browser, select the Smoke category and apply the Fog Machine clip to the sequence background.

5. In the Inspector, select the Attributes tab, click the Glyph button and rotate the clip 180°.

In my example, I then imported a snowboarder logo to use as a foreground layer. I scaled the logo to **80%** size, and then dragged it to the lower-right corner of my frame in the Canvas (**FIGURE 23.6**).

FIGURE 23.6 The imported Photoshop image was scaled to 80% and repositioned to a corner of the Canvas.

NOTE: Remember to drag the right edge of your text or image clip in the Timeline to the duration you need; by default, all new clips have an average duration of 2 seconds.

You Can Matte Video Into a Shape

One of the secrets of LiveType is that all video is matted into something. We can take advantage of this to easily matte video into our Photoshop logo—in this case, I'll use video of an actual snowboarder.

1. In the Timeline, select the track that contains the logo.

2. Choose **Inspector > Attributes**, select the Matte tab, and choose **Movie or Image** from the "Matte to" pop-up menu (**FIGURE 23.7**).

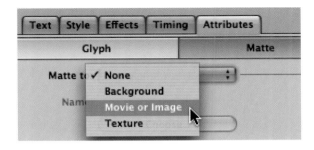

FIGURE 23.7 To matte video into a clip, choose "Movie or Image" from the "Matte to" pop-up menu.

3. Select the video clip you want to matte into your image. In this case, I used a close-up of a snowboarder (**FIGURE 23.8**).

FIGURE 23.8 Here is our logo with the video matted inside it.

NOTE: LiveType matches the In point of your video to the start of the logo. If you need the insert video to start in a different place, the easiest way to do this is to move the In and Out points in LiveType. Also, LiveType centers the clip in your image, and this positioning cannot be changed. If you need more control, create a traveling matte inside Final Cut Pro.

To make the logo stand out a bit more from the background, I added a drop shadow by choosing **Inspector > Style**, selecting the Shadow tab, and then tweaking the Blur, Opacity, and Offset settings until I liked the look (**FIGURE 23.9**).

FIGURE 23.9 Our logo with both matte and drop shadow added. The shadow settings I used are below.

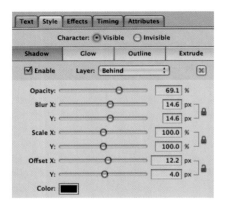

You Can Deform the Shadows

You can deform the shadows by using this strange "deform" box at the bottom of the Shadow settings window (**FIGURE 23.10**). Drag any color dot in the corners of the box and watch what happens to your shadows. (You can, if you want, type in specific pixel coordinates using the fields on the left—but that is nowhere near as much fun.)

Click in the center of the box and drag to offset the shadow. This is also a very easy way to create cast shadows—by dragging the top dots, while leaving the bottom dots alone.

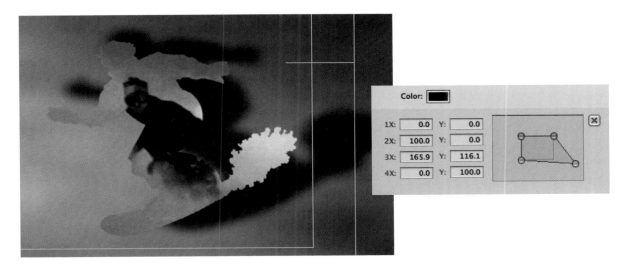

FIGURE 23.10 Drop shadows, as well as glows and outlines, can be easily deformed by dragging one of the dots in the deform box at the bottom of the Shadow tab.

In fact, LiveType carries this effect even further in that you can deform shadows, glows, and outlines. You adjust them all the same way.

NOTE: To reset a shadow to its defaults, click the black "X" button to the right of the deform dots.

You Can Create Your Own Animation Using Keyframes

Keyframes allow you to animate changes over time. If you don't need something to change, you don't need to use keyframes. In this case, however, we want our shadow to change shape over the course of this effect. Here's how:

1. Select the logo track and reset the deform dots by clicking the "X" next to the deform dots.

2. With the logo track still selected, choose **Track > Add New Effect**. A purple bar appears under your logo clip. This is the effect clip that contains all the keyframes needed for this effect. Unlike in Final Cut, where each param-eter has its own keyframes, in LiveType all keyframes for all parameters of an effect are contained in "master keyframes" stored in the effect itself.

3. Since we want the shadow to animate from the beginning of the clip to the end, drag the starting point of the effect so it starts at the beginning of your clip, then drag the end so it ends at the end of your clip (**FIGURE 23.11**).

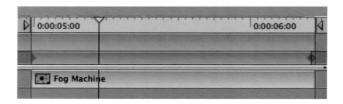

FIGURE 23.11 The length of the effect clip determines the speed, and duration, of the effect. In this case, we want the effect to run the length of the logo. Notice, also, that the In and Out points have been shifted so that the video starts at a point other than the beginning. LiveType exports only from the In to the Out point.

NOTE: The purple effect clip always displays as one frame shorter than your video clip. This is normal.

4. As we do in Final Cut, we can move between keyframes using keyboard shortcuts. Select the effects clip, or track, then press **Shift+K** to jump to the next keyframe to the right. With the effects clip or track selected, **Option+K** will jump to the previous keyframe to the left. To start creating the effect, position the playhead on the first keyframe of the effect.

5. Drag the shadow deform dots so the drop shadow looks the way you want (**FIGURE 23.12**).

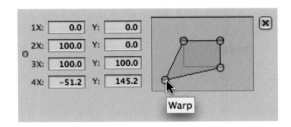

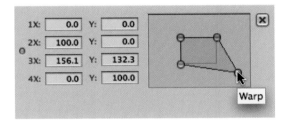

FIGURE 23.12 The starting (top) and ending (bottom) keyframe positions.

6. Press **Shift+K** to jump to the last keyframe. Again, drag the shadow deform dots so the ending position of your shadow looks the way you want.

7. Play your clip and watch what happens. Ta-DAH! Instant animation.

For all its simplicity, LiveType has a lot of depth in it. When my goal is to create animated text, LiveType is always my first choice. And, like an old friend, sometimes it can surprise you with some new tricks.

Video Tutorial: Creating an Animated Lower-Third

 LiveType can do some amazing things—if you know where to look. Visit the companion Web site to learn how to create LiveType projects for animated lower-third title keys that are easy to do and fun to watch.

Chapter 24

International Versioning and the Power of LiveType

BY MIKE KRAUSE

Multi-language international versioning can be a tedious, time-consuming, and often confusing process. It can be difficult enough to get an intricate long-format project completed on time even when you are fluent in the language it is created in, but to be given the same script translated into languages you may have never even seen before, it can be daunting to say the least. Add to that the stress of a high-profile project or a scenario where multiple producers are based on multiple continents and speaking multiple languages and the assignment becomes exponentially more complex.

I regularly work on projects destined for TVs and DVD players outside of the United States. I often face the very subjects I have already noted, but rarely with all of those complexities at once. I was recently given such a challenge: to help create thirty international versions of a long-format project loaded with text, where almost every line had been translated. With a customarily tight deadline on the horizon, a co-editor and I dove in. Right away we found a major obstacle, but one whose solution ended up saving us more time and effort than we originally thought possible.

Like with any other common online project, we received final scripts, graphics, and audio from outside vendors. Our client provided an English-language re-cut of the feature and several short bonus videos, all geared toward the international marketplace. All of the offline edits were built in Apple's Final Cut Pro. Lower-thirds and text-based effects throughout the program made extensive use of both the Boris Text plug-in and Apple's LiveType, with a smattering of Adobe Photoshop files thrown in for good measure. Complex graphics were all prebuilt in Adobe After Effects. So far, so good.

Once we copied the offline edits and got started, we learned that throughout the feature there were numerous speakers, each sharing their expertise related to the topic. Every time these speakers appeared on camera, their names and occupations were shown in a lower-third, but not just the first few times in an act, as is common in most documentary-style programs. The lower-thirds were initially built in FCP with the Boris Text plug-in. We found that even though the Boris lower-thirds were saved as master clips and then cut into the program, we couldn't just alter the master clip; instead we had to change the text in every single instance of every single lower-third on the Timeline. Put in perspective, the 90-minute program had each speaker appearing somewhere between 5 and 40 times each, for approximately 400 lower-thirds.

Manually adjusting each and every card would take hours. And all of that editing time did not include cutting in and adjusting the many other text effects and graphic clips, syncing dubbed audio, rendering, or laying off to tape. In fact, we found that out the hard way: During our first shift on the project, the other editor and I together were able to finish building only two language-versions of the feature and bonus videos. No rendering, no laying off to tape. Considering the time limit for turnaround, and the fact we had 28 more languages to go, this was unacceptable.

Although Boris Text has excellent built-in effects, for lower-thirds it was overkill. The interface was clunky for an otherwise simple duty, and it simply wasn't conducive to our workflow. Replacing them with Final Cut Pro's text generator cards had a similar clunky feeling, and the same master clip issue existed. We tested making lower-thirds in Photoshop, but it seemed to take forever when roundtripping with FCP. Since we started with a number of LiveType files already, building our lower-thirds in the same program made sense to simplify the workflow. We spent the following morning building new LiveType cards for every lower-third and text effect built in Boris Text.

A well-spent four hours later, with our retooled master Timeline as a template, we prepped a new FCP project as our first "new and improved" foreign-language master. We copied the updated Final Cut Pro and LiveType project files and named everything to match the new language. We edited all of our new cards in LiveType, pasting and adjusting the appropriate translated text. About 45 minutes later, we roundtripped back into FCP and let the Timeline update with the changes. Done.

What had taken us hours using Boris Text was done in minutes using LiveType.

Moving on, we set out to do things better and even faster. Copying the successful build, we reorganized and renamed just about everything to further simplify versioning. As each translation was delivered, we pre-edited all of our LiveType cards and copied the other graphics into our organized-by-language project structure. It became as simple as reconnecting the LiveType and graphics master clips to the prebuilt cards and saving the new language. Instead of making about 500 lower-third and text-effect edits by hand and scrolling through a long Timeline and risking making mistakes, we reduced that to about 75 text edits total.

As uncomplicated as I have made the construction of the Final Cut Pro projects sound, we still faced translation, font, and text-effects issues. There are issues common to any language-versioning project, of almost any scale.

Languages such as German, Finnish, and Portuguese often interpret with longer voicing than English, and fitting certain phrases into the same area without compromising the aesthetics often takes additional time to format.

Many languages have accent marks that ascend or descend outside of standard English text boundaries or special characters that do not exist in a standard Roman alphabet. Russian, Danish, Turkish, and Greek are all languages that require fonts including special characters.

Text with effects needed adjustments with every new language. For example, key elements of the program's discourse featured LiveType cards with a "shine on" effect that floated across the phrases, following voiceover from beginning to end in the direction they are read, during the course of the shots (**FIGURE 24.1**).

FIGURE 24.1 This is an example of the Shine On effect used to add a glow to the text.

Languages that resulted in a longer-than-English translation, as Finnish often did, had the shine accelerated. Shorter translations, such as Korean, had the shine slowed down to last the length of the shot. These we sometimes split by carriage returns, for which we had to request notes from the translators about where to split sentences.

My German is passable (barely), but beyond that we treated many cards like we were cutting mini music videos, adjusting or keyframing the effect to the timing of the shot and the beat of the spoken language.

Two languages posed yet another challenge: a right-to-left writing system. Thankfully, with proper fonts installed, Macs and Final Cut Studio are very language friendly, but in the case of Hebrew and Arabic we had to *think* in the direction of the text in order to reformat our LiveType cards. When pasting text into the LiveType Inspector, the cursor would operate in left-to-right direction but when we assigned a Hebrew- or Arabic-compatible font the cursor activity would reorient right-to-left. Editing the text took on a whole new dimension. In addition, all of the text-related effects that involved the aforementioned shine-on, type-on, and other "read-along" style reveals had to be reoriented to right-to-left as well. Thankfully it was as simple as highlighting the effect in the LiveType Timeline, going to the Inspector and clicking the Timing tab, then changing the Sequence Start to From Right (**FIGURE 24.2**).

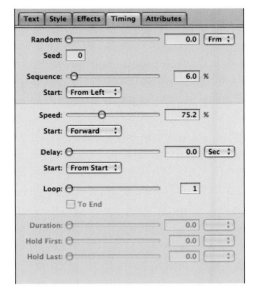

FIGURE 24.2 Sequence Start controls whether text displays from left to right, the default, or right to left.

The final obstacle came from the fonts themselves. Compatibility between languages proved inconsistent, even with expensive and specialized fonts. Several of our selected English, French, and German fonts would not work with Turkish.

Czech- and Hungarian-compatible fonts would sometimes not work with Polish or Dutch. Probably the most extreme example we found, was when versioning Mandarin from the Cantonese build, and a multitude of Mandarin characters proved incompatible with the fonts chosen to build the Cantonese Timeline—fonts preferred by our clients, of course (**FIGURE 24.3**). Not speaking either dialect, it was easy to assume, "it's all Chinese, it should just work, right?" but that certainly wasn't the case.

FIGURE 24.3 The differences between good Cantonese characters and bad ones is very, very subtle.

By the time we completed the last few languages, our system was streamlined to the point where we were able to build as many as three full deliveries in an eight-hour workday—one feature and the related bonus videos constituting a full delivery. This included time to work with the proper fonts, doctor text placement, match continuity between languages, and other aesthetics. We were able to render overnight, then spend the following day syncing audio, laying off to tape, and doing QC.

All told for this project, we constructed 30 localized language-versions, from French, Greek, and Korean to Hebrew, Croatian, and even Hindi (for a few examples, see **FIGURE 24.4**). Not counting fixes due to several re-interpretations between subtitled and dubbed translations and other similar issues, we actually pulled ahead of the incoming deliveries and presented the final masters two weeks earlier than the initial deadline. There was even time to go back and redo the original two languages we built.

LiveType proved itself to be a perfect complement to the workflow of multiple-language versioning. Neither the other editor or myself previously had extensive experience using LiveType, but we soon discovered how easy it was to integrate into our project, from simple lower-thirds to re-creating complex effects. We also found that our FCP sequences rendered much more quickly using LiveType, even when the LiveType cards included complex, multi-layered effects. To top it off, they looked great, better than we, or our producers, expected.

FIGURE 24.4 These four images illustrate how different languages take significantly different amounts of space to say the same thing.

Although Boris Text's strength might be its impressive array of integrated effects, LiveType was an unexpectedly flexible replacement, coming to the rescue of what otherwise would have been a prolonged and monotonous activity.

By taking the time to reorganize and consider alternative workflows early in this assignment, we developed a very efficient process that truly surprised us with how quickly and easily we could create numerous language masters. Instead of spending most of our time exceeding the number of clicks our mouse buttons were rated for, trudging our way through each language in a linear fashion, we were able to pay much closer attention to the quality of our work. The adage proved true: Work smarter, not harder.

I hope these pages from our versioning playbook help others who might face a similarly daunting undertaking. Now get out there and play with LiveType. You will be glad you did.

Video Tutorial: Effects in LiveType

LiveType is often overshadowed by Motion. But you can create some intriguing effects very simply using LiveType. Check out the video tutorial on the companion Web site to see how.

Chapter 25

Creating Stories in DVD Studio Pro

BRUCE NAZARIAN

On occasion you may need a way to play only a portion of a track, like when you might want to play a small segment of a travel video or one segment of a training video. On small DVDs, you can accomplish this by creating a new track in DVD Studio Pro containing only the desired segment of the track; in other words, by duplicating your video. You *can* trim the start and end points of an existing MPEG stream while authoring a track, but sometimes adding more video to your DVD project can push the total running time beyond the nominal limit, forcing you to reduce the video encode rate, and possibly reducing video quality. This might make the difference between fitting everything onto a DVD-5 or not!

Luckily, the DVD Studio Pro *story* allows you to repurpose existing content from a DVD track without duplicating that content on the disc. As you are about to see, stories are quite versatile. (DVD Studio Pro allows you to create a combined total of up to 99 tracks, stories, and slideshows.)

So, What's a Story?

A story in DVD Studio Pro is not a track or a slideshow. It's a separate item—a virtual playlist that defines the order and duration of one or more segments of a given track. If you've spent any time in Final Cut, you can think of stories as being like subclips (**FIGURE 25.1**). A story defines a specific part of a track (or all of it, if you wish).

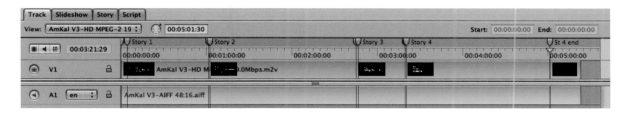

FIGURE 25.1 A track with chapter markers prepared to create stories.

Figure 1 shows a full-length track we will subdivide into individual segments using stories. In this figure, chapter markers were created that define the beginning and end of each content piece we wish to define as a story segment. A story segment may be of any length, but it *must* begin and end at a chapter marker. Each story can have up to 99 story segments that define a segment of video from within the story's parent track.

Creating a Story

Before you can define a story's content, you must first create the story inside of the track that contains the video content you want to use. Select the track in which you wish to create the story in the Outline view, and click the Add Story button, or use the keyboard shortcut (**FIGURE 25.2**).

FIGURE 25.2 Adding a new story.

Once you have created the story, it will appear in the Tracks folder of the Outline view just below the track in which it was created. (**FIGURE 25.3** shows the new story, Story 1.)

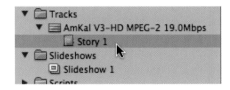

FIGURE 25.3 Story added; note that it is attached to a specific track.

At this point, you can easily rename the story by slowly double-clicking the story name in the Outline tab and changing the name of the story, or by selecting it and renaming it in the Story Inspector Name field. Additional stories can be created in the same way (remember the limit of 99, though). Note that additional stories will automatically be named and numbered: Story 2 will follow Story 1, Story 3 will follow Story 2, and so on.

Defining Story Segments

Each story can contain up to a maximum of 99 story markers, to define the story segments. During story playback, a story segment begins playing at the chapter marker that you specified to define its beginning, and the segment plays *until it encounters the **next** chapter marker*. Read that again, because this is a very important point, and something that often confuses people who are new to stories. You define *only* the *beginning* point of a story segment. The next chapter marker encountered during the playback of that segment will become the *end* of that story segment (of course, you can add additional story segments up to the limit of 99).

A new story won't play anything until at least one story segment has been defined using the Story Editor. It is here where you can select the chapter markers that make up the story entry point playlist, and define the order in which the segments will play.

To edit the story, select it, and then select the Story tab, as shown in **FIGURE 25.4**. Note that the currently selected story is shown in the View pop-up menu, and the chapters already defined in this track are listed in the Track Markers column. There's an empty list on the right for the story markers you will define in this tab.

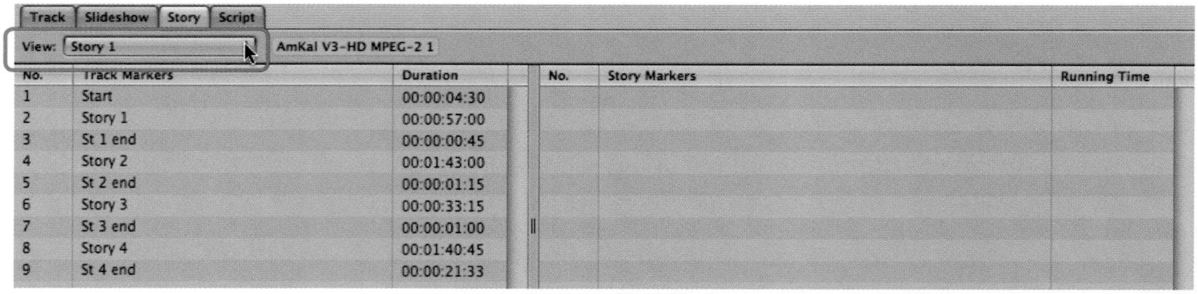
Track
Slideshow
Story
Script
View: Story 1
AmKal V3-HD MPEG-2 1
No.
Track Markers
Duration
No.
Story Markers
Running Time
1 Start 00:00:04:30
2 Story 1 00:00:57:00
3 St 1 end 00:00:00:45
4 Story 2 00:01:43:00
5 St 2 end 00:00:01:15
6 Story 3 00:00:33:15
7 St 3 end 00:00:01:00
8 Story 4 00:01:40:45
9 St 4 end 00:00:21:33

FIGURE 25.4 The Story Editor ready for editing.

To create a story segment, drag a chapter marker from the **Track Markers** list to the **Story Markers** list. For example, to create a story that begins at the Story 1 marker, drag Story 1 to the Story Markers column (**FIGURE 25.5**).

Track	Slideshow	Story	Script					

View: Story 1 ⧸ AmKal V3–HD MPEG-2 1

No.	Track Markers	Duration		No.	Story Markers		Running Time
1	Start	00:00:04:30					
2	Story 1	00:00:57:00		2	Story 1	00:00:57:00	
3	St 1 end	00:00:00:45					
4	Story 2	00:01:43:00					
5	St 2 end	00:00:01:15					
6	Story 3	00:00:33:15					
7	St 3 end	00:00:01:00					
8	Story 4	00:01:40:45					
9	St 4 end	00:00:21:33					

FIGURE 25.5 Creating the first story marker.

Clever readers may have noticed that the "St 1 end" marker was placed a little before the Story 2 marker to allow Story 1 to end neatly on a black frame (**FIGURE 25.6**). Without this marker, the Story 1 segment would play through to the first frame of Story 2, and we would see a flash-frame, which is not what we want at all.

As it is now defined, this story will play from the marker called Story 1 to the next marker in the track, called "St 1 end." At that point, the story is complete, and the story's end jump will dictate further navigation.

FIGURE 25.6 A marker to define the end of a segment.

Programming a Story End Jump

One of the powerful features of using stories is that any story's end jump can be programmed to navigate to a different location than the end jump of the track containing the story (or any other story from that track, for that matter). If needed, you can have many different stories within a track that play the same content, but each has a different end jump. Alternatively, you can leave it set to the default "Same as Track" option in the End Jump pop-up menu, as shown in **FIGURE 25.7**, and the end jump destination of the story will be the same as that of the track containing it.

FIGURE 25.7 This default setting makes the end jump the same as that of the track containing the story.

FIGURE 25.8 Four stories now defined.

However, in our example, we want to use the stories to allow for individual playback of each segment. To accomplish this, we will need to create a story to define each individual segment, set its end jump, and then create a menu with buttons where we can trigger the stories to begin playback. I'll create three additional stories (**FIGURE 25.8**) now for Track 1 using the Add New Story function, and then I'll assign each one to a different story segment within the track.

Scripting 101 in DVD Studio Pro

In DVD Studio Pro, scripts are the command elements that control DVD player navigation and presentation. Learn how you can add scripting to your projects in this online article available at the book's companion Web site.

Once the additional stories are created, use the Story Editor tab to assign one marker to each new story: Story 2 gets the Story 2 marker, Story 3 gets the Story 3 marker, and so on. So now, the content in our track has been sliced into four segments, each of which corresponds to a particular chapter of the video (**FIGURE 25.9**).

FIGURE 25.9 Four different stories, indicated by the View pop-up menu, each with a different marker setting the start for each story.

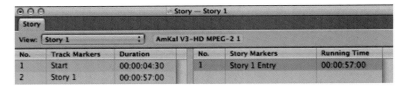

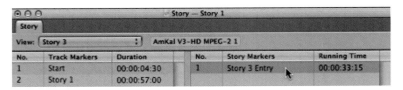

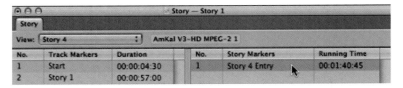

DVD Studio Pro power users *might* expect that connecting a story to a button this way would create round-trip navigation; generally, when an icon from the Outline view is dragged onto a button, both the Button link *to* that item (see **FIGURE 25.10**) and the End Jump link *from* that item back to that menu button would be connected automatically. For stories, though, this is not the case.

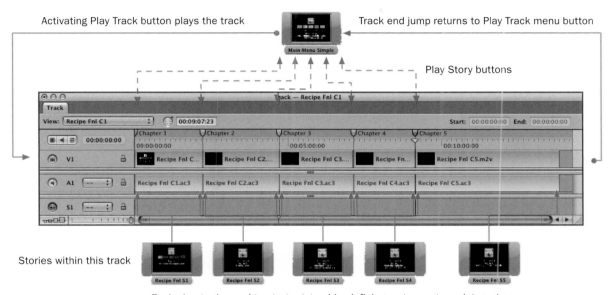

FIG 25.10 This illustrates how stories relate to tracks. A track contains stories which can have their own end jumps and buttons.

If you select and play the track, the story boundaries will be ignored and the track will play in its entirety from start to finish. If you link a story to a button and select that story, only the defined section of the track contained within that story will play, and the story end jump will control the return navigation.

I created a new menu (PLAY STORIES) with four empty buttons and dragged each story's icon from the Outline tab onto its own button in the new menu. Presto—a chapter menu! (**FIGURE 25.11** shows Story 4 being connected to its button.)

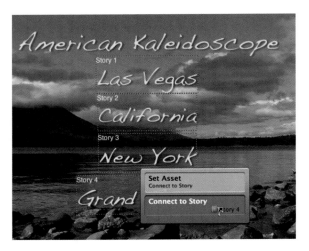

FIGURE 25.11 Connecting each story to its button (note the Drop Palette setting).

Because the story is actually a subset of a track, the "Same as Track" default will remain (**FIGURE 25.12**). But "Same as Track" will not work for us for this DVD. We want each story to return to the button that originally selected it.

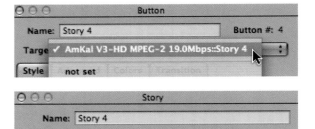

FIGURE 25.12 Button 4's target gets linked to Story 4, but Story 4's end jump keeps the default.

To fix this, use Story 4 Inspector's End Jump pop-up menu and choose **Menus > PLAY STORIES > Story 4** (**FIGURE 25.13**). This will need to be done for Stories 1, 2, and 3, as well, remembering to connect them to their proper button.

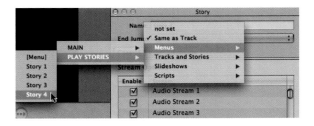

FIGURE 25.13 Story 4's end jump linked to the proper button.

If you are familiar with using the Connections tab, you can also relink them there, if you prefer. **FIGURE 25.14** shows what the connections should look like, when correctly set.

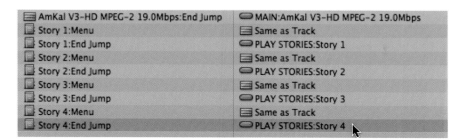

FIGURE 25.14 All stories relinked in the Connections tab.

Conclusion

So What Have We Gained Using Stories?

The original DVD had a single track of video that only played from start to finish. By defining chapters at the beginning and end of each segment and using those chapter markers to create story markers defining four individual segments, the DVD now has the ability to either play the entire movie *or* play any one of the individual segments from the movie. This was accomplished without adding any video to our existing DVD.

Stories allow us to virtually redefine the playback of the content contained within the DVD, without adding *any* additional video to the disc!

Chapter 26

Final Cut Server: Ten Ways It Can Help Manage Your Media

MATTHEW GELLER

W hen would you use Final Cut Server? When several people need to access media, when you are working with widely dispersed clients, or when staff is spending too much time doing the same repetitive media processing over and over.

Final Cut Server delivers two primary functions: media asset management and workflow automation. I like to call these two functions the "front end" and the "back end" of the program, respectively. For the most part, system administrators in large facilities will configure the workflow automation features. I'll cover Final Cut Server's media asset management features in this chapter.

A Quick Overview

Final Cut Server's media asset management function allows you to catalog every single file that has meaning to your facility. It connects to the storage systems at your facility through ubiquitous network file-sharing protocols such as SMB/CIFS, NFS, AFP, or FTP (**FIGURE 26.1**). It can also have storage systems directly attached to it, and of course it can be a client of an Xsan shared storage system. Final Cut Server recognizes each of these storage systems as a *device* (a hard drive, or folder, where files are stored).

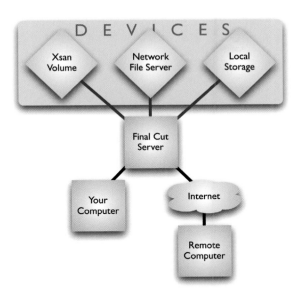

FIGURE 26.1 Final Cut Server acts as a hub connecting users who need access to media files with the devices where that media is stored.

You connect to Final Cut Server through a lightweight, Java-based client application that can run on a Mac or a PC and downloads through a web browser. Because the client application is so small and versatile, it enables just about every person inside or outside the facility to access content.

In order for that content to be accessible in a meaningful way, Final Cut Server reaches out to each device and, based on the tasks you specify, will either periodically scan these devices for new or changed material or watch specific folders on these devices for new content. As it does so, it creates catalog entries for each of these files. Metadata contained within the file is automatically transferred, or *mapped*, into Final Cut Server. Thumbnail icons are created for easy visual identification. Proxy clips (small size, low-resolution clips) are automatically created for any movie or still image file it encounters.

Proxies make that video content accessible to users who may not have fast connections to the server. Producers, clients, rights managers, and creators of closed captions are all examples of users who can access video content without having high-speed connections or specialized equipment.

Searching the Catalog

The interface of the client application is remarkably simple. The search box at the top of the main window uses keywords to search on any of the dozens of metadata fields attached to the asset (for example, filename, description, or the FCP project a clip may belong to). Because Final Cut Server provides a complete visual database of all your content, searching via keywords, along with quick visual confirmations provided by both thumbnail images and proxies of the video clips, will make finding that "needle in the haystack" clip rather effortless.

If keyword searches are not enough, a quick click on the magnifying glass, which is the Advanced Search button, to the left of the search box reveals additional search criteria to refine the search (**FIGURE 26.2**).

FIGURE 26.2 Searches can be expanded or refined using the Advanced Search button (the magnifying glass) and an almost unlimited number of search fields.

Taking a cue from iTunes, Final Cut Server even allows users to save "smart searches" on their systems to speed finding content that is searched for frequently (**FIGURE 26.3**).

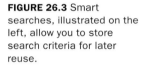

FIGURE 26.3 Smart searches, illustrated on the left, allow you to store search criteria for later reuse.

Drag and Drop Simplicity

Each asset within a search result list appears either as an icon in the default thumbnail view or as an item in a list view. These can simply be dragged from Final Cut Server's window into the windows of active applications. For example, video assets within Final Cut Server can be dragged right into a Final Cut Pro Browser for immediate use, especially when the editor's machine resides on an

Xsan volume. In this case, Final Cut Server "tells" Final Cut Pro where the hi-res version of the file exists, creating an instant link to that file.

For shops where a SAN volume is not present, or where you want to load files to a laptop for disconnected use, there's one extra step. You use the "Cache to Use" option in the asset's shortcut menu, which instructs Final Cut Server to download the hi-res file to your machine. After this process is complete, when you drag and drop the file from Final Cut Server into, say, Final Cut Pro, it links to the local file on your computer, rather than the original file stored in Final Cut Server.

As a consultant to a lot of shared storage systems, I get weak-kneed whenever I see a user with overzealous hand movements try to access files from a SAN volume in the Finder. One false move and a whole bunch of files could get moved, accidentally copied, or even deleted! Final Cut Server's drag-and-drop interface offers a coveted benefit: Creative staff will spend more time interacting with the visual catalog, rather than getting their mice into the folder structure of a SAN volume. This greatly reduces the chances of errors in copying, moving, or deleting important media files.

Accessing and Enriching Metadata

Each asset can become a repository of rich metadata, allowing others within your facility to know more about the content. This metadata can be completely customized so that the facility can enter and search for metadata that is meaningful to the workflow. Although creating custom metadata is an advanced administrative task, it's relatively straightforward, and once completed, really starts to make the app feel like it's an extension of your shop (**FIGURE 26.4**).

FIGURE 26.4 Here is a sample metadata screen showing the default settings for an asset. Additional fields can be added by an administrator.

As mentioned before, metadata can be mapped, or transferred, from a file to Final Cut Server's catalog and back. An example of mapped metadata is all the information within a Final Cut Pro project's Browser. Final Cut Pro project files map their metadata into the Final Cut Server catalog. Log notes and other "Browser column" data from the Final Cut Pro project can therefore be searched in Final Cut Server.

Remote and Mobile Edit System Workflow

Although Final Cut Server will generally discover and catalog your content automatically, files can also be added to the catalog and transferred to a shared storage device by simply dragging those files into the main Server window. Even more remarkable is that new Final Cut Pro projects that are dragged into Final Cut Server not only get cataloged and mapped, but the file itself is analyzed for connected media and compared with the current catalog, and any files not yet in the system are then automatically uploaded as well.

This opens up unique opportunities to empower remote content creators (as staff who float in and out of the facility on laptops) with media access.

However, sometimes Final Cut Pro project files of considerable complexity (such as ones that have a large number of clips and/or sequences, or ones that use embedded projects from Motion or Soundtrack Pro) tend to confuse the analyzer within Final Cut Server, which leads to project files whose media is not completely accounted for within the catalog. You would then have to manually upload those "missing" files into the catalog yourself.

Annotating Video Clips

There is a built-in annotation tool, which allows producers or clients to annotate raw content or to make comments to works in progress. This tool works with the proxies of video clips, so that even people not connected via a fast network, or even outside of the facility, can contribute annotations.

FIGURE 26.5 The data on the right side illustrate sample media annotations.

But the clear disappointment with this feature is that the information in this window cannot be printed, exported, or otherwise accessed outside of Final Cut Server, not even to other Pro apps. This forces everyone who wants to use this tool to do so within the context of Final Cut Server only (**FIGURE 26.5**).

Productions Are Virtual Folders for Assets

Assets can be grouped into *productions*, which simply act as virtual folders. An asset can appear in multiple productions without being duplicated. Productions carry their own metadata and can be searched just like the assets they contain.

Productions can also automatically be created based on Finder folder names, which allows veteran Final Cut Pro editors to work with media away from the Finder. In fact, we can add automation that changes Final Cut Server to automatically reflect changes to the contents of the Finder folder.

Check-in/Checkout

Assets can be checked out and then checked in when completed. This feature alone will be useful for collaborative teams that have tried (and often failed) to create workflows on shared storage where an individual was solely responsible for updating content and making sure it returned to the right place for the next person. Now, Final Cut Server handles this process automatically. It even has a version control system that complements the check-in/checkout system. Previous versions of files can be protected, and accessed, just in case an earlier version is needed.

NOTE: Sometimes, complex FCP files can cause problems for this system. As a workaround to the check-in/checkout process which creates a copy of the Final Cut project, the original FCP project can be accessed from inside Server by dragging the project icon to the desktop. Although doing this eliminates the benefits of the check-in/checkout system, this means we always have access to the original project file at all times.

Export

Assets can be exported out of Final Cut Server, with the added benefit of having Compressor transcode the original file to any format you specify. This allows people to keep working on their projects rather than be tied to their machines, transcoding files for delivery. Even better, these transcodes can be triggered automatically by a change in metadata status; for instance, when a movie is approved for release.

Archive Handoff

There are provisions to either manually or automatically archive assets, but I'd rather define this feature as a handoff in that it *prepares* files for archive, but really doesn't do the archiving per se. Final Cut Server can define a device as an archive device, which simply means that the device is a place where archived files get moved.

To be clear, all the archive function does is take the hi-res file of an asset from where it resides and moves it to the archive device. A restore does the opposite. That's it.

In a large facility, the archive device could be the staging storage of a very advanced Hierarchical Storage Manager, such as a StorNext, MassTech, or XenData system. To its credit, Final Cut Server can be told to run post-archive and pre-restore AppleScripts or shell scripts, so that savvy admins can create elaborate automatic archival systems when the time, brains, and money are there to do so.

However, in a small shop, I see the archive device as a FireWire drive that, when full, gets removed and replaced with another one. But when files from the missing FireWire drive try to get restored, Final Cut Server doesn't keep track of which drive is attached to the system. This means that the poor admin, or worse yet, the "smartest" of the editors, will get saddled with looking at Final Cut Server's error report, realizing which FireWire drive needs to be reattached, then retrying the restore operation.

Audio Profile

RICHARD TOWNHILL
Director of Pro Video product management, Apple

Visit the companion Web site and listen as Richard Townhill discusses Final Cut Server—what it is, who it's for, and how to use it.

Supports Both Macintosh and Windows Clients

Probably the most exciting feature of Final Cut Server is that it supports both Mac and Windows systems. And by "supports" I mean the operation, look-and-feel, and automation is identical. This means that editors can edit on a Mac while administrative staff can review and track media assets on their PCs.

For shops on both platforms, this is very exciting.

One Final Note

Amidst all this good news, however, I think a lot of folks are expecting the software to provide media management functions similar to the ones found within Final Cut Pro's Media Manager, except perhaps this time they would work. Here, then, is the greatest letdown of the 1.0 release: Although Final Cut Server allows you to work with your media files on a comprehensive level, its support for Final Cut Studio projects still needs polishing. Its process of handling Final Cut Pro projects is not rock solid, and it can't automatically import linked assets from DVD Studio Pro, Soundtrack Pro, or Motion projects.

Final Cut Server has a lot of potential, and for larger shops, it can save a lot of time. However, for smaller organizations, especially those that may not have someone in-house with strong IT skills, the first version of Final Cut Server may present some challenges.

However, its price point still makes it an attractive visual database for all your files, and with any luck, future revisions will address its current weak points.

Video Tutorial: Create a Compressor Droplet

Compressor is great for compressing video but there's a lot you can do to automate it. Visit the companion Web site to learn how to create droplets to automate your entire Compressor process.

Video Tutorial: Compressing HDV for the Web

Visit the companion Web site to learn how you can use Compressor 3 to compress your HDV footage for the Web.

Index